# ONE·HUNDRED·AND·ONE
# READ-ALOUD
# MYTHS AND LEGENDS

# ONE-HUNDRED-AND-ONE
# READ-ALOUD
# MYTHS AND LEGENDS

## Ten-Minute Readings from the World's Best-Loved Literature

By Joan C. Verniero
and Robin Fitzsimmons

BLACK DOG
& LEVENTHAL
PUBLISHERS
NEW YORK

Published by
Black Dog & Leventhal Publishers, Inc.
151 West 19th Street
New York, NY  10011

Distributed by
Workman Publishing Company
708 Broadway
New York, NY  10003

Designed by Liz Trovato

Manufactured in the United States of America

Hardcover ISBN: 1-57912-057-1
h  g  f  e  d  c  b

Softcover ISBN: 1-57912-185-3
h  g  f  e  d  c  b  a

Library of Congress Cataloging-in-Publication Data

Verniero, Joan C.
One Hundred and one read-aloud myths and legends / by Joan C. Verniero
and Robin Fitzsimmons.
p. cm.
Summary: A collection of more than one hundred traditional tales
and myths from around the world.
Hardcover ISBN  1-57912-057-1
1. Mythology—Juvenile literature.   [Mythology.]
I. Fitzsimmons, Robin, 1957.   II Title.
BL311.V48     1999
398.2—dc21                                                                98-54655
                                                                                      CIP
                                                                                      AC

# CONTENTS

# INTRODUCTION

We all remember being read to as children; a captivating story and the warmth of a reassuring voice could open up vivid imagery beyond the scope of our everyday lives. Reading can help you and your kids explore enchanting new worlds together, laugh together and share moments that you'll both cherish for a lifetime. These memories are priceless: Parents, teachers, grandparents and babysitters who take the time to read with children give the gift of discovery, imagination and learning.

Reading aloud together not only strengthens the bonds between you and your kids, it teaches and reinforces patience, attentiveness and curiosity—not to mention whetting the child's appetite for reading on his or her own.

Studies have proven that home reinforcement of concepts learned in school is an invaluable and effective educational step. Reading aloud can help demystify the reading process right from the beginning; most children learn to recognize words between the ages of four and nine. They learn and expand their skills more easily if they have shared bedtime (or any other time!) stories.

By reading stories that are interesting to kids—but beyond their reading level—you can stretch young readers' understanding and motivate them to improve their skills. Share the process with your kids—join them in their excitement as they begin to understand the relationship between printed words and contextual concepts until "reading" starts to click.

In an age when time is precious and video games and television seem to be taking over, taking the time to spend with your kids is all the more rewarding; to read, adventure and learn together. You'll be surprised how much it fun it is—for them and for you.

*One-Hundred-and-One Read-Aloud Myths and Legends* is the sixth volume in the popular *Read-Aloud* series.

## ABOUT THE SELECTIONS

*One-Hundred-and-One Read-Aloud Myths and Legends* contains stories from all over the world. Readers and listeners can explore the legacies of diverse cultural traditions, while touching on universal themes that appear in every culture. Organized in geographical sections, each tale is marked with a theme: Heroes and Heroines, Nature, Love, Fire and Lightning, Magic and Tricksters, Words and Messages, Underworld, Creation, Destruction and Immortality. As your children learn about how different peoples explain the world around them, they will be enchanted by beautiful maidens, talking animals, inspiring heroes, frightening monsters and astonishing feats of magic. Whether you choose to read a selection that will take ten minutes or several of the shorter pieces, there are appropriate stories to satisfy the attention span and interests of every age group: from four to ninety-four.

# GREEK
# MYTHS

# THE ADVENTURES OF ODYSSEUS

HE GREEK HERO ODYSSEUS WAS FAMOUS FOR HIS great skills as a fighter during the Trojan War. It was Odysseus who built the Trojan Horse, a hollow wooden replica of a soldier's steed, in which members of the Greek army hid and surprised the Trojans. He is also well-known for his many adventures during his journey home to the island of Ithaca. In Roman literature Odysseus is known as Ulysses. A great poem of his adventures was called "The Odyssey," written by Homer in the ninth century B.C.

Following the end of the Trojan War, Odysseus dearly missed his wife, Penelope, and his family. It had been many years since he had seen the land of his birth in the Aegean Sea. Weary and tired from the demands of a long, hard war, Odysseus was looking forward to being reunited with those he loved.

The voyage home, however, was fraught with dangers. Odysseus could not foresee the adventures and challenges that he would face. He left the shores of Troy with his men and set sail for Ithaca, expecting a smooth voyage.

Their first stop was the city of the Ciconians, at Ismarus. The inhabitants of this land were not friendly, and killed six of Odysseus's men.

Setting out to sea once more, the ship encountered a terrible storm. Odysseus sought refuge in the land of the Lotus-eaters. Unlike the Ciconians, the Lotus-eaters were friendly people who were only too happy to share their food with the sailors.

When Odysseus's men ate the lotus plants prepared for them, they lost all desire to return to their homes. They became lethargic and content to remain where they were. Odysseus had to drag his men back to his ship in order to continue his voyage.

The ship made way to the land of the Cyclops, one-eyed giants known for their ferocity and cunning. Despite the danger, Odysseus attempted to disembark on their island in order to gather much needed supplies. With a small band of men, he crept into the cave of Polyphemus, a fearsome, hated Cyclops.

Polyphemus trapped the sailors inside the cave by boarding up the entrance with a giant boulder. Although he had many sheep and cattle to eat, Polyphemus took delight in chasing several sailors through the cave and upon trapping them, killed and ate them.

Odysseus tried to think of a way to escape. He instructed his men to help him sharpen the end of a large log. While the giant slept, Odysseus and several men silently approached Polyphemus and gorged his eye with the point of their crudely made weapon.

Polyphemus cried in pain. Unable to see, he scrambled back and forth in the cave, trying to kill the men who had blinded him. Knowing they could only escape through the entrance to the cave, Polyphemus removed the boulder and stood alongside the opening. He waited patiently for his prey to exit.

Again, Odysseus came up with a clever scheme to trick the Cyclops. He and his men hung onto the bellies of several sheep and goats who were leaving the cave to go to pasture. Even as Polyphemus leaned down to feel the backs of his flock, he was unaware of the secret cargo being carried to freedom. Once outside the cave, Odysseus and his crew boarded their ship.

The Laestrygonians lived near the sea. Their coves and bays were inviting to weary sailors. After many more days at sea, Odysseus saw one of their harbors and instructed his crew to put down an anchor for the evening in order to rest. But that night, under the cover of darkness, the Laestrygonians descended on the ships and destroyed all but the personal ship of Odysseus, which was situated just outside the harbor. Again, Odysseus narrowly escaped harm.

The many perils that Odysseus would face were far from over. When his ship passed the land of the Sirens, sea nymphs who could cast a charm on sailors through their singing, Odysseus gave his men wax plugs to put in their ears. He allowed himself to be tied to the mast of his ship so that he would not be overcome by the irresistible song of the Sirens.

Odysseus had heard of the island of the Thrinacia, where the sun Hyperion kept his flocks of cattle and sheep. Before reaching that place, however, he and his crew would have to pass through the land of the monsters Scylla and Charybdis. Several members of the crew were killed by the six-headed Scylla, who waited patiently on the rocks for her victims. If one was lucky to escape her wrath, Charybdis, the monster of the deep, would create a powerful whirlpool to suck unsuspecting victims into the cold, dark waters of the ocean.

With little strength or morale left to them, Odysseus's men made their way to the island of the sun. They dragged their bodies to the shore and surveyed the peaceful lands, where many livestock grazed. Odysseus warned his crew not to kill any of the animals, for they belonged to the god Hyperion. But the temptation for a good meal was too much for the sailors. While Odysseus slept, his men slew several cattle and roasted the meat.

When Odysseus woke, he knew that something terrible had occurred. He urged the crew to board their ship and make way to sail. No sooner had they left the island, when a terrible storm rose from the bottom of the sea, tossing the ship about like a toy. All of the men who had traveled with Odysseus perished. Only he was able to survive by clinging to a piece of the ship's broken mast. Cold and alone in the angry waters, Odysseus drifted far over the waves.

Days passed before Odysseus's body touched dry land. He washed up on the shores of an island that was somehow familiar to him. He was certain that he had seen the trees and fields of this strange place before. But where? Suddenly out of nowhere, a large hound came bounding toward him. Odysseus yelled with joy when he realized that the animal was none other than his faithful dog. At last, he was home!

Odysseus made his way to his palace. His joyous reunion with his wife and son, Telemachus, was short-lived, however, for Odysseus had been absent from Ithaca for over twenty years. Many people were conspiring to take away his throne. No one felt threatened by the strange, old man who had climbed from the sea.

Odysseus challenged the men to an archery contest. One by one, his opponents failed to be as accurate with their bows as the mighty Odysseus. Recognizing the old man for the powerful leader he was, the men declared him king of Ithaca once more. And there, on his beloved island, Odysseus lived out the remainder of his years, delighting his followers with his many tales of adventure.

# THE LAUREL OF APOLLO

 HE GREEK GOD ZEUS WAS A POWERFUL LEADER AMONG the gods and goddesses of Olympia. He was feared and respected for his wisdom and his judgment in many situations. Despite his power, Zeus displayed humanlike qualities. He could be quick to anger, fitful, and depressed. He was often passionate, and though he loved his wife Hera very much, he was known to enjoy the company of many beautiful women.

This displeased Hera very much. It caused her to be jealous and bad tempered. When Hera learned that Leto was pregnant with a child of Zeus, she flew into a rage and pursued the poor woman to the four corners of the world. Only on the island of Delos, could Leto find a safe haven.

Leto gave birth to twins, Apollo and his sister, Artemis. Seven swans circled the area where the children were born as a sign of joy. Out of gratitude to the island for granting her asylum from Hera, Leto promised that her son, Apollo, would build a temple there.

Several of the other goddesses did not fear Hera's wrath, and soon descended upon Delos to help Leto with her babies. The goddesses washed the children in sweet water and dressed them in fine clothing. The goddess

Themis fed Apollo nectar and ambrosia, which were very special foods reserved for those who were immortal.

Apollo grew into a strong, handsome god. He could play the lyre very well. He was also adept at the art of archery. With his silver bow and arrows, Apollo killed Python, the huge dragon that plagued the inhabitants of Delos.

Apollo traveled to many places. One day, while walking in the Vale (or valley) of Tempe, Apollo saw a beautiful, young maiden partially hidden in a grove of trees. So great was her beauty that Apollo instantly fell in love with her.

The woman's name was Daphne. She had heard many stories of the god Apollo and how well he could shoot a bow and arrow and play the lyre. Daphne was very taken with Apollo's golden, curly hair and clear, blue eyes. She returned his smile.

When Apollo tried to approach her, Daphne fled into the woods. This action confused Apollo. Perhaps the young woman was shy, he thought to himself. If only he could talk to her, perhaps she would see that he was a kind and good being who did not wish her harm.

As Daphne ran into the woods, she grew fearsome that Apollo would eventually overtake her. She had vowed that no man would ever possess her, not even a god as talented and good as Apollo. She ran harder and harder, trying to elude him.

Daphne knew the valley very well. She ducked into caves and behind great trees to hide from Apollo. But it was of no use. He was determined to speak with her. No matter where she ran, Apollo was able to find her.

Finally Daphne could run no farther. Her legs were tired and her feet ached. There was no place in the woods that she loved where she could hide from the determined Apollo.

Apollo saw that Daphne was growing tired. He called out to her.

"Please don't run from me," he told her. "I do not mean you any harm. I would just like to talk to you."

Daphne could hear Apollo approaching closer and closer to her. When fatigue had completely overtaken her body, she fell to the ground. Desperate and afraid, Daphne cried aloud.

"Mother Earth, please have mercy on me! I have vowed that no man will ever take me. I would rather die than to lose my freedom and my life in these sacred woods. Please, save me!"

The moment Apollo caught up with the breathless Daphne and placed his hands on her shoulders, a very strange thing happened. The beautiful, young woman, who had enchanted the god, began to quiver and shake. Where her body had been, a tall, strong trunk began to grow from the ground. It grew higher and higher, sprouting branches and leaves as it rose upward. Daphne's slender legs descended into the earth, turning into gnarled roots that held fast to the dirt and stones.

Apollo was astonished. He watched in amazement as Daphne became a tree, forever saved from his advances. Apollo realized that despite the fact that he was a god and immortal, his will was no match for Mother Earth's love for her child, Daphne. He watched the sun as it played on the rustling leaves that had once been Daphne's hair. Sadly he reached up and took some leaves from the branches. He wove these into a laurel, which he placed on his head. For the rest of his days, Apollo would wear the laurel to remember Daphne, who chose to remain in the woods she so loved as a beautiful tree.

# THE GREAT WARRIOR ACHILLES

 HE TROJAN WAR WAS ONE OF THE MOST FAMOUS events recorded in Greek history. Many stories are written of its heroes and heroines, as well as the gods and goddesses who influenced its outcome. Here is the story of the Greek hero Achilles.

The Trojan War began when Helen, the wife of King Menelaus of Sparta, was kidnapped by Paris of Troy. Paris carried Helen far across the Aegean Sea and refused to return her to her husband. For ten years legions and armies of Greece attempted to rescue Helen from Troy in Asia Minor.

Achilles was the son of Peleus, a prince, and Thetis, a Nereid, or fairy. It was Thetis's plan to protect her child in a very special way. Since she was immortal, she decided to give her son Achilles some of the supernatural powers that she possessed. Thetis wrapped her baby in a blanket and secretly took him to the underground world of Hades. The river Styx flowed through this dark landscape where the souls of the dead came to rest after their lives on earth were through.

Thetis held her infant son, Achilles, by his tiny, pink heel and dipped him in the powerful waters of the Styx. Little Achilles let out a terrified cry, for the river was bitter cold. But it possessed a remarkable power. Upon contact, the water would form a protective covering over the baby's skin.

Thetis returned from the underworld with Achilles. Not simply content to offer her son the gift of protective armor, she vowed that she would also make him immortal. Thetis prepared a large fire. She held Achilles over it. When she was about to immerse his tiny body in the flames, her husband, Peleus, came upon her. Thinking that she was trying to harm Achilles, Peleus pushed her away from the fire. Thetis fled with Achilles.

Thetis gave Achilles to the care of Chiron, a wise centaur who had been the tutor of many Greek heroes. Achilles grew into a capable and strong, young man. When the Trojan War broke out, he was eager to go and fight for the honor of Helen. He wished to fight under the command of General Agamemnon.

When Thetis heard of her son's plans, she implored Chiron to convince him not to go to war. But Chiron would not persuade Achilles to forget about fighting. He knew that Achilles had the makings of a great warrior.

In desperation Thetis placed a spell on her son, rendering him power-less. Then she disguised him as a young girl and sent him away to the island of Scyros, where he would be under the protection of King Lycomedes.

Meanwhile, Agamemnon gathered his troops for the siege of Troy. His men were strong and willing to fight. Victory seemed certain. A seer by the name of Calchas, however, predicted that the Greeks would not win the war unless a warrior named Achilles was on their side.

Hearing a rumor that such a man was living on the island of Scyros, Agamemnon dispatched several men to find him. Among them was Odysseus.

Odysseus offered many fine gifts to the daughters of King Lycomedes. He placed precious jewels and fine cloth before them. All but one daughter was enchanted by Odysseus's gifts. When Odysseus withdrew a spectacular

sword from his belt and placed it in front of the young women, he immediately recognized a glint of delight in the eyes of the daughter who was not
impressed with his other gifts. The young girl seized the sword.

"You are Achilles!" Odysseus declared. "You can no longer live here
under the protection of your mother, who would have you be a girl. You are
destined to be a great fighter on the side of Agamemnon!"

Achilles departed with Odysseus and entered the battlefield of Troy. He
fought bravely and ferociously with his fellow Greeks, who greatly admired
his skills. Achilles even slew Hector, the son of the Trojan king, Priam.

Weary of all the fighting, and respectful of Achilles's kindness in allowing him to reclaim the body of his dead son, King Priam declared a truce.
Unfortunately, Paris was afraid that he would have to return Helen to her
husband. He did not want to see the war come to an end. From a tower
high atop Priam's palace, Paris shot an arrow at Achilles.

The arrow pierced Achilles in the back of his foot. This was the only
spot where the magical river Styx had not touched his body because his
mother had held him by his heel when she dipped him in its water. Soon
after being injured, Achilles died.

The death of the great warrior inspired Agamemnon and Odysseus to
continue to fight. After many battles and many deaths, the Greeks succeeded in defeating the Trojans and rescuing Helen. The exploits of
Achilles in the Trojan War were recorded in "The Iliad," the famous poem
by Homer, which is still enjoyed by readers to this day.

# APHRODITE, GODDESS OF LOVE

 ANY OF THE GREEK GODDESSES WERE WELL-KNOWN for their physical beauty. One was Aphrodite, the goddess of love. She was the subject of many paintings and sculptures throughout history. In Roman mythology she was called Venus.

Aphrodite means "she who was raised from the foam," since the ancient Greeks believed that the goddess appeared out of the ocean waves. She was brought ashore on the island of Cyprus, where she was dressed in finery by the daughters of the goddess Themis.

Aphrodite possessed a magic girdle that had the power to attract any man she desired. With her girdle and matchless beauty, the goddess succeeded in causing much trouble. Many men fell in love with her. The more people praised her good looks, the more vain and powerful she grew. She was not well liked by the other Greek goddesses.

One day Aphrodite wished to conduct a contest to see who among the goddesses was the most beautiful. Hera, the wife of the god Zeus, and Athena, Zeus's daughter, were the other contestants. They chose Paris, the prince of Troy, to be the judge.

The contest was to have dire consequences for everyone. Paris was instructed to give a golden apple to the most beautiful of the three women. He thought carefully about his decision. Hera was indeed quite influential because of her husband. Athena was as wise as she was attractive. And there was no question that Aphrodite possessed incredible beauty. Whom would Paris choose?

In the end he handed the golden apple to Aphrodite. As a reward for choosing her, Aphrodite assisted Paris in kidnapping Helen, the wife of a Greek king. This incident was the cause of the long, terrible Trojan War, in which the Greeks and Trojans fought for ten years.

It was not the only problem that Aphrodite would cause. She forced Eos, the dawn, to fall hopelessly in love with Orion. When she learned that the women of Lemnos would not worship her as a goddess, she placed a terrible curse upon them. They were plagued with a horrible odor that made them undesirable to their husbands. Aphrodite's mischief was legendary.

Although Aphrodite was promised in marriage to the crippled, deformed god Hephaestus, she did not love him and continued to pursue and attract many other gods and men. Poseidon, the god of the sea, tried to win her love. So did Hermes, the messenger god who promised to take her in his chariot around the universe. Even the handsome Apollo, with his talents in music and the arts, attempted to win her for his own. Aphrodite, however, desired none of these gods.

Hephaestus was aware of his wife's behavior. Her attitude toward other men displeased him. He knew he could not persuade the beautiful Aphrodite to be faithful to him alone. He was a short, ugly man with gnarled arms and twisted legs. So he devised a plan to embarrass his wife in front of all the other gods and goddesses of the kingdom of Olympus.

One evening when Hephaestus knew that Aphrodite would visit her latest admirer, Ares, the Greek god of war, he entered their meeting place before they arrived and constructed a special net that would fall down upon the two lovers and trap them. Just as the jealous Hephaestus had planned, Ares and Aphrodite were entangled in the net, unable to escape. The other gods and goddesses came to look at them and ridicule them. This upset Ares very much. He was a great warrior and very proud. He offered to pay a heavy compensation to Hephaestus in return for releasing him from the net. Believing that justice had been served, Hephaestus did just that.

Aphrodite was also embarrassed by her husband's trick. She did not remain angry for long, however. After a short period of time, she was flaunting her beauty in front of everyone, as if nothing had happened.

Of all the men Aphrodite admired, Adonis was her favorite. She had first seen him as a child. Moved by his beauty, Aphrodite gave him to Persephone, the queen of the underworld, to raise. Persephone's affection for the child grew every day. When Aphrodite returned to claim Adonis, who was now a handsome, young man, Persephone refused to give him up. The two goddesses quarreled.

The god Zeus was asked to decide who should have Adonis. In hopes of not upsetting either goddess, Zeus decided to allow Adonis to remain on his own for one-third of the year, then stay with Aphrodite for one-third of the time, and Persephone for the remainder of the year. This arrangement seemed to please the two women. Their happiness would be short-lived.

One day while hunting, young Adonis was attacked by a wild boar. Aphrodite ran to his aid, but she arrived too late to save him. As she hurried to his side, she scratched her foot on a rose bush. Out of respect for her grief for the dying Adonis, the roses on the bush turned from white to crimson red. To this day, throughout Greece, the flowers are a reminder of Aphrodite's great affection for the handsome Adonis.

# The Flight of Daedalus and Icarus

AEDALUS WAS A MASTER CRAFTSMAN WHO LIVED IN Athens. He was known for his talents in architecture and the fine arts. Everyone who saw his work praised him.

Daedalus was also a fine inventor. He invented the chisel and the ax for cutting and shaping wood. He devised the first sails for ships, thus harnessing the power of the winds to move people on the oceans.

Many men worked for Daedalus in his workshop in Athens. It was an honor to be his apprentice. Even his own nephew Talus came to work with him and learn from his skill. Daedalus was only too pleased to share his knowledge with the young people who were eager to work for him. But when he saw just how talented Talus was, and how he drew the attention of his fellow students, Daedalus became jealous.

One day Talus was working on an assignment at the Acropolis in Athens. The Acropolis was an immense temple, built high atop a cliff. As night fell, all of the young workers returned to the workshop, except for Talus. When his absence was noticed, the townspeople began to become suspicious. What had happened to the young boy who had so obviously inherited his uncle's gift of craftsmanship?

Daedalus offered a feeble explanation for Talus's disappearance. He told a court of inquiry that his nephew must have fallen from one of the cliffs of the Acropolis into the sea. The explanation seemed feasible because Talus's body was never recovered. It did not convince the court, however, and Daedalus was banished from the city of Athens. No one knew for certain if he was guilty or not.

Daedalus and his only son, Icarus, traveled to the kingdom of Crete at the invitation of its king, Minos. King Minos knew of Daedalus's reputation as an artist and builder and hoped to use his skills. Daedalus and Icarus agreed to work for Minos.

King Minos demanded a tribute from each of the cities under his rule. Every year seven young men and seven young women were offered as a sacrifice to the Minotaur, a man-eating bull who lived in a maze called the Labyrinth of Cnossus. The maze had been designed by Daedalus for King Minos a long time ago.

One year Daedalus's cousin Theseus was chosen for the sacrifice. When Theseus arrived in Crete with the other victims, King Minos's daughter Adriane saw him and instantly fell in love with him. She could not bear the thought of him being eaten by the horrible Minotaur.

Adriane knew that Theseus and Daedalus were relatives. She knew that Daedalus had created the maze. She appealed to Daedalus to help her save Theseus's life. At first Daedalus refused. He was afraid to go against the wishes of King Minos. After a time, however, he was moved by the pleas of Adriane for the life of his cousin. He confided to her the way in which to slaughter the bull. First he made her swear that she would never divulge the information that he gave her.

Daedalus told Adriane that the bull could be killed if he was stabbed by one of his own horns. Adriane passed the secret to Theseus, who was about to enter the maze.

Once inside, Theseus faced the Minotaur. Its fearsome image caused him to tremble in fear, but he did not forget the instructions that had been passed to him. He waited for the beast to charge him, then grabbed one of its curved horns and snapped it from its head. Before the startled beast could recover from its shock, Theseus thrust the sharp horn into its head, killing it.

Theseus then ran from the maze. He escaped from the island of Crete with Adriane at his side. When King Minos found out what had happened, he was enraged. He knew that Daedalus was the only person who could possibly possess the secrets of the Labyrinth of Cnossus. Thus, he imprisoned Daedalus and Icarus in a tower.

The two men were resigned to live the remainder of their lives in the lonely solitude of the tower cell. After all, they reasoned, they had each other's company. Soon, though, that would not be enough. Daedalus began to scheme of ways to escape from the clutches of King Minos.

Using his extraordinary skills, Daedalus constructed a set of wings for himself and his son. He built them from scraps of wood, tied with strings. He plucked the feathers from two eagles that he had lured to the tower window, and fastened the feathers to the wooden frames with wax. Then he built harnesses for each pair of wings.

Daedalus instructed Icarus to wear the wings.

"Follow me," he told his son. "Be certain not to fly too low, or you may crash into the ocean. Also, be careful not to fly too close to the sun, or the wax will melt from your wings and you will fall from the sky."

Icarus excitedly strapped on his wings and jumped from the tower window after his father. Together they soared over the island of Crete until they saw the vast ocean below them.

The feel of the wind on his face was very exhilarating for Icarus. After so many months of exile in the tower of King Minos, he was at last free!

Filled with a sense of joy, he rose on the strong currents of wind. Higher and higher he climbed into the air, piercing the very clouds with his great golden wings.

Icarus soon forgot his father's warning. Losing all sense of logic, he flew toward the great orb of the sun. The air grew hotter and hotter as he rose upward. To his dismay, Icarus noticed that it was becoming more difficult to fly. He glanced over his shoulder and looked at his wings. One by one they were losing the eagles' feathers as the sun melted the wax that held them to the wooden frame.

Icarus attempted to escape from the sun's heat by gliding lower toward the earth. But it was too late. The feathers began to fall from his wings at an alarming rate. Daedalus watched in horror as his son began to panic. Icarus tumbled toward the earth.

"Save me, Father!" he called to Daedalus.

Daedalus tried to reach him in vain. The young man plunged into the sea. With tears in his eyes and a heavy heart, Daedalus continued on his sad journey. He could not believe that fate would exact such a heavy price for his own freedom. Even to this very day, the water where his beloved son fell is called the Icarian Sea.

# THE WOODEN HORSE OF TROY

 ARLY ONE MORNING WHEN THE FOG HAD NOT YET LIFTED from the walled city of Troy, a sleepy guard looked over the great gates of the town and spied a terrifying sight.

A massive wooden horse, nearly as tall as the gates themselves, was positioned outside. Its cold stare and massive size frightened the guard, who picked up his horn with trembling hands and sounded a warning.

Troy had been under attack by the Greeks for many years. The Greek army had sailed across the sea from their homeland to fight a battle in retaliation for the kidnapping of the Greek queen Helen, by Paris, the prince of Troy.

Stirred by the sound of the guard's horn, the people of Troy woke from their beds. They were always prepared for an attack by the armies of Greece. Today was no different from any other day. They scrambled for safety inside their homes. The men of the Trojan army quickly found their weapons.

The guard called to the people, "Behold a strange object that is left outside our gates!"

When the people heard him, they shook their heads in wonder. What sort of joke was this? They hurried to the top of the high walls and looked down to where the guard was pointing.

To their amazement they saw a replica of a soldier's steed constructed of wood. It was perched on a large wooden platform with wheels. No one spoke.

Cautiously several soldiers climbed down off the walls and approached the statue. A small plaque on its side read, "In honor of Athena."

The Trojans were confused. As far as they could see, in every direction there was a calmness and tranquillity to the landscape that they had not experienced in years. There were no Greek soldiers to be seen; no smoking camp fires, no calls to arms or battle cries.

Inspecting the massive horse from every angle, the soldiers could find nothing unusual on its surface. They prodded and poked it with their spears. They tapped on its hooves. They clamored upon its back, examining its thick neck and stiff mane. Its glass eyes gave no indication of danger. The wooden steed was silent and still in the morning air.

A soldier suggested that the horse was a request for peace from the Greek army, and that the people of Troy should consent to bring it within the gates of the city. The people argued back and forth. Could it be true that the Greeks desired peace after so long and terrible a battle? Finally all agreed to allow the horse to be brought inside, since it was a tribute to the great goddess Athena and appeared to be harmless. Tying a rope to its neck, the soldiers pulled the horse on wheels through the gates of Troy. They displayed it in the city's center. Then the soldiers closed the gates again, still slightly baffled at the unexpected gift left outside their city that morning.

In the evening the Trojans gathered once again around the base of the wooden horse. They lit bonfires and offered tributes to the goddess Athena. They played musical instruments and danced. A great feast was held with food enough for the entire army and townspeople. Vats of wine were opened, and everyone drank and sang. The Trojans were eager for peace and eager for the opportunity to celebrate and be joyful.

After several hours passed, the people began to get tired. They collapsed from drinking too much wine and from dancing too long and hard. They were soon gathered in heaps, here and there, all over the city. The moon rose high in the sky, and the stars shone down on the sleeping revelers of Troy.

As they slumbered, a small wooden panel slid open beneath the belly of the horse. One by one, a group of armed men jumped down onto the platform and crept among the sleeping people. With swords drawn and ready to fight, a fierce contingent of Greek soldiers had stolen into the heart of Troy, undetected.

Horrified, the Trojans woke up from their feast to find themselves under siege. They scrambled to find their weapons, but it was too late. The Greek army clearly had an advantage. They opened the once-protective gates of Troy and allowed their fellow soldiers to enter. They began to slay the Trojans without mercy. Even the city's army could not organize itself in time to defend the people.

When the surprise attack was over, hundreds of Trojan soldiers lay dead within the walls of the great city. Women and children were taken as prisoners of the cunning Greek army. Helen was rescued from her captors and returned to her husband.

To this day the phrase "Trojan Horse" still refers to a suspicious gift that is given to someone in order to trick them.

# HERMES, MESSENGER OF THE GODS

ODAY IT IS EASY TO SEND MESSAGES AROUND THE world. We have electronic mail through our computers, telephones, fax machines, and delivery services like those used by the Post Office. In ancient times, however, messages were conveyed in a different way. They were delivered by heralds, or messengers, people who were hired or appointed to bring special news from one person to another.

Imagine a man dressed in white with a round hat on top of his head. In his hand he carries a staff with white ribbons, and on his feet he wears a pair of sandals with golden wings. This was the messenger Hermes, who was appointed by the most powerful god of Greek mythology, Zeus.

Zeus did not choose Hermes because of his speed or agility. He chose him because Hermes was a clever individual—capable of tricking people in a playful sense. He earned Zeus's admiration through a series of events that unfolded when he was very young.

Hermes was the son of Zeus and Maia, the daughter of Atlas. He was born in a cave on Mount Cyllene in Arcadia. Hermes was anything but an ordinary immortal baby! He was extremely inquisitive and wished to know everything about the world firsthand. Though Maia had wrapped him tightly in a blanket and placed him in his cradle for safekeeping, Hermes managed to escape—undetected by his mother—and set out for adventure.

Descending down the mountain, Hermes saw a herd of white cows. He wanted to have some fun. He decided to play a trick on the owner of the animals. Hermes herded the cows into a pen and tied their hooves with long reed grass that he had gathered from the riverbed. Then he led the cows to a deep ravine, where it would be difficult to find them. With their hooves covered with reeds, no one would be able to tell from what direction they had come.

The herd of white cows belonged to the god Apollo. When he discovered that they were missing, he searched for them throughout the countryside. After several days of searching, he came to a cave. Apollo heard the sound of beautiful music coming from the mouth of the cave and decided to investigate. He found the young Hermes playing a crude instrument made from a tortoiseshell.

"Where did you get that musical instrument?" Apollo asked the young boy.

"I made it!" Hermes declared proudly. "I used the shell of a tortoise and the dried intestines of a white cow for strings. I call it a lyre."

Apollo hesitated for a moment. "The intestines of a white cow? You didn't happen to come upon *my* white cows, did you?"

Hermes was surprised by Apollo's question. He had no idea that the cows belonged to the god.

"I'm sorry," he said, "I didn't know they were yours. I'll lead you to them right away!"

Apollo pretended to be mad at the young boy, but in reality he was quite amused by the child's inventiveness and bravery.

He decided to take Hermes with him to Olympus. Perhaps the god Zeus would enjoy the story of what his son Hermes had done.

Indeed, Zeus was amused by the tale. He found Hermes clever and playful. He admired his sense of adventure. Zeus asked Hermes to be his messenger.

"By this post you will deliver my word to all the gods and goddesses on my behalf. You will protect travelers and merchants." Then the great god smiled as he added, "I hope you will not be too mischievous in your job."

Indeed, Hermes did his job well. Zeus provided him with a special staff that would announce that he was the messenger of Olympus. He also gave him swift sandals for his feet, with a pair of powerful wings attached to each one.

Among his responsibilities, Hermes was in charge of guiding the souls of the dead to the underworld kingdom of Hades. He brought them to the dark land beneath the world, to the banks of the river Styx, where the ferryman Charon would conduct them across the water to their final resting place.

Hermes was also famous for many other things. Not only had he invented the first lyre, but he discovered how to make a fire from dried kindling. He devised a method for measuring and weighing grain. He is credited with creating the alphabet for writing words, as well as a system for studying the stars. He even became the patron of the art of wrestling, for it was said that he brought good luck wherever he traveled.

Throughout his career, however, he still enjoyed a bit of fun whenever he could. With his winning ways and carefully constructed arguments, Hermes found it easy to trick people, though he always told the truth and delivered Zeus's messages in a timely manner.

# LIFE AFTER DEATH: THE UNDERWORLD

EATH WAS NOT THE END OF ONE'S EXISTENCE, according to the ancient Greeks. They believed that when people died, their souls traveled to the underworld. The underworld was not necessarily a place of punishment where the dead were sent to atone for their sins. Rather, it was a final destination for the souls of mortals and immortals alike. Some souls were punished in the underworld, such as those who had displeased or insulted the gods and goddesses during their lives on earth.

There are countless stories in Greek mythology involving the underworld. One of the most famous stories is that of Demeter and Persephone. Demeter was the Greek goddess of agriculture and the harvest. No doubt, she was a very important deity. When her only daughter, Persephone, was abducted by the king of the underworld, Hades, Demeter was filled with grief and sorrow. She withheld her blessing from the earth, and consequently, no crops grew. Finally the great god Zeus intervened in the quest to rescue Persephone by asking Hades to release her to her mother for part of the year. Thus, Persephone remained with Hades to be his queen, except in springtime when she would return to Demeter. This myth helps to explain the seasons of the year. Whenever Persephone was reunited with Demeter, the earth experienced springtime and became green and fertile again. As soon as she took her place on the throne next to her husband, Hades, the world experienced winter and became cold and barren.

To reach Hades's kingdom, the souls of the dead would travel to the river Styx. This river was one of several rivers that flowed through the underworld. The others were known as Acheron, or the river of pain, Cocytus, the river of groans, Phlegethon, the river of fire, and Lethe, the river of forgetfulness. Once on the shores of the Styx, the dead would wait to be ushered into the underworld by the ferryman Charon. Charon was an old, withered man, who piloted his barge with great seriousness. Charon would only accept the souls of those who had been properly buried. He would ask for the fee of an *obolos*, or penny, for the journey. If people had not been buried with the proper rites, or could not pay for the ferry crossing, they were doomed to wander along the riverbanks for one hundred years.

Charon's barge would float on the Styx until it arrived at the entrance to Hades's kingdom. Along the way the souls of the dead would witness many frightening sights. Monsters and beasts, like the Hydra and Chimera, would pose on the riverbanks. The three Furies—Tisiphone, Alecto, and Megaera—might make an appearance to the newly dead. One might also get a glimpse of the hounds of hell, or the Keres, which were fierce canines that pursued those souls who had committed crimes and attempted to escape punishment. It was the responsibility of the Furies to intervene in disputes between mortals and to settle the affairs justly. Thus, they were a powerfully respected trio, even though their black deformed bodies bore bats' wings, and they possessed wriggling snakes for hair.

Charon delivered his charges to the great gates, the entrance to the kingdom of Hades and Persephone. These grotesque, twisted gates were guarded by Cerberus, a dog with three heads and three serpents' tails.

Cerberus made certain that only the dead entered Hades. No living person was allowed in, although there are a few stories of individuals who convinced Charon and Cerberus to allow them to pass through the gates. Charon was also assigned to prevent anyone from leaving.

Certain souls were judged for their behavior on earth. They were brought before a council of the three judges: Minos, Aeacus, and Rhadamanthus. If the dead souls had angered the gods or goddesses during their lifetime, they were sent to an area in Hades known as Tartarus. It was in Tartarus that the gods had their vengeance on the poor unfortunates who had crossed them. Tityus, the giant who had attacked the mother of the god Apollo, was chained and tortured there, as well as Ixion from the kingdom of Thessaly, who had dared to flirt with Zeus's wife Hera.

The souls of those who had lived valiant lives were sometimes sent to the glorious Elysian Fields. Here, they were allowed to exist in harmony and peace, honored for their actions in battle. The many soldiers who had fought during the Trojan War were ushered to the Elysian Fields, where they were rewarded with blue skies, sunshine, ample food to eat, entertainment, and beautiful meadows in which they could wander and roam.

It was unusual for a soul to appear directly to the king of the underworld, Hades. Occasionally a petition, or request for mercy, was brought before Hades's queen, Persephone. She was well-known for her compassionate ways and her ability to convince Hades to intervene on behalf of a troubled soul.

Thus, the world that followed death was as important to the ancient Greeks as the realms of the earth, sea, and sky. The many colorful personalities who dwelled there, and the souls of those who were carried there, are the subjects of many fantastic stories, which are told to this day.

# PHAETHON AND THE SOLAR CHARIOT

 HAETHON WAS THE SON OF THE GREEK GOD APOLLO and the nymph Clymene. His mother had told him many wonderful stories about his ancestry, and about the exploits of the gods and goddesses who dwelled on Olympus. Phaethon loved to hear these stories, for they made him feel important, even royal. He tried to boast about his royal lineage to his schoolmates. No one believed him, however. They looked at the awkward, skinny boy and could see nothing in his appearance or personality that suggested that he was the son of a god. Especially not a god as powerful as Apollo!

Phaethon was deeply troubled by his friends' refusal to accept his stories. He complained to his mother. Clymene felt sorry for her son and tried to console him. "Phaethon," she reassured him, "Apollo is indeed your father. Please, believe me when I tell you this. Do not pay attention to the other children."

Phaethon tried hard to believe what his mother had said. He tried to ignore the jeers of his classmates, but it was too difficult to bear.

"I need proof that I am the son of Apollo," he told his mother one day. "Surely, if he is my father, there must be some way that I can prove who I am."

Clymene thought for a moment and then answered Phaethon.

"Go to the sun Helios, the great god in the sky. He is a witness to all that happens in the universe. He can see everything that transpires as he rides his golden chariot across the skies each day. Surely, he will be able to prove your claims."

Phaethon did as his mother suggested. He climbed to the realm of the sun, high above the world. Helios's palace was a sparkling, dazzling building, colored in every shade and hue of gold imaginable. Jewels and precious stones adorned the walls and roof.

Phaethon ventured inside the palace. There he saw Helios seated on his throne. He was surrounded by the four seasons, the hours of the day, the days of the month, and the months of the year. Each was dressed in magnificent robes with symbols of the measurements they represented. Spring was crowned with tiny green buds; summer in glorious red and yellow blooms. The months of November and December wore heavy fur gowns with halos of ice and light around their heads. Phaethon had never seen such a sight!

Overcome by all the beauty around him, the young boy could barely speak. Helios smiled at him, and asked him why he had ventured to his palace. Finally Phaethon took a deep breath and explained what he wished the sun god to do for him.

"You have my word, as a witness to all that happens in the universe, that you are the son of the god Apollo," Helios told him.

Phaethon was not satisfied with the god's reply. "Helios," he pleaded, "it is not enough that you say I am who I am. I must have proof that I can show to others. I would ask you if I could drive your great chariot for one day in order to show my friends that I am indeed the son of a god."

Helios was shocked at Phaethon's bold request.

"This I cannot do for you, Phaethon," he told him. "My steeds are swift and dangerous. They are accustomed to my skilled hands. I am afraid of what would happen if I entrusted them to you."

Phaethon was filled with sorrow. His eyes filled with tears.

"Then you cannot help me, Helios," he answered sadly. "Without such proof, no one will believe my story."

Helios thought for a moment. Although it was a difficult decision to make, he eventually agreed to allow Phaethon to drive his chariot.

"Just for one day!" he cautioned the boy. "And you must do everything I tell you to do. You must follow my instructions very carefully. Do not be foolish or attempt to do anything on your own. I follow the same path every morning. You will do the same and follow the constellations that I instruct you to follow."

"I will!" Phaethon agreed joyously. "I will do as you say!"

Helios led Phaethon to the stables where he kept his horses. He lifted the boy into his magnificent chariot and handed him the reins. Once again he instructed Phaethon to be careful.

When it was time to depart, Phaethon took control of the sun god's chariot and began his famous journey. He watched for the constellations in the sky and carefully steered the golden chariot along its path.

Below him Phaethon could see the houses in his village. He cried out to his friends so that they would look up and witness the wonderful thing that he was doing that morning.

However, no one could see who was driving the sun chariot, for it was too high in the sky. Phaethon grew angry. How could he make them see him?

An idea came to him. If he drove the horses lower in the sky, perhaps his friends would recognize him. He took the reins and told the horses to descend closer to the earth.

The horses did as they were instructed. They drew closer to the earth. As they did, several trees and houses caught fire, for the chariot of the sun was too close to the ground. Phaethon saw what was happening and tried to pull the horses back. But it was too late. The steeds were now well aware that Phaethon did not know what he was doing. They rose and fell in the sky like two wild steeds, burning up towns and villages as they went along.

Phaethon called to Helios to help him. There was nothing Helios could do. He called to his horses, but they would not listen to him. Finally the god Zeus saw what was happening and threw a thunderbolt at the chariot to stop it. The bolt struck the chariot, and Phaethon was thrown from his seat. He fell many feet to his death.

Phaethon's mother ran to her son's side and cradled him in her arms. Several nymphs came to console her on the loss of her beloved Phaethon.

Helios was also overcome by grief at the death of the young boy. Sadly he caught up with his golden chariot and subdued the wild horses by shielding their eyes with a blanket and speaking softly to them.

It is believed that the driest deserts on our earth were created during the ride of the careless youth Phaethon in the chariot of the sun god, Helios.

# IN THE BEGINNING— CREATION OF THE WORLD

 HE ANCIENT GREEKS ASKED THEMSELVES MANY OF THE same questions we ask ourselves today. "How did I get here?" "Who were the first people?" "Who made the stars and the sky and the world?" While we may rely on scientific knowledge to help us answer some of those questions, the Greeks, like many of our ancestors, invented stories, or myths, which explained the creation of humans, the world, and the natural events that took place in our universe.

The Greeks believed that at the beginning of time, there was nothing. That is, the universe was in a state of chaos. Chaos is a word that means great confusion. The universe did not obey any laws or logic. Nothing organic existed anywhere.

One story of creation stated that a great black bird called Nyx laid an egg in the darkness. From this egg came Heaven, Earth, and Love. Heaven and Earth were joined and gave birth to twelve gods and goddesses who ruled the universe.

Another version stated that from the state of chaos, great clouds of gases swirled through the universe. Massive and ghostly, they were divided into strata, or layers. The uppermost layers were destined to become the sky.

The middle layers would one day form the earth. The lower layers would become the underworld.

The layers became more and more defined, giving birth to Uranus (sky), Gaia (earth), and Erebus (underworld). From this organization the element of Eros, or love, was born. It was Eros that gave to the universe its meaning, or force.

The three divisions each created the world we know today. Gaia formed the mountains and fields, as well as the vast oceans. Erebus created Night, who in turn gave birth to light. The creation of the celestial bodies in the sky, such as the sun, the moon, and the stars, came much later.

Through the assistance of Eros, the Sky and the Earth married. This union would produce twelve children, or Titans, who would rule the universe. Their reign would last until Cronus, a mighty Titan, would cause the downfall of his own race, and would therefore allow the rise of the Olympian gods like Zeus, Hades, and Poseidon.

The union of the Sky and the Earth created many other marvels, as well as the Titans. It created the Cyclops, or storm-spirits, Arges, Steropes, and Brontes. Three fierce monsters with hundreds of hands were also given birth. They were known as Cottus, Briareus, and Gyges.

The task of creating soon tired Gaia, who appealed to her son Cronus to help her. She wished for him to scare away his father, Uranus. She knew that Cronus was brave and fearless and would accomplish the feat. She also knew that Cronus wished to be the father of all creation.

Cronus attacked Uranus with a knife and warned him to keep away from Gaia. The blood from Uranus's wounds fell upon the world. Giants, nymphs, and all types of creatures populated the earth from the drops of blood.

Cronus was delighted with what he had done. He desired to have the power of the universe to himself. He imprisoned his brothers, and with

Rhea, a daughter of Gaia, he produced six children. These children would one day become the Olympian gods, ruled by Zeus.

When Gaia learned what Cronus had done, she became angry. She cursed her son, telling him that one day one of his offspring would overthrow him. This prediction so frightened Cronus that he killed all of his children, but one. Rhea managed to hide the infant Zeus. It was Zeus who grew up to lead a successful rebellion against his father, Cronus. His brothers eventually helped him rule the universe: Hades was the god of the underworld; Poseidon, the god of the seas; and Zeus took his place as master of earth and sky. A new generation had been born.

The Greeks have many stories of the creation of humans. In some cases it is just assumed that humans always existed. One story, the story of the god Prometheus, states that he took some clay and created the human form. Another story relates how humans were the result of the union between the nymphs and the gods and goddesses. The human Phoroneus was the child of the river god Inachus and Melia, a tree nymph.

No matter which story is told, the existence of humans in the universe affected the actions of the gods and goddesses. They were constantly intervening in the lives of mortals, either by helping them or punishing them. It was the god Prometheus who granted the gift of fire to human beings. Zeus created a woman named Pandora to unleash disease and unhappiness on the world. He wished to punish the humans, who he believed were becoming too mighty.

Though we may find the Greek myths of creation and the first humans amusing as stories, they offer us explanations for all of the phenomenon in the universe. The concepts of day and night, the sun and moon, rain, thunder, life after death, and love are told in these great tales.

# ATHENA AND THE SPIDER

 HE GOD ZEUS WISHED TO MARRY METIS, A GODDESS from the Titan race. Metis tried to elude the powerful god by turning herself into a fish and then an eagle. Each time, Zeus was able to find her. Finally Metis relented and married him.

Zeus went to the Oracle at Delphi, a shrine to Apollo, to ask the priests and priestesses to foretell his future. Zeus was pleased to hear that a daughter born to him would be a brilliant and gifted child who would bring him much glory. However, he was very anxious when the seers told him that Metis would also bear him a son that would someday overthrow him.

When Zeus learned that Metis was pregnant with their first child, he panicked. He followed Metis as she took her morning walk in the countryside. He called to his unsuspecting wife and asked her to come to him. Metis ran to Zeus, expecting him to enfold her in his arms in a loving embrace. Instead, Zeus flew into a terrible rage and swallowed Metis whole. Although his actions were appalling, Zeus found comfort in knowing that Metis would never bear a child stronger than he.

Zeus sat down on his throne to rest. His head began to throb. The more he tried to relax, the more his head hurt. The pain was so bad that Zeus could hardly see. Hours went by, and still the headache did not subside. The physicians could not help him with his terrible headache. Finally, in desperation, Zeus took an ax to his head to relieve the pressure.

From the spot where the ax broke through his skull, a fully formed young woman sprang from his head. Her hair was golden blond and fell in curls at her shoulders. She possessed crystal-blue eyes and high cheekbones. The mysterious woman was as intelligent as she was beautiful. Her presence stunned everyone in Zeus's palace.

Despite his fear that a child would someday grow to be more powerful, Zeus could not reject his daughter. He called her Athena.

Athena was a skillful artisan who could weave fine cloth. She instructed people in how to make axes, wheels, plows for the fields, and sails for ships. She was asked to sit in judgment at trials because her wisdom was prized among her companions.

One day Athena journeyed to Lydia, a land of exceptional weavers who knew how to create the most beautiful purple dye anyone had ever seen. Athena had heard that a woman from that village named Arachne had created a magnificent tapestry that told the strory of the gods and goddesses of greece. They were brilliant images of the sea god, Poseidon, riding the waves in his golden chariot, and the goddess Demeter searching for her only daughter, Persephone, in the darkness of the underworld.

People in the village remarked at how the figures portrayed in the Arachne's tapestry were so lifelike. Athena had come to see them for herself.

Arachne was proud of her achievement—perhaps a little bit too proud! She grew vain as she received praise from the villagers. But when one of them remarked that Arachne's talent was a gift from the goddess Athena, also well-known for her skill as a weaver, Arachne flew into a rage.

"I can weave a tapestry that is more beautiful than anything that Athena can produce," she boasted.

Although Athena was wise, she could not bear this self-centered comment from a mere mortal. Additionally, when she saw how grand the tapestry really was, she was plagued with jealousy. As one would expect from the daughter of the passionate god Zeus, Athena seized the tapestry from the wall where it was displayed and shredded it into a thousand tiny pieces.

Arachne regretted her boastful words. She cried when she saw how the goddess had destroyed her work of art. Heartbroken, she disappeared into the woods.

In time Athena's anger subsided. She realized that Arachne was only human in displaying her emotions of pride and vanity. She decided to search for the missing Arachne and forgive her.

In the deep woods Athena spied a horrible sight. Hanging from the gnarled branch of an oak tree was the body of Arachne, who had hung herself in sorrow. Athena was overcome by feelings of guilt. Quietly she took Arachne's lifeless body from the limb of the tree and placed it on the ground.

Stroking Arachne's hair, Athena placed a spell upon her. The dead woman's body shriveled beneath her flowing garments until it was no longer visible. In its place, a tiny creature with eight legs crawled from the folds of the dress. Arachne had become a spider!

"You will weave with thread finer than anything else in this world," Athena promised her. And from that time on, spiders have inhabited our world, spinning their intricate webs in fields and corners everywhere for us to admire.

# DEUCALION AND PYRRHA SURVIVE THE FLOOD

ANY CULTURES THROUGHOUT THE WORLD HAVE A story concerning a great flood that covered the earth. Here is how the ancient Greeks explained it.

The powerful god Zeus looked down from his home on Mount Olympus and watched the human race develop. First there was a time known as the "Golden Age." All humans were at peace with each other. There was no fighting or quarrels of any kind. Therefore, there was no need for weapons. The earth was abundant with tall trees, pure lakes, and fields of grain and corn to eat. The climate of the earth was temperate, allowing every variety of flower to blossom throughout the year.

As time passed, Zeus divided the year into seasons, creating a period of cold and ice known as winter. People had to find ways to stay warm when winter was upon them. They took shelter in caves and constructed dwellings to protect themselves from the cold. It was necessary to plant seeds because the soil no longer yielded crops without the help of humans. This was known as the "Silver Age."

The "Bronze Age" followed next. This was a time of unrest and strife on earth. People began to disagree about things. They built forts to protect themselves and armed the forts with weapons. Still, the Bronze Age was not as bad as the next era that appeared on earth.

The people who lived during the "Iron Age" forgot the wonderful gifts they had received from earth. People lost their respect for the land and cut down trees faster than young trees could grow and replace them.

Men and women did not share the fruits of their harvest and became concerned with possessions. War broke out throughout the land, and children went hungry.

Disgusted, the gods abandoned the human race. Even Astraea, the goddess of innocence and purity, left her place on earth and retreated sadly to the skies, where she became the constellation Virgo.

All of this angered Zeus so much that he decided to destroy the world. He wished to create a new race of people. Zeus went before the council of gods at Mount Olympus and announced his plan.

"I will send a thunderbolt to the earth and burn it," Zeus declared.

The gods warned Zeus that such a fire would not only destroy the earth, but would touch the heavens, as well, and cause the skies to burn out of control.

"Then I will send water to destroy the earth," Zeus decided. "I will flood the earth until the fishes swim among the tops of trees and mountains."

And so he did.

Zeus called upon his brother Poseidon, the god of the seas, to help him. Poseidon pointed his trident, a three-pronged staff, at the earth and caused the oceans to rise high above the land. Rivers flooded their banks, and the skies were black with storm clouds. The clouds dumped torrential rains on the earth.

Everything on the surface of the world was covered with water. Buildings and homes were washed away. Crops in the field were drowned, and birds had no place to rest during their flight, since the trees were well below the water.

The only mountain peak that remained above the rising waters of the floods was Parnassus. On top of Parnassus, Deucalion and his wife clung to life. Zeus saw them and felt pity for them. He knew they had lived good lives and had remained faithful to the gods.

Zeus instructed Poseidon to command his waters to recede. Then Zeus dispelled the dark clouds from the skies and allowed the sun to shine on the land.

As the earth slowly returned to normal, Deucalion and Pyrrha found themselves alone. There were no other humans left alive after the flood.

"What do you desire?" Zeus asked the pair.

"We wish to have companionship," they answered.

"Throw the bones of your mother over your shoulders and you will find what you need," Zeus replied.

Pyrrha was horrified by Zeus's words. She said to Deucalion, "We cannot dig up the bones of our mother! How can Zeus ask us to do this?"

Deucalion thought for a while and then answered his wife.

"Zeus is talking about our mother, the earth," said Deucalion. "Take stones and sticks, for these are truly the bones of our mother, and throw them over your shoulder."

Deucalion and Pyrrha tossed stones and sticks over their shoulders. Behind them Zeus transformed the objects into humans. A new race of people was born.

# THE FAMILY OF GODS AT OLYMPUS

HE ANCIENT GREEKS WORSHIPPED A FAMILY OF GODS who ruled the universe. The gods lived atop Mount Olympus in northern Greece. It was believed to be the highest point in the world.

Olympus was truly a paradise. It was never cold there. It never rained. Fragrant flowers grew everywhere, and the strains of beautiful music filled the air, day and night. The entrance to Olympus was a "gate of clouds," which was tended to by the goddesses of the seasons. The gates opened to allow the gods and goddesses to journey to earth and return to Olympus.

Of the gods who dwelled on Olympus, no one was more powerful than Zeus. He lived in a magnificent palace where all the other gods gathered at his request. In his great hall the gods feasted on nectar and ambrosia, a delicious food that was only eaten by those who were immortal.

Zeus's architects created magnificent buildings as dwellings for the gods. Golden shoes for the gods and goddesses were fashioned by Zeus's smiths. Even the horses that pulled the chariots of Olympus were shod in brass shoes that gleamed as they trotted along the streets.

The gods were dressed splendidly in gold and silver robes. They lived in their own palaces, surrounded by magical gardens and streams. The gods liked to travel to earth and become involved in the lives of humans. Occasionally they protected people from danger or misfortune.

Among the most powerful gods that surrounded Zeus were Poseidon, god of the sea, Hephaestus, the smith, Ares, the god of war, Hermes, the messenger of Zeus, and Apollo, the god of music. Athena, goddess of wisdom, and Hera, Zeus's wife, also lived there along with Aphrodite, the goddess of love, Artemis, the goddess of the hunt, Hestia, the goddess of the home, and Demeter, the goddess of agriculture.

There were also lesser gods who gathered at the request of Zeus in Olympus, such as Hades, god of the underworld, and Pan, a goat-horned, goat-legged god of the countryside.

Where did these powerful gods come from?

It was believed that at one time the universe was in a state of chaos, or confusion. From this state, Mother Earth appeared. She had a consort, or mate, Uranus, who created everything in the universe.

With Uranus, Mother Earth bore twelve children known as the "Titans." Of these children, the youngest son, Cronus, became a leader in an uprising against his own father, Uranus.

Cronus took Rhea as his wife. He feared that their children would one day overthrow him as he had done to his father. To prevent this, Cronus swallowed each of his children after they were born. Rhea managed to save one child from Cronus's horrible actions. She took her baby Zeus to Mount Lycaeum and hid him in a cave.

Cronus became suspicious. He searched for Rhea's child. Zeus was moved from place to place to save his life. Finally Rhea decided to wrap a heavy stone in a blanket and present it to Cronus as her baby. Cronus, thinking that he had found Rhea's child, swallowed the stone and was convinced that he was safe from the threat of an uprising by his offspring.

Zeus grew into a powerful god. He was the god of the sky, the thunder, and the rain. He became known as the first of a race of new gods. Zeus took Hera as his wife, and together they had many children. Zeus also had many children with other wives. His children included the gods and goddesses who lived with him in Olympus.

Despite his wisdom, Zeus often fell prey to jealousy and fits of rage. He tried to keep his children in line and often quarreled with Hera. Zeus enjoyed the company of beautiful women, and this angered Hera. He enjoyed teasing Hera. Once he created a statue of a woman that he placed in his chariot as he drove through the streets of Olympus.

Thinking that her husband was being unkind to her, Hera stopped the chariot and threw herself at the woman she believed to be Zeus's latest love. How foolish Hera felt when she discovered that the woman was made of stone!

When humans became greedy and selfish, Zeus decided to flood the earth and create a new race of people. From his throne on Mount Olympus, Zeus ruled the universe with passion and anger, delight and concern. Many myths tell of the colorful deeds and enormous power of the father of the Greek gods.

# HERACLES AND THE AMAZONS

 HERE ARE MANY STORIES OF THE LEGENDARY HERO Heracles. He was the son of Zeus and Alcmene, a mortal. Despite his father's lineage, Heracles was only a mortal, too. His incredible exploits, however, have made him one of the most famous figures in Greek mythology. To the Romans he was known as Hercules.

Heracles demonstrated his remarkable strength at a very early age. Jealous of Alcmene's position, Zeus's wife Hera tried to gain revenge by placing two deadly snakes in baby Heracles's cradle. The tiny infant crushed the serpents with his hands.

When he set off to make his way in the world as a young man, Heracles was confronted by two figures, Pleasure and Virtue. They each offered him the opportunity to choose a life based on instant gratification, or one that entailed sacrifice and courage. Heracles chose the latter.

This decision would affect the rest of Heracles's life. In the end it would change his destiny. But at the time it was difficult to see what impact his choice would have on his life.

Heracles married the daughter of Creon, the king of Thebes. He was content to live with the lovely Megara and their children. Hera, however, was not content with the way the hero's life was unfolding. She wished to introduce him to misery.

Hera placed a spell on Heracles that drove him insane. He did not recognize his own family. Thinking they were an enemy force that wished him harm, he slaughtered his wife and children. When he finally discovered what he had done, Heracles was crushed by feelings of intense grief. He journeyed to the Oracle at Delphi, a magical shrine, to ask one of the priestesses for assistance.

The priestess instructed Heracles to go to the city of Tiryns and present his services to the king, Eurystheus, for twelve years. Although the sentence would be full of danger, Heracles was happy and willing to seek forgiveness for the unspeakable act he had committed.

King Eurystheus was a weak and foolish king. He put many tasks before Heracles, each one more dangerous and challenging than the one before. Several times he tricked Heracles into believing that he had not done his service properly or within the rules that the sly, old king had determined. Yet, each time Heracles returned to Eurystheus to complete another service.

To his dismay, the king could not stump Heracles. When he asked the hero to slay a man-eating lion, Heracles returned from the task with the skin of the deadly beast wrapped around him like a cloak. At the king's request Heracles captured the golden-horned deer of Cerynea, and the wild boar of Erymanthus. He slaughtered the man-eating birds of Stymphalus. Heracles did battle with the ferocious Hydra, a sea serpent with thousands of snakes coming from its head. He cleaned out the stables of King Augeas, removing years of stench and waste from the area, permitting crops to grow in the barren, trash-laden fields surrounding the stable house.

On the island of Crete, Heracles was asked to remove a large and menacing bull who had escaped from its pen and was killing innocent residents with its sharp horns. Heracles bravely tackled the bull and snapped its neck.

The Amazons were a race of warrior women who lived along the shores of the Black Sea. They were known for their cunning ability to do battle, even with the most ferocious enemies. Heracles approached their homeland. One of the Amazons rode toward him on a magnificent white steed. It was a messenger of the queen, Hippolyte. She asked Heracles to follow her.

Heracles was astounded by the appearance of Queen Hippolyte. She was very tall, wearing an iron crown on her head, and a bronze girdle around her hips. Her expression was stern and serious.

"Why have you come here?" she asked Heracles.

"I have been sent on a mission to retrieve your girdle," he told her.

"I do not wish for there to be war in my lands," Queen Hippolyte announced, "therefore, I will give you the object that you seek, and you will leave my kingdom peaceably."

Then Hippolyte took off her girdle and handed the armor to Heracles. He thanked her and started to leave, but not before the goddess Hera could cause some mischief. Disguised as an Amazon, she convinced the other women that Heracles was sent to kill Hippolyte. The women warriors mounted their horses and set out after Heracles.

Fortunately, Hipppolyte found out about Hera's foolish trick, and convinced her troops that Heracles did not mean her any harm. They retreated back to their homeland with the tall, beautiful queen of the Amazons, while Heracles continued on his many quests.

# MONSTERS OF GREEK MYTHOLOGY

 MAGINE THAT YOU ARE INVITED TO VISIT THE GREEK gods and goddesses at their home high atop Mount Olympus. You find everything in this special world exciting and breathtaking. The music playing lightly in the air is the sweetest you have heard. The food is so satisfying and so delicious that you can't wait for the next course to arrive from the kitchens. Sweet nectar is poured from bejeweled chalices. There are overstuffed chairs and stools for you to sit on and rest your feet.

As you walk along the streets of Olympus, admiring the spectacular architecture and fragrant gardens, suddenly someone taps you on the shoulder. You turn to face a young man who asks you for directions. Glancing down at his feet, you notice that he is walking on hooves! Although he is a man from the waist up—his lower body is that of a horse! You have come in contact with a centaur—a creature who is half human, half horse.

If Olympus had a zoo, it would be filled with other amazing beings, as well. There would be sea nymphs and wood nymphs, fairies and ogres, great horned monsters and tiny elves.

Perhaps you would find yourself staring at Cerberus, the three-headed dog who guards the gates of the dark underworld. Next to him would be the fascinating and frightening Chimera—a beast who is half goat and half lion, with the tail of a powerful viper. Above you the silent air is disturbed by the thrashing of mighty wings. It is only Pegasus, the flying horse.

He warns you to take care not to stand too close to the Hydra, a beast with thousands and thousands of deadly snakes writhing from its hair. Then he flies high in the sky to pursue the Harpies, birdlike creatures who possess the faces of ugly, old women. The Harpies enjoy stealing food from people and tormenting them. They scatter, however, when they see Pegasus coming for them.

The beasts and monsters of Greek mythology had many powers. Though they were not as powerful as the gods and goddesses who dwelled on Olympus, they could definitely disturb the plans and actions of the gods and mortals.

Among the monsters you might encounter would be the Gorgons. These were three-headed females with huge razor-sharp teeth, needlelike claws, and snakes for hair. If someone dared to look directly at them, they turned the unfortunate observer into stone. Most famous of the Gorgons was Medusa, who had once been a beautiful woman. From her severed head the swift Pegasus was born.

When humans could not find a suitable solution to a problem, they might call upon the avenging Furies, who lived in the underworld of Hades. Alecto, Megaera, and Tisiphone would often achieve justice in a difficult situation. The Furies looked like black dogs with bats' wings. They carried whips, which they used when someone broke the law.

High atop the mountains of ancient Greece, one might stumble upon the gigantic nests of creatures called Griffins. The Griffin was a monster with the body of a lion and the head and wings of an eagle. Its back was covered with long feathers. Since Griffins liked to build their nests near deposits of gold, they were often followed and hunted by plunderers and thieves. It was not easy for them to hide their rooks from the greedy.

Near the source of the great Nile River lived a nation of very small people known as Pygmies. A Pygmy was only thirteen inches tall. Though they were small in stature, the Pygmies were fierce warriors. They even did battle with the Greek hero Heracles. They did not win, however, for Heracles managed to subdue them by entrapping them in a lion's skin.

The Sphinx is certainly one of the most famous monsters in Greek mythology. With the body of a lioness and the upper torso of a woman, the Sphinx would lie quietly in the sand, waiting for her next victim. It was customary for her to pose a riddle to whoever happened to venture too near to her. The clever Sphinx often outwitted those she challenged. According to legend she was unable to trick a man called Oedipus who happened to come upon her one day.

The Sphinx asked Oedipus if he knew what thing walked on four feet in the morning, two feet in the afternoon, and three feet in the evening. Oedipus looked around him at the skeletons of those who had not guessed correctly the answer to the riddle. He thought for a moment, then responded to the great beast.

"It is man who first crawls on his hands and legs when he is a baby. When he is grown, he walks on two feet. But in his old age he may have need of a cane or walking stick, and so walks on 'three legs.'"

The Sphinx had no choice but to let the clever Oedipus continue on his way, for he had answered her riddle.

Be certain not to wander into the land of the Sphinx, unless you are prepared to take up her challenge. Then, you can only hope that the winged horse Pegasus will be prepared to swoop down and rescue you if you happen to answer wrong!

# ORPHEUS IN THE LAND OF THE DEAD

RPHEUS, SON OF THE GOD APOLLO, LOVED TO PLAY his lyre, a small, stringed instrument that resembled a harp. The strains of his beautiful music enchanted both gods and mortals. It calmed the wild beasts and birds. Even the streams and rocks absorbed the wonderful noise like warm sunshine.

Apollo blessed the marriage of his son to the lovely wood nymph, Eurydice. Although Eurydice and Orpheus were very much in love, Eurydice occasionally grew weary of the great palace in which they lived. She longed for the fragrant fields and woodlands of her home.

One day, while playing with her sister nymphs in a grove of trees, Eurydice was spotted by the god of the hunt, Aristaeus. Upon seeing the beautiful woman, Aristaeus dropped his bow and arrow, forgetting all about the agile deer he was pursuing.

"You are every bit as wondrous as I was told!" Aristaeus declared to Eurydice.

Eurydice was startled by the handsome god, who had appeared suddenly in the woods. She blushed.

"Please, sir," she responded. "I am not flattered by your speech. Be on your way."

Aristaeus could not believe his ears. "You dare speak that way to a god?"

"Sir," Eurydice said matter-of-factly, "you may be a god, but my husband is Orpheus, son of Apollo. He would not be pleased by your lack of manners."

Aristaeus laughed. "I am not afraid of Orpheus, who loves music above all things." He moved toward Eurydice.

Frightened by his boldness, Eurydice fled into the woods. She ran as fast as her nimble legs could carry her. But it was difficult to elude Aristaeus, who was used to chasing prey through the thick underbrush.

Eurydice looked for a place to hide. She climbed a rocky slope and jumped down into a clearing, alarming many birds, which quickly took to flight. She did not look back at the figure of Aristaeus. Finally, overcome with fatigue, Eurydice slowed down long enough to realize that the god of the hunt was no longer pursuing her.

She fell into a heap on the ground. In no time her eyes closed with sleep.

Eurydice did not see the tiny viper that crawled among the surrounding rocks. She did not feel his bite on her bared leg. Within minutes the viper's deadly poison spread through Eurydice's body.

Orpheus was concerned that his wife did not return from the fields. He paced through the great halls of his palace. Finally he commanded several servants to comb the countryside in search of her.

With terrible sadness the servants returned the body of Eurydice to Orpheus. The sight of his dead wife caused Orpheus to become filled with inconsolable grief. Nothing could calm him. Day after day he played sad songs on his lyre inside the palace walls. He would not eat, nor could he sleep.

"I must go to the underworld and retrieve my one true love," Orpheus declared to his father.

Apollo was greatly distressed at his son's reaction. "Don't be foolish, Orpheus," he told him. "You cannot undo what has been done. Leave Eurydice to the land of the dead."

But Orpheus did not listen to his father's counsel. Taking his lyre, he left his comfortable palace and began the long journey to Hades, the under-world. Near the Ionian Sea, Orpheus found a deep chasm that led him to the river Styx. It was here that he found the ferryman Charon, who carried the dead across the river to the land of Hades.

Charon refused his services to Orpheus. "I can only carry the dead," he told him.

But Orpheus was not discouraged from his quest. Fueled by his longing for his wife, Eurydice, Orpheus began to play sweet songs on his lyre. So touching were the songs he played, that neither Charon nor the creatures that dwelled in the land of darkness could resist their effect.

Orpheus boarded Charon's ferry to the throne of Persephone, queen of the underworld. Even she was moved by the notes that danced from his lyre.

"Please return my wife to me," Orpheus begged Persephone. "I cannot imagine life without her."

Persephone thought of the consequences of such a bold move. Finally she gave in.

"Take Eurydice back with you to the land of the living," she told Orpheus. "But remember my warning to you. If during your ascent to the land of light you turn around and look at your wife, she will be forced to return to Hades."

From the shadows of hell, Eurydice was reunited with Orpheus. She held him to her and was filled with joy.

"Follow me back to our home," Orpheus instructed her.

The two began the long climb to their home. Eurydice could not climb as quickly as Orpheus. She struggled to keep up with him.

Near the opening that led from Hades to the world of the living, Orpheus was overcome by feelings of great joy and accomplishment. He had managed to rescue his beloved wife from the jaws of death. He felt the faint touch of sunlight on his skin, and the promise of their life together.

In his excitement Orpheus reached back behind him for Eurydice's hand. "Look, look!" he exclaimed to her. "We are almost there!"

But when he turned to encourage Eurydice to come quickly to the light, Orpheus realized what he had done. The figure of Eurydice, slightly behind him, turned to a pale shadow. She fell back into the horrible chasm, which cut sharply into the earth, until he could no longer see her.

Orpheus raced after the vision of Eurydice. When he again reached the shores of the river Styx, he told Charon what had occurred. But this time Charon was not moved by his story. He refused to bring Orpheus a second time to Hades. Heartbroken, Orpheus exited the underworld without his wife.

# TROUBLE AND HOPE: PANDORA'S BOX

 HE GREAT GOD ZEUS WAS THE MOST POWERFUL GOD in the Greek pantheon, or family of gods that ruled the universe. Despite his wisdom and compassion for his creations, Zeus could be jealous, petty, and cruel. He punished his wife Hera for plotting to dethrone him, and was equally harsh with his sons and daughters.

When the god Prometheus angered Zeus by giving the gift of fire to humans on earth, Zeus had him chained to a cliff where an eagle would viciously attack him each day. But even this punishment did not satisfy Zeus, for he wished to inflict more pain on the humans, who now owned the secret of fire.

Zeus thought of a very clever way to get revenge on the mortals and teach them a lesson. He asked his son, the god Hephaestus, who was an artisan to the gods, to sculpt a woman from clay. When Hephaestus had finished, Zeus took the sculpture to the goddess Athena and asked her to breathe life into it. Zeus called his creation "Pandora," or "all-endowed." From every god of Olympus, Pandora received many favorable gifts, such as the ability to sew, to entertain, and to cook. She was given beauty, grace, and charm. Her wardrobe was woven from precious metals and jewels, and flowers adorned her long blond hair.

Zeus was involved in a long-standing feud with the old gods of Greece, or Titans. Part of his plot to teach the humans a lesson included taking revenge on the brother of Prometheus who was a Titan. Epimetheus was dim-witted and easily flattered, unlike his brother.

Zeus instructed Hermes, the messenger god, to deliver Pandora to Epimetheus. Before he sent her, however, he gave the beautiful woman a box, or a "dowry," which contained untold wealth.

"Do not open this box, Pandora," Zeus told her. "It is your dowry, which contains many, many treasures."

Pandora excitedly took the box from Zeus. She wondered what magnificent things it contained.

Hermes led Pandora to Epimetheus. When he first saw her, Epimetheus was overcome by Pandora's many charms. He could hardly take his eyes away from her. He lost all sense of logic. He forgot that he had been warned by his brother, Prometheus, not to accept gifts from Zeus. He even forgot that it was Zeus who held his poor brother in captivity, bound to the jagged cliffs above the sea. Epimetheus was too overtaken by the beauty and grace of Pandora.

Pandora was briefly occupied with all the attention she received from Epimetheus. She enjoyed the flattery and the compliments that he gave her, but the thrill of his advances did not remain with her for long. Soon she tired of it all. She began to think of the box that Zeus had given her. She wondered what it contained and why she was not allowed to open it. After all, it was her dowry. Didn't she have the right to show Epimetheus what was inside?

Innocently Pandora began to play with the lid of the box, gently prying it loose with her fingers. She wiggled the lock. Nothing happened. Finally, in frustration, she gave the lid a strong tug. It popped open.

Strange sounds and smells filled the air. Black-winged creatures poured forth from the box like a swarm of locust. They filled the land and sky and spread across the water until the earth was darkened with their presence. The creatures were called "agony" and "pain," "suffering" and "regret." The earth had not known these things until Pandora opened the box that Zeus had given her. Now there was hunger and suffering everywhere. Children cried, and husbands and wives quarreled bitterly.

When Pandora realized what was happening, she tried to close the lid of the box. It was difficult to do, but after hours of struggling with it, she managed to slam it shut. Unfortunately, it seemed that all the ills of the world had escaped.

Epimetheus was horrified when he realized what Pandora had done. "Now no one will remember me as the brother of Prometheus who gave the world the gift of fire! They will only think of me as your husband—the husband of the woman who gave the world all its pain and misery!" Epimetheus was no longer charmed by Pandora. He left her alone.

However, Pandora looked closely at the box. One thing was not released from its contents. Just inside the lid a glimmer of hope remained imprisoned in the box. Pandora knew that it was important that she keep the lid sealed so that humans would never lose the gift of hope.

Looking down at her from his home with the gods, Hephaestus took pity on his lovely creation. He traveled to the earth and took Pandora back with him to Olympus.

# POSEIDON, GOD OF THE SEA

HE SEA WAS OF SPECIAL IMPORTANCE TO THE ANCIENT Greeks, who fished in its waters and sailed from the rocky coasts in great ships. They believed that the god Poseidon ruled over the waters of the world, riding the waves in a horse-drawn chariot.

When Zeus, Hades, and Poseidon overthrew their father, Cronus, they decided to divide the universe into kingdoms of water, earth, and sky. Poseidon chose the sea; Zeus chose the sky; and Hades, the earth.

Others had ruled the sea before Poseidon. Oceanus had created the great river that circled the earth and lapped the shores of ancient Greece. Nereus, a kindly, old man, was another god who helped sailors in peril. He was the father of the sea nymphs, beautiful creatures who dwelled beneath the salty waves.

Poseidon, however, was the greatest ruler of the oceans. Off the coast of Euboea, south of the city of Athens, Poseidon lived in his palace under the sea. Made of mother-of-pearl, glistening seashells, and dark-colored coral, the palace rose from the ocean floor like a beautiful jewel. Its white turrets gleamed in the crystal-blue waters. Portraits of fierce sea monsters hung on the castle's walls.

Poseidon visited the creatures of his kingdom in his chariot. His horses wore shoes of gold, and their bridles were decorated with silver and shells. He held a three-pronged trident in his hand as he rode along. His eyes were as dark and blue as the cold waters of the sea. Seaweed clung to his beard, and tiny crabs and starfish crawled through the ringlets of his shaggy hair. Sometimes Tritons, creatures who were half man and half fish, swam alongside Poseidon's carriage. Sea nymphs offered urchins and exotic flowers to the god of the seas.

The whales and walruses, dolphins and seals bowed as Poseidon went by. Even the most mighty of sea serpents feared the god. They crawled timidly back into their murky caverns as his chariot churned up the sand below the waves. Yet, with all his power, Poseidon desired much more. He wished to rule the land, as well.

Poseidon set his sights on the city of Athens. Athens was situated in the province of Attica. Poseidon plunged his trident into the rocky top of Athens to show that he wished to claim the land as his own. Water sprang from where he had pierced the ground.

Athena the goddess was the guardian of Athens. She attempted to plant an olive tree in the very spot where Poseidon had created a spring of running water. Poseidon found Athena's attempt to discourage him from taking over Attica, to be very humorous. He knew that he was much stronger than the goddess.

Zeus, however, was not amused by Poseidon's antics. He called on all the gods and goddesses of the universe to join him at his palace, where he put before them the problem of subduing the mighty Poseidon.

It was not easy to choose between Poseidon's ambitions and the wise nature of Athena. The gods of Zeus's council voted in favor of Poseidon. The goddesses voted in favor of Athena. Zeus could not vote; therefore, the goddesses won. It was decided that Poseidon's efforts should be stopped.

The vote angered Poseidon. He wished to destroy Athena's temple. As revenge he sent the surface of the sea over the lands, flooding crops and homes. Despite the destruction, Poseidon would not stop. He tried to overtake the city of Torezen, which belonged to Athena, and the island of Aegina, which belonged to Zeus. When he went after land that belonged to Hera, Zeus could not ignore his brother's behavior.

Zeus attempted to reason with Poseidon. But Poseidon's pride was injured by the vote of the council. He believed the goddesses were against him.

Zeus remarked that the river gods Inachus, Asterion, and Cephissus would sit on a new council in judgment of Poseidon. Poseidon was encouraged by the news, since he knew that his power over the waters of the world was unsurpassed. Surely, the river gods would vote in favor of his views. Imagine how he felt when the new council still voted against him!

Again Poseidon vowed revenge. This time he did not flood the earth as he had done in the past. Instead, he dried up the lakes and rivers and streams. Boats and ships were stranded in the dried-out beds. Fish gasped for air with their withered gills. The sea nymphs were left high and dry on the rocky shores of the oceans. The scales of the Tritons became dull and flaky.

Poseidon sulked for many years. Finally he relented and allowed the winter rains and snows to replenish the waterways of the worlds. In the summer, though, he restated his displeasure by causing droughts to plague the world.

# PROMETHEUS'S GIFT TO HUMANKIND

HE GREEK GOD PROMETHEUS LOOKED DOWN AT THE earth from the world of the gods on Mount Olympus. He pitied the humans that lived below.

When the strong gusts of winter winds blew across the mountains and seas of the earth, the people had no fires to warm them. They ate their food cold and uncooked. There were no flames to help them to shape metal into weapons for defense, or tools to assist with harvesting grain. The human race was in need of fire, and Prometheus knew that the most powerful god in the universe, Zeus, had no plan to share this element with the mortals he had created.

Zeus feared that one day human beings would rise like disobedient children against the gods. Zeus behaved like a jealous, strict parent who demanded loyalty from his offspring—in this case, the human race.

Prometheus, however, did not agree with Zeus's treatment of humans. He believed that they could be guided with love and affection to do the right thing. He appealed to Zeus to share the gift of fire with the mortals on earth. Zeus refused to listen.

"Suppose I share fire with them, and they rebel against me?" Zeus asked

Prometheus. "With fire they could eat well, keep warm, and create powerful weapons. Why would they continue to obey me?"

"I believe you can trust them," Prometheus answered. "If they are treated with respect and kindness, they will return it to you."

"I cannot do that. Do not share the power of fire with humans," Zeus warned.

Prometheus found it difficult to obey Zeus's command. During the many festivals that were celebrated on earth, the people were required to share the best selection of meat and other foods with the gods. Prometheus secretly taught them how to disguise their offerings by wrapping bones and fat in the hides of animals so it would appear that they were giving a true sacrifice to the immortals of Mount Olympus.

Zeus eventually discovered what Prometheus was doing. He attempted to keep his anger to himself.

Not content to leave well enough alone, Prometheus thought long and hard about the humans' need for fire. Eventually his compassion for the people of earth won out. He dared to disobey the all-powerful Zeus.

On a dark evening Prometheus ventured to the part of Mount Olympus where the orange, red, and golden flames of eternal fire were dancing on the mountaintop. Unnoticed by the other gods, Prometheus took an ember of the precious fire from the flame and hid it in a stalk of fennel, which is an herb. He hid the ember in his cloak. As he stole away from the home of the gods, he could feel the heat of the ember warm his side.

On earth Prometheus showed the glowing ember to several humans, who delighted in its powerful warmth. Soon they ignited logs and branches and sticks with the ember and passed the gift of fire from one to the other until the earth was lighted up by dancing flames.

It was now possible for men and women to cook their food and to gather around the fire to warm themselves. Prometheus instructed them on how to fashion tools from heated metal and how to make weapons.

Zeus soon spied one of the burning fires as he looked out on the world from his palace among the gods. Enraged, he summoned Prometheus before him.

"What have you done?" he screamed.

"I have given to humans the one thing they always should have owned," replied Prometheus.

"Then you shall be punished for your disobedience!" Zeus cried.

He ordered Prometheus to be taken to an outcrop of cliffs above the sea, and to be chained to the rocks. Every morning a giant eagle would descend from the clouds and attack the helpless Prometheus by devouring his liver. Every night Prometheus's liver would grow back in time to be consumed by the eagle after sunrise.

Prometheus endured this torture for centuries before he was eventually freed. Despite the ghastly punishment of Zeus, Prometheus was fondly remembered for sharing the power of fire with humans on earth.

# DEMETER AND PERSEPHONE

ERSEPHONE WAS THE BELOVED DAUGHTER OF Demeter, the goddess of the harvest. She lived with her mother on the island of Sicily, off the coast of Italy. Every day Persephone would play among the vines of grapes and rows of grain that her mother had blessed. She was enchanted by the beauty of nature, the warmth of the sun, and the bounty of the earth. The people of Greece were grateful for Demeter's goodwill, for it assured a fruitful harvest.

One evening Persephone did not return to her mother after a day of playing in the fields. Demeter grew concerned. It was not like Persephone to come home late. Demeter began to search for her daughter. She asked everyone she met if they had seen Persephone, but no one could help her.

Finally Demeter appealed to Hekate, the goddess of the moon. "From your position high in the sky, Hekate, perhaps you've seen my Persephone."

Sadly, Hekate had not seen the girl. She suggested that Demeter go to the god Helios—ruler of the sun—and ask him. Demeter approached Helios, who was about to embark on his daily journey across the sky. Helios calmed the high-strung horses that were eager to pull his chariot, and listened to the pleas of Demeter.

"Your daughter has been abducted," he told Demeter. "Hades, god of the underworld, came upon Persephone while she was picking flowers. He has driven her in his carriage to the dark world beneath this world, where he wishes for her to sit next to him on his throne."

Demeter was heartbroken. She knew that the mighty god Zeus was aware of Hades's actions. This angered her so much that she refused to go to Olympus with the other gods at Zeus's request. She refused to bless the crops and promote a good harvest. All that concerned her was finding her daughter.

Demeter wandered aimlessly through town after town, lost in thought. She sat near a well one day and closed her eyes to rest. A local girl from the village saw Demeter by the well, but did not recognize the powerful goddess.

"Old woman," the girl asked, "why aren't you at home with your family at the end of this day? It's getting late."

Demeter did not answer.

"If you have nowhere to go," the girl continued, "please, come with me to my house. We have need of a nursemaid for my newborn brother."

Demeter was touched by the girl's concern. She followed her to her home and tended to the infant, who was called Demophon. In a short amount of time, Demeter's sorrows were softened by the baby's smiles. She grew attached to little Demophon and wished to bestow upon him the gods' gift of immortality.

As Demeter began the ceremony to give Demophon the right to eternal life, the baby's mother walked into the room. She saw Demeter lowering her child over an open flame and began to scream.

"No, no!" Demeter cried as the woman took Demophon away. "You shouldn't have done that! You misunderstand what I am trying to do."

With that, Demeter stood before Demophon's family and unveiled her fine robes and let her golden hair spill around her shoulders. Everyone gasped as they looked upon Demeter, for they realized that she was a goddess.

"I must leave you," Demeter told them. "I must continue my search for my own daughter, Persephone. But before I leave, I will bless your fields and they will continue to give you a bountiful harvest."

Demeter continued her sad journey alone. Everywhere she traveled, people begged her to bestow her powers of life on their crops. But Demeter refused.

The people finally appealed to Zeus for help. Afraid that Demeter's actions would stop the daily flow of offerings he received from the farmers, Zeus commanded Hades to release Persephone. He sent Hermes, the messenger god, to retrieve the girl. "As long as she has not eaten anything while in the realm of Hades, she may return to her mother," Zeus told Hermes.

Hermes traveled to the dark underworld and crossed the river Styx. He found Hades sitting on his throne, with a pale and undernourished Persephone by his side. Hermes told Hades what Zeus had commanded.

"Very well," Hades responded. "But you must know that Persephone has eaten the seeds of a pomegranate."

Demeter appealed to Zeus to intervene. She could not bear the idea that Persephone would remain forever with Hades in the underworld.

Zeus proclaimed that Persephone would stay with Hades as his bride for two-thirds of the year.

During the spring, however, she would be able to rejoin her mother.

This solution pleased Demeter, who celebrated her reunion with her daughter by placing her blessing on all growing things. The ground sprang forth with all types of flowers and blossoms. Young seedlings pushed through the dark soil to find the sunlight.

When Persephone returned to Hades, however, Demeter withdrew her magic from the earth. Then the trees dropped their leaves, and a snowy frost covered the ground, as Demeter waited again for her beloved daughter.

# DIONYSUS, GOD OF VEGETATION AND WINE

IONYSUS WAS KNOWN AS A DEITY OF VEGETATION, wine, and ecstasy. He was often portrayed as a rampant bull, a sign of fertility. He was the son of Zeus and Semele, the daughter of King Cadmus.

Hera, Zeus's wife, was not pleased that Zeus had been with Semele. She learned of their newborn son and set out to find him to kill him. Knowing this, Zeus hid the infant Dionysus in an incision in his thigh. He stitched the wound closed, and was able to sneak past Hera with the baby. He carried Dionysus to Mount Nysa, where Dionysus was raised by nymphs and taught how to make wine from grapes. They crowned the young boy with wreaths made from vines and followed him into the woods and valleys.

Dionysus loved to travel to faraway places. Once, as a young man, Dionysus was captured by a band of pirates, Tyrrhenian sea rovers. Dressed in a purple robe, with his long flowing hair, he resembled royalty. The pirates tied him to the mast of their ship. The captain of the pirates was particularly pleased with his catch, because he imagined that Dionysus was the son of someone important. Little did he know!

The captain calculated aloud what he would do with Dionysus. He speculated about selling him as a slave, or asking an enormous ransom for him.

The navigator of the ship approached the captain.

"I think this young man is someone very powerful, someone whom we should fear. If I were you, I would let him go."

The captain just laughed at the navigator and thought him an old fool.

This angered Dionysus, but he did not speak, nor did he reveal his true identity.

While the ship was at sea, the aroma of fermenting grapes began to fill the air. The men could not determine the source of the smell, for they were not carrying any vats of wine with them. Slowly the clouds and the water began to take on a purple hue. The purple color washed up on the side of the vessel and spilled along the deck, the mast, and the sails. Again the sailors were perplexed by what had happened.

Finally one of them shouted, "I think the boy is really a demon! He is causing all this magic to occur! We should kill him!"

All but the navigator agreed. "Leave him alone! He has done no wrong!"

The sailors refused to listen and went to find Dionysus. Imagine their surprise when they found that the boy they had kidnapped was gone, and in his place stood a roaring lion! The lion broke free of his bonds and leaped out at the sailors. They fled in fear and jumped overboard—all but the navigator, who knew then that the young man was truly a god.

Dionysus returned to his true form and asked the kindly navigator to take him to Naxos. When he reached his destination, Dionysus married Ariadne, the daughter of King Minos. Following his marriage, Dionysus traveled to India and Egypt and was received by important people in each place. He journeyed all over the world, instructing every culture in the art of growing grapevines and making wine.

Dionysus had a curious following. The satyrs, creatures with the upper body of a man and the lower torso of a goat, were great admirers of the god. Silenus, an old, grotesque satyr, was in charge of Dionysus's education.

Many women also followed the travels of the handsome god Dionysus. They enjoyed drinking the wine he made and dancing throughout the night, sometimes in a wild frenzy. Their behavior frightened many people. Among them was Pentheus, the cousin of Dionysus. Pentheus was destined to become king. He felt that Dionysus was becoming much too powerful. Threatened by Dionysus's popularity, he forbid the growing of vines in his kingdom and outlawed dancing and celebrating. He announced that he would punish anyone who dared to follow Dionysus. But even these actions did not satisfy Pentheus for long. Eventually he imprisoned Dionysus.

Pentheus secretly followed a gathering of women one night to see if they would continue drinking and dancing. He wished to expose their ridiculous behavior and have them sent to jail. Pentheus climbed into a leafy tree, out of sight. As the moon rose in the sky, the women started their celebration. They began to drink and to dance. A sound in the branches of the nearby tree alerted them that something was wrong. One of the women looked up and discovered that someone was spying on them. She recognized Pentheus. Angry that he had taken Dionysus away from them, the group of women dragged him down out of the tree and killed him. Then they went to find Dionysus and set him free.

# ROMAN MYTHS

# THE GOLDEN BRANCH

 HEN HIS SHIPS TOUCHED SHORE IN ITALY, AENEAS went to locate the Sibyl. The ancient prophet was already hundreds of years old in the time of Aeneas. The god Apollo had given her the gift of prophecy and longevity. Though he gave her a very long life, Apollo deprived the Sibyl of everlasting youth and beauty because she refused to be his lover.

Aeneas hurried to the cave where he knew the Sibyl lived. The cave was set within a grove near a temple dedicated to Apollo and the goddess Diana. The warrior stood in reverence to the god and goddess for a few moments. He looked toward the opening of the cave and wondered whether the Sibyl would honor his request.

"Do not yield to the disasters, but press forward that much more bravely," said the ancient voice.

Aeneas had come to ask the Sibyl to accompany him to the Land of the Dead to visit his father, Anchises. He had been told in a dream to take the trip. According to the dream, his father would reveal Aeneas's future and the fortunes of the Roman people. Anchises would instruct Aeneas about what to do to accomplish this destiny.

The Sibyl began to speak of the Underworld before Aeneas even had the opportunity to state his request. In a trancelike state the prophet foretold of the difficulties and dangers on the road to his father. Many perils awaited Aeneas.

"I have prepared myself for these," said Aeneas.

"The descent is easy. The gate of Pluto is open night and day. The toil is to retrace your steps and return to the upper air," warned the Sibyl.

She told Aeneas he must procure a golden branch as a gift for Proserpine, queen of the Underworld. He would find it in the forest upon one of the trees. If his fate was to be prosperous, the tree would yield the branch easily. No force could tear the branch away. Even if it were possible to break the branch from the tree trunk by force, the effort would be wasted. If the branch was broken from the tree, someone other than the person who tore it off would succeed in that person's place.

Aeneas heeded the Sibyl's solemn words and set off for the forest. A short distance from the cave, he noticed two doves. They belonged to his mother, the goddess Venus. The doves directed Aeneas to the tree that bore the golden branch. The branch came easily away from the trunk when Aeneas touched it. He hurried back to the Sibyl with it.

In the region of volcanoes, near Mount Vesuvius, the countryside rippled with chasms. Flames of sulphur burst forth accompanied by hollow roars from the earth's foundation. In an extinct volcano lay Lake Avernus. The lake was half a mile wide and very deep. Beyond the volcano's steep banks was a dense, gloomy forest. No wildlife sweetened the area, and no birds flew overhead nor dared to light upon the strange trees.

The cave through which to enter the Underworld was on the lake's banks. At the direction of the Sibyl, Aeneas offered sacrifices to Proserpine, to Hecate (goddess of sorcery, and Proserpine's attendant), and to the Furies, the spiteful female deities who existed to seek revenge. When he finished, the earth resounded with a great bellowing that shook the hilltops. Howling dogs announced the presence of the deities Aeneas had worshipped.

"Summon your courage. Now you will need it," proclaimed the Sibyl. She descended into the cave. Aeneas followed in her path.

They passed a cluster of beings, called Griefs, Cares, Diseases, Age, Fear,

Hunger, Toil, Poverty, and Death. The beings were horrible to behold, and Aeneas had to look away. Next he saw monsters. Briareus had one hundred arms. The Hydras, with their huge doglike bodies and many snake heads, hissed at him. The lion-headed, goat-bodied, serpent-tailed Chimeras breathed fire. Aeneas was so revolted that he drew his sword, but before he could strike, the Sibyl restrained him.

They moved on to the black river called Cocytus. The ferryman Charon was waiting. Charon was very old, but still strong. Eager to board the ferry were many and all types of passengers, including glorious heroes, young boys, and maidens with hair of all colors. The ferryman accepted only those passengers he chose.

The Sibyl explained the reason to Aeneas. "Charon takes only those passengers whose souls have received proper burial rites. The others must wander for a hundred years before he will take them."

When Charon saw Aeneas, he asked, "By what right do you approach this shore? You are armed and still alive."

"He will commit no violence," answered the Sibyl. "He wishes only to see his father, Anchises."

Aeneas held out the golden branch for Charon to observe. Seeing it, the ferryman turned his back to Aeneas and the Sibyl, and cooled his anger. Subsequently he invited them to board his boat. The ferry buckled under the weight of the living Aeneas, for it was so accustomed to transporting the light souls of the dead.

As the ferry approached the opposite shore, the three-headed dog Cerberus awaited them. His necks bristled with snakes. He held his ground, barking furiously out of all three throats. The Sibyl threw the dog a med-icated cake, which he devoured. When Cerberus retired to his cave for a nap afterward, Aeneas and the Sibyl disembarked safely upon the far shore of the Underworld.

# Aeneas in the Underworld

ENEAS AND THE ANCIENT FEMALE PROPHET, THE SIBYL, disembarked from the ferry on the shore of the Underworld. They sought Aeneas's father, Anchises. The first sound they heard were the wails of the children who had died at birth. Alongside the children were people who had been put to death under false charges. Minos, the son of Zeus and Europa, who had been king of Crete, heard each of the cases of the falsely accused as their judge.

Aeneas and the Sibyl next traveled past the souls of the people who had taken their own lives.

"How willingly would they now suffer poverty, hardship, and other inflictions if they could return to life," advised the Sibyl.

Aeneas felt the heaviness of sadness as they progressed. From the groves of myrtle trees, radiated numerous paths. On the paths humans who had been disappointed in love roamed endlessly. Even death had not cured their heartache. Could it be? Aeneas thought he saw the figure of Dido. She bore a recent wound. Dido had been queen of Carthage, and Aeneas's lover for one year before the god Mercury had instructed him to depart for Italy. At Aeneas's departure Dido killed herself with her own sword.

"Could that be you, unhappy Dido? Was I the reason you perished? I left you only at the request of the gods. I did not think my absence would harm you so deeply. Please, do not refuse me one last farewell," cried Aeneas.

Dido continued to move on the path she had chosen. Momentarily she stopped and looked to the ground. Silently she began to walk again. Aeneas pursued her for a short distance. With a disappointed heart he turned around and rejoined the Sibyl.

They passed through the fields where the heroes who fell in battle gathered. The Trojan heroes flocked to the living Aeneas in his shiny armor. The Greeks, on the other hand, fled from him as they once had done on the plains of Troy. Aeneas wanted to linger with the dead Trojans, but the Sibyl hurried him away from the fields.

The road was divided at the next place they encountered. One road led to Elysium, the destination of the blessed. The other road progressed to the regions where the condemned dwelled. The fiery waters of the Phlegethon surrounded the walled city of the condemned. The avenging Fury Tisiphone kept watch from an iron tower by the gate. Tremendous groans emerged from the city. The creaking of iron and the clanking of chains rose from the background.

"What crimes have they committed?" Aeneas asked the Sibyl.

"This is the judgment hall of Rhadamantus, who illuminates the crimes that they thought they had hidden so well during their lifetime. Tisiphone whips them with scorpions. Then she hands the offenders over to her sister Furies," the Sibyl explained solemnly.

Just then, the gates flew open. Aeneas observed a Hydra with fifty heads guarding the entrance. Some of those inside sat at tables that were heavy with savory things to eat. A Fury stood ready to snatch away the food from the lips of anyone who dared to try to taste the delicacies. Over the heads of others were gigantic rocks that threatened to crush them at any moment.

The Sibyl explained that these people had hated their siblings, injured their parents, or were disloyal to their friends when they were alive.

She pointed out several figures. One was Sisyphus. Time after time he rolled a tremendous stone up a hill until he almost reached the summit. Each time he was about to roll it up to the crest, a sudden force repelled the rock and pushed it back to the bottom of the hill.

She showed Tantalus to Aeneas. Thirsty, Tantalus stood in a pool of water up to his chin. Time after time he lowered his head to take a drink. When he did, the water disappeared beneath his feet. Around him were trees heavy with pears, pomegranates, apples, and plump figs. Whenever the hungry Tantalus reached to pluck a piece of the fruit, a fierce wind blew the fruit-laden branch out of his grasp.

"We must turn away from this region of the melancholy for the city of the blessed," advised the Sibyl.

Even as they traveled through the middle region of darkness, Aeneas was grateful. They emerged upon the Elysian Fields, where the souls of the happy rested. A purple light cloaked everything that Aeneas saw in these fields. The city of the blessed had its own sun and stars. Inhabitants played games on the grass. Others danced. Still others sang. The renowned musician and poet Orpheus played sweet music on his lyre for all to enjoy.

In a laurel grove, the source of the great River Po, Aeneas witnessed the founders of Troy. Nearby were their resplendent chariots and armor. Their horses freely roamed the plains. Here dwelled also the poets and priests who had sung the glories of the gods. Here, too, rested the people who had lived their lives in the service of humankind. Aeneas knew he would find his father, Anchises, nearby.

# A Father's Message to His Son

 HE OLD WOMAN PROPHET CALLED THE SIBYL LED Aeneas to the city of the blessed in the Underworld. They traveled through the groves of the Elysian Fields and witnessed the souls and the trees there bathed in a purple hue. The place was called Elysium and it was the paradise where the souls that were saved went after death. The inhabitants were the founders of the Trojan state, old heroes, priests, and other blessed souls who contributed to the happiness of their fellow humans during their lives in the upper world. Strains of sweet music penetrated Elysium.

"Where is the soul called Anchises?" inquired the Sybil of a group of inhabitants.

The Sybil and Aeneas turned down to a rich, green valley. Under a tree sat Anchises. He was deep in thought until he recognized his son, Aeneas.

"You have come at last. I was contemplating posterity, my ancestors, and my descendants. I have worried over your well-being as you've lived the career of a hero of Troy," said Anchises to his son.

"My father! Your image guided me throughout my adventures," proclaimed Aeneas. He reached out to embrace his father. But his arms enfold-ed a mere image and not the substance of the body he remembered when Anchises was alive.

Aeneas soothed his disappointment by looking out over the wide, tranquil valley. A gentle summer wind danced through the trees. The River Lethe cut through the landscape like a ribbon. Aeneas noticed a multitude of forms on the far bank. They reminded him of the insects he might find on a summer's day on earth.

"Those souls will receive bodies in time. In the meantime they reside on the bank of the Lethe. They are engaged in drinking oblivion of their most recent lives. They must forget in order to be born fresh once more," explained Anchises.

"Father, how can it be possible for souls to love the upper world so much that they would depart from this tranquil valley?" asked Aeneas.

"I will relate for you the plan of creation in order to explain," answered his father.

Aeneas listened as Anchises told his story. "The Creator originally made souls from the four elements, which are fire, air, earth, and water. The four combined into the most excellent element, which is fire, and they became flame. The Creator scattered this flame like seed among the sun, moon, and stars.

"The inferior gods took the seed and made human beings and the other animals. To do this, they mixed in different proportions of earth to reduce the purity of the seed. The more earth they put into the composition of the human or animal, the less pure that individual became. You have seen that men and women in their adult bodies are far less pure than they were in their childhood.

"After death the impurity must be cleaned away. Souls purge away the earth that composed their bodies by airing themselves in the wind. Or by washing in water. Or by burning in the fire. Only a few souls like myself are immediately admitted to Elysium without cleansing. And only a few souls remain here forever.

"The rest of the souls return to earth again after they are cleansed of the impurities of their last life. They return with new bodies. And they return without any memory of the life before. That memory they have washed away in the River Lethe."

"What about the animals?" asked Aeneas.

"Some human souls have been so corrupted by their past deeds that they are unfit to return to the upper world in human bodies. These souls are reborn as the brute animals. They become lions, cats, monkeys and the like. The natives of India do not destroy the life of an animal, because the beast might be a relative in a different form," explained Anchises.

The father showed his son which of the souls waiting by the river would become his relatives in their next lives. Anchises related what these souls would accomplish on earth when they were born into new bodies. He shared with him what Aeneas himself would do when he returned to the upper world. He would fight battles and win wars. He would find a bride to wed and found the Trojan state. Out of that state, the Roman state would become the most powerful sovereign in the world.

It was time for Aeneas and the Sibyl to return to the upper world. They bid farewell to Anchises. The Sibyl led the path back to earth through a secret shortcut.

"I will build a temple to your honor and bring you offerings," said Aeneas to the Sibyl upon their return.

"I am no goddess, nor do I have any claim to offerings," she answered. "I am a mortal. I did not accept the love of Apollo when he claimed me. Instead, I took a handful of sand and asked to see that many birthdays. Unfortunately, I forgot to ask for eternal youth. So far, I have lived seven hundred years. I have still to experience three hundred springs and three hundred harvests. In time I will be lost to sight. But my voice will stay behind, and future peoples will respect my words."

# GALATEA AND ACIS

 ALATEA WAS A SEA NYMPH. THE ONE-EYED GIANT Cyclops Polyphemus was in love with her. But Galatea loved the sixteen-year-old mortal named Acis.

"What is stronger? My love for Acis? He is so beautiful, his cheeks covered in down with scarcely a beard. Or my hatred of Cyclops? With a sickle he trims his shaggy beard," lamented Galatea.

So piercing was Cyclops's love for Galatea that he took to looking at the reflection of his unkempt self in the waters of the sea. He wanted to please the object of his affection. He combed his matted hair with a rake, and tried to shape his mangy beard with a sickle. He left his flocks of sheep untended to spy upon Galatea. All day long he kept watch for a glimpse of her, and he only returned to his dark cave to sleep.

One day Cyclops climbed up the side of a rocky mountain to a point high above a wedge-shaped piece of land that jutted out into the sea. He used his staff for support. The staff was a pine tree as tall and sturdy as the masthead of a ship. At the top of the hill, he rested his staff against the rock. He took up his pipe, which was made of one hundred reeds, and began to play a ballad to his would-be lover, Galatea.

"Fair Galatea, whiter than the snow,
Taller than alders, flowerier than the meads,

Brighter than crystal, livelier than a kid,
Sleeker than the shells worn by the ceaseless waves,
Gladder than winter's sun and summer's shade,
Nobler than apples, sweeter than ripe grapes,
Fairer than lofty planes, clearer than ice,
Softer than down of swans or creamy cheese,
And, would you welcome me, more beautiful
Than fertile gardens watered by cool streams....

Now, Galatea, raise your glorious head
from the blue sea; spurn not my gifts, but come!
For sure I know—I have seen—myself
Reflected in a pool, and what I saw
Was truly pleasing. See how large I am!
No bigger body Jupiter himself can boast ...

Why prefer Acis, Acis's arms to mine?
Acis may please himself and please, alas,
You, Galatea. Give me but the chance,
He'll find my strength no smaller than my size
I'll gouge his living guts, I'll rend his limbs
And strew them in the fields and the sea—"[1]

"I have heard his words. How pitiful am I?" pondered Galatea.

She lay within the arms of the mortal Acis, whom she loved as much as the sea. They were hidden behind a rock upon the shore. Hopefully, thought Galatea, Cyclops would not see them. What did it matter to her all of the gifts that the giant offered? Of what did she need noble apples or

---

1 Ovid, *Metamorphoses*, trans. A.D. Melville, (Oxford, New York: Oxford University Press, 1986), pp. 319-321.

ripe grapes? What did she care for the down of swans or creamy cheese? Or fertile gardens? She loved another, not the ugly Cyclops.

He lived in dark caves where the summer sun never entered. Nor did the winter's cold penetrate. His flocks roamed the woods or found shelter in the same caves. What gifts could he give her, Galatea, that mattered? Deer or goats or hares? Doves or gulls? Shaggy bears that rested with him in his caves?

And his hair was like a grove of rough trees! His coarse, giant face looked as though it was carved from a rock! One eye with which to see! Like the grossest shield on his forehead!

As Galatea thought these things, she did not feel that eye upon herself and Acis. Cyclops stood suddenly from the rocky mountain upon which he had been sitting and playing his pipe. Embracing one another, Galatea and Acis had captured his attention. His raging anger was more fierce than caves of bulls.

"I see you now. This loving embrace is your last," shouted Cyclops. His voice shook the mountain that supported his great weight.

Frightened, Galatea dove into the sea to escape. Acis turned to run.

"Help me! Galatea! Mother! Father! Help!" he cried.

Cyclops tore a boulder from the mountain and hurled it at Acis as he fled. Poor Acis lay crushed beneath the rock. Only the love of Galatea saved him. She watched as his blood flowed crimson beneath the boulder. With her powers as sea nymph, she changed its substance. Now it flowed like a stream that rushed after a heavy rain. Then, the water stopped. Into the rock, a deep crack began to grow. Out of the fissure grew a tall, green reed. The sound of water emerged from the hollow. In the water, waist deep, stood a youth. He had horns woven through with rushes. Though he was now larger, and his face was sea-blue, he was surely Acis. Galatea changed him into a river god.

# SCYLLA AND GLAUCUS

IKE GALATEA, SCYLLA WAS A SEA NYMPH, A NEREID.
The Nereids were the fifty daughters of Doris and Nereus.
Their mother, Doris, was an Oceanid. She was one of the
three thousand daughters of Oceanus, who was the ancient
god of the river that circled the earth at the beginning of time. Their
father, Nereus, was a minor god of the sea. He also was called Old Man of
the Sea.

One day Scylla found that she was swimming too far out to sea, and she
did not feel safe. She turned back to the shallow waters near the shore.
From time to time she strolled along the beach naked. When she tired, she
took a dip in the sheltered cove.

A lesser sea god named Glaucus happened upon the same beach. When
he saw Scylla, he was enraptured with her beauty. His heart throbbed in his
chest, and he wanted her to stay with him forever.

Glaucus started to talk to the sea nymph. He said everything that came
into his mind to try to keep Scylla on the beach. "Beautiful day, isn't it? I
love this beach. I've never seen another like it. The sun casts a more radiant glow with you here than it did yesterday." Glaucus could not believe
the silly things he was saying.

Scylla fled to a cliff high above the shore. She could not discern whether Glaucus was a god or a monster. He had a bronze-green beard and blue arms. His hair draped upon his shoulders and climbed down his back. His thighs twisted into a fish's tail. Glaucus could read Scylla's thoughts. Leaning on an outcropping of rock, he explained his appearance.

"Fair maiden, I am not a monster or a beast. I am a sea god. On the open sea, no other has greater power than I. I did not always appear in this form. I used to be a mortal, a fisherman. One day while I was counting my fish, they began to move on the grass as though they were swimming. I watched as they continued their movement back to the sea. Amazed, I wondered whether a god or the juices of some plant had allowed them to do this. I picked the stalks of a plant that grew nearby, and I chewed until the juice ran down my throat. No sooner had I swallowed, then I longed for the world of the sea. I plunged into the waves. The sea gods welcomed me, and their chanting took away my sins. When I recovered my wits, I looked like I do now," explained Glaucus.

Rather than be moved toward affection for the strange-looking god, Scylla fled once more. Glaucus took to the sea. With mighty strokes he swam through straits that had destroyed hundreds of ships. The most dangerous was the strait between Italy and Sicily. Across the Tyrrhene Sea, he went, propelled by the cause to make Scylla love him. He found the famous sorceress he sought in her magic halls. She was surrounded by phantom beasts. Glaucus prayed to Circe, the same goddess who had turned half of the crew of Odysseus into swine. Her father was Helius, god of the sun.

"O Circe, daughter of the sun, hear me. Goddess, make Scylla share the hell of this love I feel," pleaded Glaucus.

"You would do better to woo a willing lover," responded Circe to his prayer. "Trust in your looks and be brave. Pray instead that I be your lover. Welcome me, the one who wants you."

"Before I change my love for Scylla, green leaves will grow inside the sea, and seaweed will take their place upon the hillside," answered Glaucus to the goddess's offer of love.

Rage filled Circe, but she had no desire to turn it against Glaucus, whom she loved. Scylla was the object of her anger. Therefore, Circe donned a deep blue robe and made for the water where Scylla swam. The goddess crossed the strong waves of the ocean by walking upon them. Circe carried potions of ill-intentioned herbs, and she sang rounds of demon spells. When she reached the bay in which Scylla bathed, she dropped her potions into the peaceful water. She recited the same wicked incantation nine times.

Scylla suddenly saw barking beasts around her stomach and legs. She tried to flee them, but she brought them with her. Then, looking down and expecting to see her legs and feet, she found a pack of outraged dogs. Their jaws were open wide, and their teeth were poised to bite. The jealous goddess had changed her into a dangerous reef. Choosing not to die from the reef like the sailors in the fleet of Odysseus, mariners today still steer away from Scylla.

As for the weeping Glaucus, when Circe came to embrace him, he fled from her arms.

# Picus and Canens

ING PICUS OF LATIUM WAS THE SON OF SATURN, WHO was thrown out of Olympus by his son Jupiter, the greatest of the gods. From Olympus, Saturn settled in the territory he called Latium. It was the land south of where Romulus would found Rome.

Picus was a young king. He had not yet lived twenty years. Mortal women, wood nymphs, water nymphs, and fountain sprites admired him for his good looks and youthful spirit. Picus despised all of his admirers except his queen, who was the nymph Canens. She was named after the word cano, which meant to sing.

Her voice was as rare as her beauty. Her song delighted the woods and the rocks. Wild beasts were tamed by it. Rivers changed their courses to hear the strains of her song. Birds stopped their wanderings to listen.

One day Picus bid his wife farewell and went off to hunt wild boars in the countryside surrounding his castle. He was radiant in his purple cloak with its clasp of gold. He sat tall upon his young bay steed. The goddess Circe, the sorceress daughter of the sun god, was, by coincidence, in the same woods into which Picus rode. The hills were fertile, and Circe was digging for the herbs she used in her potions.

When the goddess saw Picus, she released the plants in her hands. She was filled with a longing for him. She wanted to tell him of her love. But Picus rode so quickly through the woods that Circe was unable to catch up with him.

"You will not escape me," she said outloud. "Even if the wind should whirl you far away, my magic herbs will return you close to me."

Circe conjured up a phantom boar to attract Picus's attention. When the boar raced past the king, he followed. The phantom darted into a spinney, a thorny thicket with heavy undergrowth that did not allow a horse to enter. Picus pursued the boar to the spinney. He dismounted and followed on foot deep into the thicket.

The sorceress Circe began to chant to gods both known and unknown. The incantations eclipsed the pale face of the moon and reined in layers of clouds to obscure her father's orb. The king's guards searched for him in the woods, but they could not find the spinney that obscured him.

"With the lovely eyes that captured mine, look upon me, beautiful King. I, a goddess, kneel before you. By my father, the Sun, who sees everything, swear your love to Circe," the goddess ordered Picus.

"As long as the Fates keep my Canens safe, my love will never betray her," responded the king.

"Then, you will pay. Canens will never again have you home," shouted Circe. "You and she will know the result of another woman who is betrayed by love."

Circe turned eastward twice. Twice she rotated westward. Three times she sang a spell. With her wand she touched Picus three times. The king fled from her. How could he run as fast as he did? Wings sprouted from his shoulders! They were the same purple as his cloak. Where the brooch had closed the cloak, a gold band of feathers now circled his neck. His hard beak pecked the rough barks of the oaks in the woods he knew so well. The love-scorned sorceress had turned him into a woodpecker! From this moment forward, his name would mean woodpecker.

The guards searched for their missing king. They happened upon Circe as they rode. They aimed their spears at the sorceress, suspecting her hand in the king's disappearance. Circe sprinkled evil drugs and poisoned essences about them. She summoned Night and the gods of Night and cried to Hecate, the attendant to Proserpine, queen of the Underworld. The very woods leaped away from the spell. The ground emitted a deep, hollow groan. Stones hurled themselves far away to escape from her. Dogs bellowed, and snakes floated through the air.

The horrified guards stared in disbelief at the happenings. Circe touched their faces with her wand of poison. At the wicked touch, each of the guards changed into the magic form of a different wild beast.

Canens, meanwhile, was desperate for her husband to return. The entire royal household was searching the woods with torches for signs of Picus. Unable to bear the separation from her husband any longer, Canens began to roam the woods and the countryside like a madwoman. For six nights and six days, she covered hill and dale in her search. Finally she lay her head by the River Tiber. Through sobs she breathed her final breath. Slowly she vanished into the air, taking the song she sang with her. To this day, it is believed, no one has forgotten its strains.

# Juno Versus the Destiny of Aeneas

 UNO WAS THE GODDESS OF WOMEN AND MARRIAGE. SHE was married to Jupiter, ruler of the worlds of gods and humans. The Trojan hero Aeneas was part mortal and part immortal, having the human father Anchises and the goddess of love, Venus, as his mother. He was to become the father of the Roman people. But Juno tried to stop him for a number of reasons.

It all began at the wedding of Peleus and Thetis. Thetis was one of the fifty Nereids, or sea nymphs, a daughter of the minor sea god Nereus and the sea goddess Doris. Jupiter himself had once wooed Thetis. But when the god learned that her future son was to become greater than his father, he decided that Thetis should marry a mortal. Jupiter chose Peleus, king of Phthia, to wed Thetis.

Nearly all the gods and goddesses attended the wedding. But Eris, the goddess of discord, however, was not invited. To cause havoc Eris inscribed "For the Fairest Goddess" upon a Golden Apple. She threw the Golden Apple into the reception. Immediately a dispute arose among Juno, Venus, and Minerva, the latter being the goddess of wisdom and war.

"Surely, this is meant for me," proclaimed Juno.

"Absolutely not. It is mine," declared Venus.

"I own this Golden Apple," boasted Minerva.

Jupiter ordered the goddesses to take their dispute to the walled city of Troy, which was located on the coast of the Aegean Sea in Asia Minor. He selected Paris, the very handsome Trojan prince, to decide which goddess deserved the Golden Apple. One by one the three goddesses tried to bribe the prince.

"Choose me and you'll rule the world," declared Juno.

"You'll be victorious in every battle if you name me," offered Minerva.

"Select me and you'll have the most beautiful woman in the world," tempted Venus. She referred to the notoriously beautiful Helen, who was also a daughter of Jupiter.

Paris awarded the Golden Apple to Venus without hesitation. Unfortunately, Helen was married to the Greek king of Sparta. His name was Menelaus. Paris stealthily made off to Troy with Queen Helen while he was a guest in the house of Menelaus. Juno now had two reasons to hate Aeneas. He was the son of her rival Venus; he was from the same land as Paris.

King Menelaus named his brother Agamemnon as commander-in-chief of the forces he organized to wage war against Troy. The bloody war would end with the surprise defeat of Troy by the Greeks, who hid inside the wooden Trojan Horse and tricked the Trojans into admitting them inside their city.

Aeneas served under Prince Hector, the leader of the Trojan forces, during the war. He escaped from the siege of Troy with his lame father upon his shoulders. He held his son Iulus and his wife Creusa by the hands. During their escape his wife was lost and was never found. Aeneas now led the only Trojan survivors in a fleet of twenty ships to search for a new home. It would take him nearly ten years to find a home upon the land that is now Italy.

As Aeneas neared the end of his journey to his destined land, Juno took her revenge. She had added one more gripe against him. The city of Carthage was her favorite city. It was located south of Rome, across the Mediterranean Sea on the northern shore of Africa. Juno looked into the future and saw that the Roman descendants of Aeneas would destroy Carthage.

"In heavenly minds, resentments such as mine dwell deeply," vowed Juno to herself.

The goddess commanded Aeolus, the keeper of the winds, to destroy the Trojan fleet. Aeolus obediently commissioned his sons, Boreas, Typhon, and the other winds, to fiercely toss the ocean in all directions. The Trojan ships were set wildly off course. It looked like they would be destroyed.

Only Neptune retaliated against Juno's orders. He had not sanctioned the disturbance, and he was annoyed by the goddess's interference in his realm. Raising his head above the waves, he was able to see the Trojan fleet. He reprimanded the winds. He soothed the waves. And he swept away the clouds that obscured the face of the sun. He took up his trident, the three-pronged spear of the god of the sea, and he pried the ships off the rocks upon which they had been thrown. Neptune's son Triton, a minor sea god, and one of the sea nymphs lifted the other endangered ships upon their shoulders and steered them to safety. In this miraculous way, all of the Trojan ships were saved.

Aeneas was to wander for several more years. When at long last his Trojan ships touched upon the shore of the land called Latium. King Latinus had a daughter named Lavinia. He had been told by an oracle that she would marry a foreign prince, so Latinus welcomed Aeneas and his countrymen.

The path was clear for Aeneas to marry the princess, except that Juno was not through with her revenge. One of the spiteful Furies, who was called Alecto, brewed up trouble between the Latins and the Trojans at the goddess's command. Alecto spoke against Aeneas to Lavinia's mother and nephew Turnus. Turnus was the king of the neighboring state of Ardea. He had wooed Lavinia for some years, so he declared war against Latium. When a single-handed battle was fought between Turnus and Aeneas, finally Juno did nothing to interfere. With a single blow Aeneas killed Turnus, and the war ended.

Aeneas married Lavinia and became the new king of Latium. Iulus, his Trojan son, succeeded his father to the throne. Other sons of Aeneas also ruled, including Silvius, the first child in the new Roman race. The line of Iulus was called the Julian House. Among the rulers to follow in this house for the next four centuries were Julius Caesar and Augustus Caesar.

Jupiter honored the request of Venus to have her son Aeneas become immortal. Once his mortality was cleansed in the waters of the sea, Aeneas became the minor god called Indiges.

You can see that this myth contains some history of Rome and its rulers. The poet Virgil created his hero Aeneas within the world of the gods and their powers in order to emphasize the importance of the Roman state.

# The Children of Mars

lba Longa was an ancient Latin city, which named itself in honor of the dawn. It was situated along a ridge behind which the sun seemed to rise each day. Silvius was the first king to reign in Alba Longa. His name came from the Latin word for forest, which is where he was born. Silvius was the son of Aeneas and Lavinia, and he was the first child of the new people who were to be known as Romans.

After Silvius died, two kings also took his forest name. These were Aeneas Silvius and Latinus Silvius. Proca was the next king, and his reign was supposed to pass to his son Numitor. But the succession of the throne from one king to the next within the Silvan dynasty stopped moving smoothly after Proca's death.

Numitor had an evil brother called Amulius. When Proca died, Amulius drove the rightful heir to the throne, his brother, Numitor, from the royal house. He then ordered Numitor's young sons to be killed. The maiden Rhea Silvia was the last of his brother's children. As evil as he was, Amulius was afraid to have Rhea Silvia killed. He knew the people of Alba Longa would turn against him if he ordered the death of an innocent maiden.

Amulius disposed of Rhea Silvia in a different way, seeing to it that she never married nor had any children. To make certain that no heir of Numitor's would someday challenge his right to rule, Amulius placed his niece among the women who did not marry. Rhea Silvia became a Vestal Virgin, one of the women who tended the sacred fire of Vesta, the goddess of hearth and home. Amulius told everyone that he did this as a means of honoring his brother's daughter, and the people believed him.

One day, while she went about her duties as a Vestal Virgin in the woods, Rhea Silvia came upon a man. A wolf and a woodpecker accompanied him. The man was Mars, the war god, and he forced Rhea Silvia to marry him. Because she broke her vow never to marry, Rhea Silvia was condemned to death by her uncle, who gladly took the opportunity to be rid of the last of his brother's children. Amulius had one more decree. While in prison, Rhea Silvia had given birth to twin boys. The angry king ordered the babies to be drowned in the river.

In the old days the river was called the Albula. After King Tiberinus of Alba was drowned there, its name was changed to the Tiber. In the time of the year when Rhea Silvia gave birth, the Tiber spread beyond its banks, creating shallow, stagnant pools. When the slaves of Amulius brought the twin boys to the river, they left the basket that held the babies among the grasses on the banks. When the water resumed its normal flow, the basket rested in the mud that remained.

A she-wolf found the babies inside, and she gave them some of her milk to drink. A woodpecker dropped food into their small mouths. The wolf and the woodpecker had saved the babies at the request of the infants' father, Mars.

Sometime later, a shepherd named Faustulus came upon the basket. He brought the twins to his hut, where they grew as his own children. The youngsters, who were named Romulus and Remus, were not content to be only with their sheep. As the sons of Mars, they ventured, too, over the mountains and through the forest during their days. Other boys accompanied them, and the twins became the leaders among their peers. They hunted wild beasts. They attacked gangs of robbers, took the spoil, and shared it.

Romulus, Remus, and the other boys attended the festival of the Lupercalia, on the hill now called Palatine. A gang of robbers, avenging the booty taken from them, stole Remus. Romulus followed from a distance, and he saw Remus thrown into the king's prison.

"My brother is in the prison of King Amulius," Romulus told the shepherd Faustulus.

"I have something to tell you, my son," answered Faustulus. "I was once the shepherd of Numitor. I saw him driven from his throne by his wicked brother. I witnessed the murder of his sons and the death of his daughter. Since you and your brother were babies, I have wondered when I would tell you. I see now is the time."

And Faustulus explained to Romulus that he had found a basket with two babies. He believed that the boys were of royal blood. But he had sheltered them because of the wrath of Amulius. He told Romulus that he and his brother were, in all likelihood, the grandsons of Numitor. And he sent him to speak with Numitor.

One look at his grandson told Numitor, who was now an old man, that Romulus belonged to the line of Silvan kings. Numitor swore to help him free his brother. They devised a plan.

Romulus and his shepherd friends armed themselves and went to Amulius's house. Numitor had traveled ahead of them. He told the king's defenders that enemies were invading the citadel, the fortress that protected the city. When the king's guards rushed to the citadel to prevent the feigned invasion, the shepherd boys freed Remus from prison. Amulius had no army to protect him, and Romulus slew him for his evil deeds against the family of Numitor.

The people hailed Numitor as their rightful king. They recognized Romulus and Remus to be of the royal house. For their part, Romulus and Remus swore allegiance to their grandfather and vowed to serve him.

# THE FOUNDING OF ROME

OMULUS AND REMUS LIVED WITH THEIR GRANDFATHER, King Numitor, in Alba Longa. But they were young, and Alba Longa was crowded. The brothers decided to found a new city. They shared their plan with the young men whom they had known when they lived with the shepherd Faustulus and his wife in the days before they were reunited with their grandfather.

The group of shepherd youth, with Romulus and Remus as their leaders, chose for their city the hills where they were accustomed to grazing their sheep and the open spaces surrounded by woods where they chased robbers and hunted game. Romulus selected Palatine Hill for his quarters. Remus took Aventine Hill for his.

Remus received the first augury, a sign that was believed at the time to predict the future. One day he saw a flight of six vultures. The vulture was considered a sacred bird because it did not prey on other birds, but only fed on dead things.

"Surely, I am the one destined to found the city and give it a name," exclaimed Remus to Romulus and the shepherds.

Nearly as soon as Remus had spoken the words, Romulus observed a flight of twelve vultures!

"It is I who has been selected. I saw twice the number," boasted Romulus.

Immediately he set out to build a wall around the city to protect it, convinced that it was indeed he whom the gods had chosen. Remus ridiculed his brother. Laughing, he leaped over the wall into the city. Romulus struck down Remus and killed him on the spot.

"So will perish all who leap over my walls," declared the proud Romulus.

He called the city Rome after himself and became its king. But the city of Rome had very few people. The surrounding population had shown no interest in joining the followers of Romulus and Remus in the new city.

So Romulus founded a sanctuary between two groves partly up the slope that is now called Capitoline Hill. He invited men who had committed dangerous crimes to the sanctuary. He also sent the word out that debtors who could not meet their obligations were welcome. Anyone who was being pursued for whatever reason could come. What the newcomers would find in the sanctuary, promised Romulus, was safety and protection.

The population of the new city upon the hills soon became a strong and daring bunch. Now there was another problem. Few women resided in the city of Rome. The fugitives did not have wives, and without the birth of children the city would not endure.

Romulus sent messengers throughout the land to the neighboring states and cities. He asked the heads of the states and cities to enter into marriage alliances with the men of his city. But the neighboring rulers and peoples considered Rome to be more a camp of outcasts than a city that deserved their respect. In fact, it could be said that most of them wished the city to perish for its lawlessness.

One neighbor responded, "Unless you have a sanctuary for runaway women, you'll have no wives."

The statement drew the wrath of Romulus and the residents of Rome. Romulus became determined to find wives for the men through trickery and force. It was the time for the harvest and the festival of Consus, the god who helped the people to gather and store their crops. Romulus sent an official invitation to the people of the closest neighboring state. He promised a great spectacle if they attended the celebration of the festival of Consus in Rome.

The neighbors Romulus invited were the Sabines. Despite their dislike of the Romans, they could not resist a good spectacle. The Sabines came to Rome in droves. Most of the men brought their wives and children. When they arrived, they marveled at the wall around the new city and at the new building that had been constructed. The Romans invited the Sabines to stay with them in their houses, and they treated their guests to all manner of food, drink, games, and music. The Sabines began to lose their distrust of the residents of the new city.

The day of the spectacle dawned at last. Finely clad, young Roman men seated upon wondrous horses delighted the crowd. They paraded the horses in formation and demonstrated how well the animals responded to command. The crowd applauded and cheered for more. But the spectacle changed from the parade to something unexpected.

On cue the horsemen galloped among the Sabines. The surprised crowd scattered in all directions. Parents and older brothers did not have time to protect the young women. One by one, the Sabine maidens were swooped up by the young Romans on horseback, who desired them as wives.

"A curse on this city for the crime of violating the code of hospitality," said the spokesman for the Sabines.

Romulus dispatched a messenger to the Sabine king. He promised that the maidens would be given an honorable ceremony of marriage. They would then share in the riches of Rome. As for the Roman husbands, Romulus himself would see that they consoled their wives for the loss of their home and families. What Romulus promised did come to be. The maidens were treated respectfully by their new husbands after a proper ceremony. But, back in their land, the Sabine fathers donned the robes of mourning and stirred up the sympathy of the people, who vowed to punish the Roman people for the crime.

# NUMA, THE LAWGIVER

HE PEOPLE OF ROME DECIDED THAT THEIR SECOND KING would be someone who was born on the same day that the building of their new city had begun. Numa was the person born on that day. The Romans knew Numa did not have a human wife when they pledged their allegiance to him. He loved a minor goddess named Egeria, who was a wise nymph in the service of Diana, the goddess of the hunt and the moon. The Romans recognized that their second ruler would be a great king because of the counsel he received from Egeria.

Numa and Egeria were accustomed to meeting in the woods, near a clear spring of water, to talk. One day they spoke about the plague that had started to ravage Italy. Numa confided in Egeria the people's worries that their beautiful, new Rome would perish as the population in the city would surely die.

Suddenly a shield descended from heaven to the floor of the forest. Numa heard the message: "As long as this shield is among the Roman people, they will be prosperous."

He ordered eleven shields identical to the divine one to be forged. When the twelve shields stood one by the other, no one, not even King Numa, could discern which one had come from heaven. Only, then, was the king satisfied that no enemy would be able to steal into the city and take the precious shield that had been given to the Romans. The population grew comfortable in their prosperity, and the plague soon left the land.

Numa next drafted laws for his people to obey. He began with the two commandments that Egeria counseled him in making: "Thou shalt not drink wine from an unpruned vine"; "Thou shalt not make any sacrifices without grain." Through these first laws that required the people to care for their vines and harvest their grain, Numa encouraged the Romans to cultivate the land.

He introduced arts and crafts, too. Companies of musicians, goldsmiths, metalworkers, carpenters, dyers, shoemakers, and potters established themselves in Rome. Each company had its own council. Depending upon the art, the companies prayed to their special gods.

Temples were built in the land. The first temple was dedicated to Vesta, the goddess of the sacred fire. The circular building housed an ever-burning fire. To the Romans, Vesta's fire guaranteed that their fortunes would never die. The second temple in Rome honored Janus, god of peace. (Originally Janus was referred to as Ianus, but contemporary scholars always classify him with the "J" spelling.) The building had two faces because Janus was believed to have two faces. The temple's gates were built to be open during war and closed during peace. During Numa's reign the gates were always closed because there was not a day without peace.

King Numa organized the months in the beginning of the year after he built his temples. The month of January was deemed first because it celebrated the god Janus. February, the month of the festival of Lupercalia when the Romans purified themselves, was second. March, the month of Mars, the god of war, came safely next.

One day Numa called upon Jupiter, the god of the sky and of thunder. "Please, make it so the lightning and thunder do no harm to Rome," asked Numa.

"The only way to remove the spell is with heads," answered Jupiter.

"With the heads of onions," offered Numa.

"No, of men," demanded Jupiter.

"Hair of men's heads, then," suggested Numa.

"No, with living ...," began Jupiter.

"With living pilchards," interrupted Numa, and he had the last word.

Thus, the Romans began to charm away the thunder and lightning of the great Jupiter with the heads of onions, the hair of humans, and living pilchards, which are a type of fish from the herring family.

As Numa was able to charm the gods, he also charmed the Romans under his rule. He once invited the elders of the city to his house for a feast. They found a very modest house and a table and benches made of humble wood. Nothing ostentatious presented itself to the elders. Wooden dishes were placed on the table before them. Upon the dishes were set only bread and fruit. Plain goblets presented them with milk and wine.

A wonderful brilliance entered the humble room. The light transformed the wooden dishes and goblets into vessels of gold and silver. The simple cuisine became the rich foods of the world's most powerful sovereigns.

The elders then overheard a conversation between Numa and Egeria. Some of the words they understood, while others were of a language unknown to their ears. The familiar language told them the life of their king was to end soon. Shortly after the banquet in his house, Numa died.

According to the wishes of their king before his death, the Romans constructed two coffins. In one they placed the body of Numa. In the other they laid the sacred books that contained his laws and writings. The Romans put the two coffins of stone under the hill Ianiculum.

The nymph Egeria dissolved in tears at the passing of Numa. And the goddess Diana transformed her into a natural spring.

# THE SIBYL

N OLD WOMAN PRESENTED HERSELF AT THE COURT of King Tarquin the Proud. Wrinkles that could only have been earned over many centuries traced her face. A wooden staff supported her. Heavy gray hair lay like a tremendous weight upon her shoulders. Under one arm she held a large, cumbersome bundle. Her eyes glowed with light and purpose.

"Bring me before the king," said the old woman at the door of the king's house.

"You have no place here," responded the doorkeeper.

"I must see the king," demanded the woman.

King Tarquin the Proud was seated upon his throne when the doorkeeper startled him with news of the insistence of the would-be visitor. The doorkeeper described the woman's aged countenance. The king had dreamed the evening before of an ancient woman, whom he did not know, but who matched in appearance the woman of whom the doorkeeper spoke. Neither the king nor the servant knew that she was a prophet. The god Apollo himself had given her the power of prophecy. He had also bestowed upon her the gift of a very long life. Apollo had offered her youth and beauty, too, if she would have agreed to become his mistress. But the woman, who was called the Sibyl, had refused Apollo's request.

The king, robed in purple and seated upon his ivory chair, with his protectors about him, pondered the situation a moment. Then he instructed the servant to admit the stranger. She proceeded, supported by her staff and carrying her great bundle, until she stood directly before Tarquin the Proud. She opened the bundle and carefully extracted its contents. She held before the king nine books.

"These books I would sell to you, O King," she said.

Her voice quaked when she spoke. The sound alarmed all those who were present. They could not discern whether the strangeness was because she had not used the voice in a very long time. Or, was it due to the fact that this woman was not like any human they had ever encountered.

"What do your books contain?" asked Tarquin the Proud.

"A foretelling of the events that will occur and how to deal with the events for the safety and greatness of Rome," answered the Sibyl in her shaky, hollow voice.

"What is the cost of your nine books?" the king demanded.

"Half of the king's treasury," she responded.

"Preposterous! You crazy old crone," ridiculed the king.

The woman asked that the brazier of burning coals in the room be brought to her. The king nodded to several people in the room to carry it over. Then she lifted three books from the pile. With surprising strength she threw the books into the fire. Everyone in the room watched as the flames consumed the volumes. They observed the burning until the leaves turned to ashes.

Once more the woman, who was now leaning more heavily upon her staff than she had before, spoke in the strange voice. "I have books for sale. It is for you to buy them, O King."

"How much, then, do you ask for the six remaining books?" demanded King Tarquin the Proud.

"Half of the king's treasury," she responded.

"That is what you asked when you had nine books," said Tarquin.

"I ask the same price for six as I did for nine," insisted the woman.

"She must be the craziest woman in Rome," said one of the king's advisors.

"She is not from Rome," corrected another advisor.

"Indeed, she is a stranger," said someone else.

"I cannot pay the price you ask for your books or anyone's books," roared the king.

The Sibyl took three books from her pile of six, lifting them above her head for all in the room to see. The flames lit up her aged face so that every wrinkle captivated their eyes. Assured that she held everyone's attention, she cast the three books into the brazier. Tarquin looked at her with respect.

"Half of your treasury, O King, for the three books that are not yet burned," said the Sibyl.

Laughter filled the room, but the king did not join the others in the merriment. He knew that once she threw the last three books into the flames, he would never see this woman again. The realization filled him with worry. He told her to come closer. She hobbled toward him until she stood next to his ivory chair.

"Leave the books. For your payment you will take half of the king's treasury," commanded Tarquin the Proud.

The keepers of the treasury escorted the Sibyl to the treasury. When she had departed with her payment, the king ordered the last three volumes to be put into a shrine in the temple of Jupiter. Fifteen priests guarded them for one thousand years. The priests' duty was to consult the books whenever the Romans had the need to speak with the gods regarding the welfare of their city. The books were called the Sibyline Books, after the woman who brought them to Rome.

# POMONA AND VERTUMNUS

OMONA WAS A NYMPH, ONE OF THE MINOR GODS WHO became known as maidens that dwelled in the forests, trees, or waters. She never went near the springs, lakes, or rivers in the land. She stayed away from the woods, for she cared not for hunting. Only near the trees that bore fruit could Pomona be found. Her implements of choice were the spade and the pruning hook.

She loosened the earth around the roots of her beloved fruit-bearing trees. She cut away any growth that had become too luxurious so it did not sap too much energy from the trees. She grafted a twig from one tree onto a cut she made in a different one. After a time she rejoiced to see the tree bearing two types of fruit. On other days she might train a vine to grow alongside an elm tree. She dug small canals so water could flow by the roots in her orchard. She was careful to destroy any insects that threatened the leaves.

In the springtime Pomona enjoyed watching Flora, her sister nymph, at work in the fields giving color and fragrance to the flowers, sweetness to the honey in the combs, and grace to the children who ventured near her presence. But Pomona never left her fruit trees to call upon Flora. Nor did she call upon the shrine of Venus, the great goddess of love. When she caught a glimpse of the goddess, Pomona was most pleased but she would not leave the comfort of her trees.

Pomona did not adorn herself with any ornaments. She wore a plain, brown dress, no ribbons in her hair, nor even flowers. The wreath of leaves about her head was to keep the sun from burning her face, not as decoration. Yet, word of her beauty spread throughout the world of the demigods, the mythological beings who had more power than mortals but less than gods.

The first demigods to notice her were Silvanus and Picus. They discussed Pomona's fine qualities among themselves.

"She's becoming more good-looking with each season," said Silvanus.

"She's shy, but as ripe as an apple," said the bolder Picus.

"She has much to share with her garden of fruits of every kind," said Silvanus.

He was the first to try to visit Pomona. He donned a hunter's dress, carried a spear in his hand, and a recent kill in the bag at his side. Pomona was not impressed, and Silvanus was forced to hide behind tree after tree with the nymph in hot pursuit until he was gone from her orchard. Silvanus waited one whole season before renewing his attempt to woo Pomona. This time he came dressed as a shepherd. Pomona was as disinterested in the shepherd as she had been in the hunter, and she drove him away once more.

Picus took up the chase that same day. He came wearing a scarlet cloak, and he felt proud. He knew he was handsome to women, and he trusted his good looks and smooth ways, which had won him success with other women, to win over Pomona. What he found, instead, was his face doused with stream water that Pomona flung at him.

Running from the orchard, Picus observed Silvanus dressed as the shepherd. He surmised that Pomona must have treated him in his fine cloak so poorly because she favored Silvanus. So Picus began to hurl insults at Silvanus. Silvanus retaliated with a series of blows. Then he ripped the red cloak from Picus's shoulders. They kept at their fighting until they exhaust-ed themselves.

Pomona decided to build a wall around her trees. In it she placed a gate through which she would not exit. Vertumnus, another demigod, younger and more innocent than Silvanus and Picus, observed Pomona through the gate. He knocked to gain entrance, but Pomona refused to admit him. He returned as a reaper with a basket of barley ears, but she would not accept the gift. Next he came as a mower, with grass on his brow, but that disguise received the same negative response from Pomona. He came as a plough-man, carrying a goad that was used to drive oxen. Still, Pomona refused him entrance. Finally he arrived with a ladder, in the hopes that she would consider him a fellow tree-lover, but that plan failed, as well.

A few days later Pomona encountered an old woman at the gate. "I have heard of you, dearest. Everything I heard about your beauty pales before you," said the woman. Then she kissed Pomona.

Pomona opened the gate and invited the visitor into her garden. They walked from tree to tree in peace, marveling at the splendor of the place. The old woman stopped before an elm.

"Look, if that elm tree had not mated with the vine, its only value would be as timber. If the vine had no elm tree to grow upon, it would lie flat on the ground and not flourish," she said to Pomona.

She continued, "If you refuse to be wedded, so will be your fate. Choose Vertumnus!"

As the old woman spoke the words, her headdress fell to the soft earth. Her eyes glowed with love, and her face softened. Her cloak disappeared.

"You are Vertumnus," cried Pomona.

She smiled into the youth's face, and she shared his love. When the evening star appeared among the trees, Pomona promised to marry Vertumnus.

LOVE

# Psyche and Cupid

SYCHE WAS THE YOUNGEST OF THREE DAUGHTERS BORN to the king and queen of a faraway country. Her beauty was so great that any of the words that were spoken to describe her appearance sounded empty and meaningless. Men came from great distances, not as suitors but as worshippers, to gaze upon her. Rumor spread that Venus had left her immortal home in heaven to become mortal in the form of the girl named Psyche. Shrines to Venus soon emptied of the mortal worshippers now enthralled with Psyche. Before long, Venus got word of the happenings.

"Shall I who am judged the fairest among the immortal goddesses be challenged by an earthly girl? This Psyche will have little joy from her loveliness," she challenged.

Venus called her son Cupid to her. He was the winged boy who flew at night, armed with his bows and arrows, inflicting the pain of love upon unsuspecting mortals. Venus and Cupid traveled together to the faraway country to observe Psyche.

"I pray you, allow your mother a fitting vengeance. See to it that this Psyche becomes slave to an unworthy love," Venus instructed Cupid.

Once his mother was off to her purposes, Cupid wounded himself with his own arrow, so overcome was he with the maiden's loveliness. For her part, Psyche was desperate with the attentions of so many men. Her sisters had both wedded before they reached Psyche's age. Psyche fell into a deep sorrow.

Her parents left at once to consult an oracle about their youngest daughter's future. "Dress the maiden for a wedding and for death. Place her on top of a mountain. Do not search for a son-in-law of mortal blood. Her husband will be the serpent whom even the gods fear, who makes the bodiless ones on the Styx shrink in terror," said the oracle.

Beneath her yellow veil Psyche wept. The torch that was lighted upon the mountain gathered ashes, and an ominous dark smoke replaced it. What should have been the joyous strain of the pipe sounded like a wail. Psyche's family held their heads low as they would at a funeral.

"Do not waste your tears by weeping for me," Psyche told them. And she said good-bye and asked them to leave her alone upon the mountaintop.

When they had departed, the gentle breeze Zephyrus lifted Psyche from her perch. He set her softly among the flowers in the valley beneath the mountain. When Psyche awoke, she saw a fountain as clear as ice next to a golden dwelling place supported by golden pillars and ivory arches. Silver latticed the walls. The wild creatures of the wood frolicked about the dwelling, and the air hung with the music of more birds than Psyche had ever heard.

Psyche entered the house, sure that it was the abode of a god who had rescued her from a miserable life. A banquet was laid in the great room. Beautiful goblets and vessels adorned the table. A multitude of fine tastes and textures presented themselves for her pleasure.

A voice said, "Lady and mistress! I am your servant. This is your feast, which is fit for a queen." No one appeared to claim the voice or to share the feast.

She heard a song played by harp and sung to honor her, but the bearer of the song was invisible. Unseen hands lit the lamps. When she finished eating, the same unseen hands extinguished the light. Exhausted, Psyche wandered to her bed. Her bridegroom came to her, but he departed before the dawn.

During the next day and the days that followed, Psyche was cared for as she had been the day of her arrival. One evening her husband spoke to her for the first time. "Psyche, my life and my spouse! Ill-favored fortune at the hands of mortals is harkening toward us. Your sisters are seeking after you. You will hear their cries. If you must, answer them. But do not yield to their counsel about my form. If you do, we may never embrace each other again."

Psyche wept at his words. To live without him would break her heart. Trustingly, she admitted her sisters to her dwelling. They marveled at the luxuries that belonged to her. And they were very jealous. While they had been properly married by arrangement as was the custom of the time, their husbands were poor by comparison. They prodded Psyche about the location of her husband. She responded that he was away hunting. But they knew she was withholding something from them.

"Let us scare her, if not into revealing the secrets that live here, then at least we can bring her down from her high spirits," said the oldest sister. The other sister agreed with the plan.

"You exist in the midst of a danger you know nothing about. You have never seen your husband. We know that. Remember what the oracle spoke. You are destined to be devoured by none other than a beast. The beast waits for you to bear a babe so he can devour both of you. While nothing can be done to save you, at least know that we have warned you," said the sisters. They took turns saying the words.

That night Psyche bore their false message in her heart. While she was alone, she hid a knife in her bed for protection. Behind her curtain she concealed a lighted lamp. When her husband was sleeping soundly, Psyche arose from the bed. She held the knife in her right hand above her head, ready to strike him if necessary. She suspended the lighted lamp over the form of her husband.

Before her, she saw Love himself. She trembled at the sight of his golden hair, his soft, ruddy cheeks, and his white throat. His skin was fresh with dew. At his feet lay his bow and arrow. Psyche bent to kiss his red lips. A drop of the burning oil from the lamp fell upon his shoulder and burned him. Understanding at once his wife's faithlessness, Cupid rose from the bed and flew away.

# PSYCHE AND VENUS

HE GODDESS OF LOVE, VENUS, CURSED THE MORTAL maiden called Psyche because the girl's beauty was claiming the attention of the godddess's mortal worshippers. Hoards of foolish men flocked to the home of Psyche to gaze upon her, instead of paying their respects at the shrines of the goddess. So the angry Venus demanded that Psyche become the slave to an unworthy love. She entrusted her son Cupid, the boy god of love, to carry out her mission. But Cupid fell in love with Psyche. He enticed her to a beautiful palace filled with luxurious things. In the evenings he treated her like his queen. The only condition Cupid placed upon the arrangement was that Psyche promise never to investigate what he looked like. When Psyche, encouraged by her jealous sisters, broke this vow, the god of love fled from her.

This is a myth about how Psyche confronted the anger of Venus. No immortal being would give her aid outright because Venus was one of the most venerated immortals. However, Psyche did receive help from the blessed forces of nature in fulfilling the impossible tasks that Venus put before her.

Poor Psyche wandered from the castle in search of her husband, her heart aching for him. One day she came upon a temple. She looked inside for Cupid. What she saw instead were ears of wheat and barley strewn on the temple's floor, as well as sickles and other tools.

"While I am overcome with my desire for my husband, I must not neglect the shrine of any god or goddess," she said to herself.

So Psyche tidied up the shrine, putting everything in order. The goddess of the harvest, Ceres, came upon Psyche at the shrine. She knew the visitor as the wife of Cupid.

"While Venus tracks you, noble Psyche, I find you here in my service," said Ceres.

"Please, Goddess, conceal me here until I can recover some strength after my long wandering," pleaded Psyche.

But so adamant was the wrath of Venus, that Ceres refused. Psyche had no recourse but to continue on the journey to find her husband. She came upon a second shrine. This one was richly adorned with offerings and priceless garments. In the trees letters of gold spelled the name Juno, the great goddess of women and marriage. Psyche entered the temple and lay herself upon its altar in prayer.

"O Juno, spouse of Jupiter, you who are the helper in childbirth. Deliver me, Goddess, from the danger I face," prayed Psyche.

Juno answered, "If only I could answer your prayer, but I cannot. Venus is one I have loved as a daughter. I will not go against her wishes."

Leaving the temple of Juno, Psyche decided to face Venus directly. When she arrived at Venus's house, the servants mocked her. One of them dragged her by the hair to their mistress.

"You dare at last to greet me as your mother-in-law!" laughed Venus. "I will see whether you are a dutiful daughter-in-law."

The goddess took heaps of barley, millet, and every other grain she had in her fields and mixed them together into a tremendous mound. Then she sent Psyche to sort out one grain from the next into neat piles. Psyche knew the task was impossible and could do nothing but stare at the giant mound. After some moments an ant who had watched her all morning spoke.

"I have harnessed an army of ants to help you, wife of Love," said the ant.

When Venus returned that evening to find the grain carefully sorted, she was certain that her son had helped Psyche. She ordered the mortal as her next task to gather shreds of gold from the fleece of sheep that grazed on the land found on the other side of a rushing river.

Early the following morning Psyche came upon the torrent. It was useless to try to win the forgiveness of Venus, she thought. She was about to cast herself into the river to drown, when she heard a whisper.

"Dear Psyche, stop before you poison this water with self-destruction. Instead, rest beneath the plane tree until nightfall. You will find shreds of fleece left in the trees by the flock," said the whisper. It belonged to the green reed, the maker of music.

When Psyche gathered the shreds according to the reed's instruction and presented them to Venus, the goddess once again suspected that Cupid had given his assistance. She handed Psyche a crystal vessel. With her other hand she pointed to a high mountain.

"I am not finished with you yet. A dark stream runs down from the peak of that tall mountain. You must fill this crystal with water from its innermost source," demanded Venus.

Psyche climbed the mountain, fighting to keep her footing on its treacherous slope. At the top she found a rocky gulf that was invisible from the mountain's foot. Serpents with long necks, and eyes that never blinked, jutted out from among the rocks.

They spoke to Psyche in voices muffled by their surroundings. "Why did you come here?" hissed one of them.

"You are bringing destruction upon yourself," echoed the chorus of serpents.

Psyche lost any sense of purpose. Fatigue and despair filled her veins. She stood at the edge of the gulf as though she were of the same substance as the rock.

The eagle that belonged to Jupiter, the ruler of all gods, took pity on her. He swooped down for the crystal vessel and flew with it to the source of the stream. Filling it, he returned to Psyche.

"Go to Venus," said the eagle.

The serpents raised their heads and hissed, but they were unable to stop Psyche. Her legs were hers again. She raced down the strange mountain and gave the spiteful Venus the water she demanded.

# PSYCHE IN HADES

HE GODDESS OF LOVE, VENUS, WAS ANGRY WITH THE beautiful mortal named Psyche. Cupid, the son of Venus, and the boy god of love, had pierced himself with his own arrow in order to fall in love with her. Now Venus had a daughter-in-law against her wishes. She resolved to put Psyche to a test that would most likely kill her. Venus sent her to the Kingdom of the Dead, named for, and ruled by, the god Hades.

"Take this tiny casket to Proserpine, the queen of Hades. Tell her that Venus wishes for her to fill it with enough of her beauty to use for one day. Bring the casket back to me when she has filled it," Venus ordered Psyche.

Psyche understood that Venus intended to send her to her death. She set out for the tower she could see in the distance. Climbing to the top, she prepared to jump. Thus, she would quickly enter the Kingdom of the Dead.

"Wretched Psyche! If you die in the jump, which you surely will, you will indeed enter Hades. But you will never be able to return," scolded the stones of the tower.

"What does it matter whether I enter alive or dead. I will never accomplish what Venus demands," complained Psyche.

"I will guide you in what you must do," said the tower. "But you must not go empty-handed. Find two morsels of barley bread, one for each hand.

Soak the bread in honey. Procure two pieces of money. Hold both in your mouth." Psyche listened carefully and obtained what the tower described. She departed for Hades further armed with the tower's instructions.

Not far into her journey, as the tower had said, Psyche came upon a mountain. She searched until she found an opening in the mountain's side. Through the hole she traveled the rough, dark course downward until she emerged in Hades. She looked for the castle of Orcus in the distance, like the tower had instructed. She walked in its direction. On the path she came face-to-face with a lame donkey carrying wood. The animal was driven by a lame master.

"Kind mortal, please hand me the cords that have slipped from the donkey's pack. If you do not, the burden he carries will be lost," implored the lame man.

But Psyche ignored him as the stones of the tower had directed her. She passed the man and the donkey in silence, then continued toward the River of the Dead, called the Styx. The ferryman Charon, who transported the dead across the river, ferried Psyche to the other side. As they came close to the far shore, an old man rose partially from the water and begged Psyche to help him into the boat. She was careful not to pity him, as the tower had instructed. When the ferry beached on the far shore, Psyche edged one of the two pieces of money out between her lips, and the ferryman grasped it with his fingers in payment.

"Lend us a hand in our spinning," cried a group of women with long, gray hair.

Psyche knew from the tower that if she helped them, she would have to drop one of the two pieces of bread she carried. She ignored their pleas and held fast to the bread that she would need to survive Hades. Psyche drew near at last to the isolated house of Proserpine. A watchdog bared his teeth at the entrance. Psyche gave one piece of the honey-soaked bread to the dog, and he closed his fierce mouth long enough for her to enter the house.

"What is it that has brought you to Hades?" asked Proserpine, the queen.

"I have come from Venus to ask you to fill this casket with beauty to last a day," answered Psyche.

"Have a seat while I do as Venus has requested," invited Proserpine.

When the queen took leave to stock the casket in private, Psyche sat upon the floor. She did not sit upon the couch, nor did she eat or drink anything that was left for her. To have done either would have confined her forever to the Kingdom of the Dead. When Proserpine returned, she handed Psyche the casket with the lid shut fast. At the door of the house, Psyche gave the watchdog the other piece of barley bread soaked in honey. She paid the ferryman Charon with the remaining piece of money when he left her on the opposite shore.

Psyche emerged from the vent of the mountain into the light of life. She rushed to the house of Venus with the casket filled with the beauty of Proserpine. An impulse to raise the lid and touch herself with a speck of dust from the beauty it held, and thus please Cupid, rose in Psyche. But when she opened the casket, its content was only sleep. And it was the sleep of the dead that felled Psyche to the ground. She could not move.

At that moment Cupid flew from the house of Venus, where he had been healing himself. With the point of one of his arrows, the god of love woke his mortal wife from the deep sleep. He ascended to the highest heavens and presented himself to Jupiter, ruler of the gods.

"You have upset the harmony of things," scolded Jupiter. Then he kissed Cupid's face. Jupiter commissioned his messenger Mercury to call the gods and goddesses together for a wedding. Once the immortals were assembled, Jupiter sent Mercury for Psyche.

"Drink this and live forever, married, with Cupid," said Jupiter to Psyche.

# THE SABINE WOMEN

HE SABINES LIVED IN THE STATE NEXT TO ROME. KING Romulus of Rome had invited all of his neighbors, including the Sabines, to marry their daughters to young Roman men. Young men had founded the new Roman state. They had built remarkable buildings and a citadel. They had established a government of senators. What were missing were young females to wed. The neighbors had mocked the invitation from the Roman king because they considered Rome to be a state populated by criminals and ruffians. So King Romulus had tricked his neighbors, the Sabines, and they were angry. He had invited the Sabines to the festival of Consus, god of the harvest, promising a great spectacle for all who attended. Whole families of Sabines had crossed into Rome to see the spectacle. Little did they know—the fine Roman horsemen would capture all the Sabine women of marriageable age as the grand finale to their performance and make them their wives.

This is a myth about war. It is about how the brave Sabine women turned the war of the Sabines against the Romans away from bloodshed. The myth begins with an act of treason by the daughter of a Roman commander, one of the few women of Latin descent in the new state of Rome. It ends with an act of power by the god of war, Mars.

The name of the Roman commander's daughter was Tarpeia. She was approached by the king of the Sabines, Titus Tatius.

"I'll give you anything you want if you open the gates of the citadel of Rome on the Palatine Hill for the Sabine army to enter," offered Titus Tatius.

"What every Sabine soldier wears on his left arm is my price," responded Tarpeia.

"You shall have them," promised the Sabine king. He agreed to give the girl the gold bracelets worn by his men. These bracelets were very thick and served as shields.

Tarpeia opened the gates of the citadel to the invaders, and she was ready to accept the bribe. First, Titus Tatius removed his shield. He tossed it upon Tarpeia, and she fell to the ground. One by one, the Sabine soldiers followed suit, covering Tarpeia completely with the gold shields. The weight of the shields crushed her to death.

The Sabines continued their advance upon the Roman forces. King Romulus and his army were taken by surprise, and their losses mounted. Romulus cried out to Jupiter, the ruler of the gods.

"O Jupiter, you sent to me an omen of twelve sacred vultures, the birds that do not prey upon other birds, and I founded this city. Deliver us now from the invaders. I will proclaim to all how you saved the city of Rome," prayed Romulus.

Then the king spoke to his demoralized men. "Hear me, Romans, Jupiter will protect us if we stand firm in this battle," he proclaimed. And the Romans found new strength to fight against the invaders.

Meanwhile, the Sabines were certain they would be victorious. "We will show these Romans the difference between carrying off helpless maidens and fighting against men," said Titus Tatius.

As he spoke, though, a squad of young Romans pushed the Sabine forces back into the valley between the two hills. Both sides faced each other with the fire of blood in their eyes. They were prepared to fight to the death for victory. Into the valley advanced the Sabine women. They had loosened their hair, which hung to their shoulders. In the gesture of mourning, they had torn their clothing. The women took a position between both armies. On one side they faced their fathers and brothers. On the other, they confronted their new husbands.

"Better for us to die here than to live without either one of you," said one Sabine woman.

"Yes, what is our choice? To watch our fathers and brothers die? Or our husbands?" said another.

The women's pleas moved the armies to drop their weapons. The enemies declared a truce right there in the valley. Romulus and Titus Tatius agreed to rule the combined city states of Rome and Sabine together. The new people were to be called Quirites.

After a time Titus Tatius died. Romulus ruled alone in his absence. Rome's power in the region grew, and the state became greatly feared by other states. Even the once dominant Etruscans were weak by comparison.

Romulus was proud of his army. One afternoon he sat upon his royal chair on the Campus Martius, the playing fields dedicated to Mars, to review the soldiers. As they advanced for review, a great cloud obscured their king from them. Tremendous peals of thunder silenced the drums. Finally it was quiet once again. But when the clouds lifted, the chair of King Romulus was vacant. One of the senators who had been standing close to the king spoke to the soldiers and the other spectators.

"Hear this, Quirites. Romulus, father of this city, said this to me, 'My father, Mars, has made me immortal in heaven. Know from this day that Rome will be the chief city in the world. Teach the children to cherish war so that no army will be able to resist Roman arms,'" proclaimed the senator.

And the Roman people renamed Romulus "Quirinus." They worshipped him as a minor god of war and built temples in his honor.

# PYRAMUS AND THISBE

YRAMUS AND THISBE LIVED NEXT DOOR TO EACH other in the city of Babylon. They became acquainted as children, passing on the street as they entered their houses. Over time a fondness developed between them.

Thisbe knew Pyramus to be the most handsome young man in her city. Pyramus appreciated Thisbe as the most beautiful maiden in all of the East. Pyramus and Thisbe would have asked to be married, had they been born to different fathers. As it was, their fathers hated one another. Suspecting their offspring's affections, the fathers forbid Pyramus and Thisbe to see each other any longer.

Between the two houses was a high brick wall. There was no kindly servant or acquaintance to act as go-between from one house to the other, exchanging the youths' messages of affection. Still, even the wall did not squelch their love.

When the thick obstruction was built long before Pyramus and Thisbe were born, a slight imperfection was overlooked. A narrow chink between the bricks had gone unnoticed. The tiny slit permitted a small shaft of light. From their separate courtyards Pyramus and Thisbe peered through the slit. If they squinted into the light, they could take turns looking at one another. When they whispered, they could hear each other.

"O jealous wall," spoke Pyramus. "You make it impossible for us to meet."

"You block the sweetness of our kisses," said Thisbe.

But Pyramus and Thisbe were nonetheless grateful that the pathway in the wall allowed them to share their words of love. They spoke until nightfall came, and they departed with a quick kiss through the chink. They found each other again each morning, with the rising sun.

One day they changed things. "Let us meet tonight," resolved Thisbe.

"Yes, at the tomb of Ninus," agreed Pyramus.

"Near the spring, beneath the mulberry tree," said Thisbe.

That evening Thisbe carefully released the lock on the front door of her house. Wearing a shawl to hide herself from anyone's recognition on the street, she stole her way outside and to the spring. The water smelled fresh. The evening was delightfully cool. The snow-white fruit of the mulberry beckoned to her. But what did she see in her path? A lioness with her jaws bloody from a recent kill sprang to the water to satisfy her thirst.

Thisbe ducked into the shadows of a cave to hide. As she did, she unknowingly dropped her shawl. The lioness, upon finishing her long drink, discovered the shawl. She sniffed until she had her fill, then she tore the material with her bloodstained paws.

Pyramus hurried toward the meeting place. As he ran, he saw the animal's footprints in the deep dust of the path. He quickened his pace, now worried about Thisbe's well-being. When he came within sight of the mulberry, he found the shredded and bloody shawl of his lover.

"O Thisbe, you should have lived a long, happy life. The guilt for your death is mine. I made you come to this dangerous place. I should have come first," cried Pyramus.

Next he spoke to the lioness. "Rend my body. Devour my guilty flesh with your fierce fangs. Drink a draught of my blood, too."

Pyramus kissed the ravaged shawl. He reached for his sword and plunged it into his side. Blood burst forth in long jets into the air. The berries of the mulberry tree colored purple as the tree's roots quenched themselves.

Thisbe looked out from the cave to see if it was safe to exit. The lioness was nowhere in sight. She longed to tell Pyramus about her narrow escape. She ran to the tree, but it could not be the same tree! The stained berries told her to beware. She saw Pyramus's twitching leg. Thisbe screamed. She held her lover's head in her shaking hands, and she kissed his cold lips.

"What evil has done this to you? Pyramus, lift your head and answer Thisbe!" she cried.

At the sound of Thisbe's name, Pyramus lifted his head. He opened his eyes, then he died. Thisbe noticed the empty ivory scabbard where Pyramus's sword should have been. She recognized her shawl in his limp hand.

"O Pyramus! Your hand and your heart have destroyed you. Mine are brave enough for this deed, as well. Death has no power to part us any longer. Love, give me strength to strike. O Gods, grant that we may share the same tomb. O tree, mark our death with your fruit funeral. May our twin blood be a pledge of our grief," cried Thisbe.

Thisbe grabbed the warm, bloody sword. She fixed its point beneath her breast, and she fell upon it. The berries of the mulberry deepened their purple hue in answer to her cry. Thisbe's parents, guided by the gods, lay the bodies in the same tomb.

To this day the mulberry celebrates the lovers with its purple fruit.

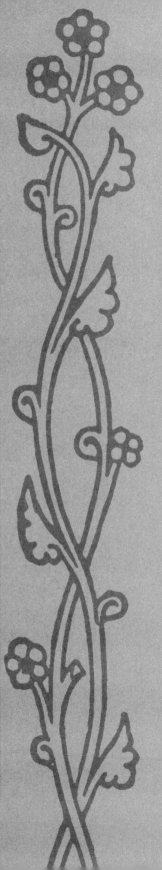

# CELTIC
# MYTHS

# TUAN MAC CARELL

## *Ireland*

 HIS STORY DATES FROM THE SIXTH CENTURY. TUAN mac Carell was chief of his clan. In those days and in those parts, the clan chief was a very powerful warrior who owned a vast amount of land.

St. Finnen was an abbot. His monastery was at Moville, County Donegal, and not too far from the castle of Tuan mac Carell. When the saint arrived at Tuan's castle, he asked to be allowed to stay there as a guest. But Tuan refused him.

In the custom of the day when someone was wronged by a person in power, St. Finnen sat upon the chief's doorstep. He began to fast. Magical power was attached to the custom, and it was held that the wronged individual would fast until right was done to him. Then the denier of the right would fast, so the wrong would be undone altogether.

Finally the chief opened his door to the saint. The saint stayed with the chief, and the two men resolved their conflict. Most probably, the chief also fasted. After the stay the saint returned to the Monastery at Moville.

"Tuan is a fine man. He will come to you, and he will tell you the old stories of Ireland," said St. Finnen to the other monks when they greeted him.

The monks received the saint's words with interest. They looked forward to the chief's visit, because they were eager to hear the old stories. Shortly afterward, Tuan came to the monastery with an invitation to his castle for St. Finnen and the other monks.

"Tell us the history of Ireland," the saint requested of Tuan.

Tuan began the tale. "The first man to settle in Ireland was Partholan. My father was the brother of Partholan. A great pestilence scoured the land, and I was the only person to survive. For there is never a slaughter where one person does not survive to tell the tale.

"I was alone in the land, wandering from one unoccupied castle to another. I traveled from rock to rock. I sought shelter from the wolves. For twenty years I lived like this until I was very old and decrepit. My hair was gray and long. I was clawed, naked, and miserable.

"I saw Nemed, son of Agnoman, also my father's brother, take possession of Ireland. When the Nemedians embarked for Ireland, they filled a fleet of thirty-two ships, with thirty people on each ship. When they arrived after a year and a half on the rough seas, they were only Nemed himself with four men and four women. Over the course of time, they grew to number eight thousand sixty men and women. I watched from the cliffs, and I avoided Nemed. One morning when I awoke, I had changed into a stag. I was young once more, and my heart was filled with gladness. My song was of Nemed's coming, of the new race of people in the land, and of my own transformation from human to deer.

"I was king of all the deer in the land during Nemed's rule. Over the course of time all of the Nemedians mysteriously died. I grew old and decrepit once more. One day I stood at the mouth of my cave, and I realized I had become a wild boar. And I sang a song about it. I was young again, and I was glad.

"The next to come to Ireland was Semion, from whom the Firbolgs and two other tribes descended. When I grew old and decrepit, I changed into a great eagle of the sea. Next the people of Dana came. They were both gods and false gods, and everyone knows the Irish people of learning descended from them. Then the Sons of Miled conquered the people of Dana. Throughout this time I kept the shape of the sea eagle.

"One day, when I was again old and decrepit, I found that I could not undergo another transformation. I fasted for nine days, and I fell asleep. When I awoke, I had changed into a salmon. I escaped the nets of fishermen for many years, until one day I was caught. The fisherman brought me to the wife of the chief of the country. She ate me whole, and I passed into her womb. I was born again as Tuan with all of the memories since the days of Partholan. I remember in order to teach these things to the monks, who carefully preserve them."

St. Finnen spoke to the other monks when Tuan had finished the story. "Did I not tell you he would tell you the old stories?"

Sawan, and Goban the Smith. The last was the land's great maker of armor and crafted arts. Kian owned a magical cow. The cow's milk flowed so freely that everyone in the land was eager to possess her. For this reason Kian kept close watch over the animal.

One day Sawan and Kian traveled to the forge to ask Goban the Smith, their brother, to construct weapons for them. Kian carried the steel they brought for the weapons into the forge, and he appointed his brother Sawan to guard his precious cow. King Balor wanted the cow. So he changed himself into a redheaded boy. He told Sawan a lie about how he overheard the brothers decide to use all the fine steel for their swords. Sawan's sword, Balor said, would be made of base metal. Upon hearing the untruth, Sawan placed the cow in the charge of the young boy, and he hurried into the forge to confront his brothers. Seizing the opportunity, Balor stole the cow and brought her across the sea to Tory Island.

Kian discovered Balor's trickery. He enlisted the help of a Druid wisewoman named Birog to take revenge on the king. Birog dressed Kian like a woman. By means of a magical spell, the wisewoman transported herself and Kian in disguise across the sea. They told the guardians of Ethlinn, Balor's imprisoned daughter, that they were two noblewomen who had been abducted to the island but they had escaped their captors. They begged entrance to the tower, and the guardians granted the request.

The wisewoman Birog cast a spell that put the guardians into a deep sleep. While they slept, Kian went to Princess Ethlinn, and he and the princess fell in love. In the morning Kian, Birog, and the magical cow were gone. Soon the guardians found that Ethlinn was pregnant. Fearful of Balor's wrath, they convinced her that her evening with Kian had been merely a dream. However, when it was time, the princess gave birth to three sons.

When Balor discovered the event, he commanded that the three babies be drowned in a whirlpool at sea. Despite the obedience of the soldier who was given the horrible duty, only two babies died. One dropped from the sheet in the soldier's grasp when a pin opened to make room for him to fall into the bay. The bay was afterward named Port na Delig, or the Haven of the Pin. It is called by that name to this day.

While his brothers drowned, the lucky baby was found by Birog and she gave the child to Kian. Kian in turn handed the baby over to Goban the Smith. Goban taught the child the fine details of his craft, and when the child grew, he was as talented an armorer and artisan as his uncle. The child was called Lugh. The Druids called him the sun god.

# LUGH, THE SUN GOD

## *Ireland*

UGH, THE SUN GOD, WAS APPOINTED BY HEAVEN TO save his people, the Dannans, from their enemies, the Fomorians. As an infant he escaped the death sentence of the evil Fomorian king, Balor. He had been placed with his two brothers in a bundle to be drowned. But one of the pins that held the bundle together opened, and Lugh escaped. The bundle was hurled into a whirlpool at sea by King's Balor's order. But Lugh had been found in the nearby bay, which was afterward named Port na Delig, or the Haven of the Pin. The bay is called the Haven of the Pin to this day.

When he was pulled from the water, Lugh was given by the wisewoman Birog to his father, Kian. The child was raised by Kian's brother Goban the Smith, the armorer and craftsman. Lugh learned his uncle's arts at an early age. Still a youth, the Dannan elders gave him to Duach, or "The Dark" king of the Great Plain, which was also known as the Land of the Dead. Lugh lived in the Great Plain until he grew to be a man.

The myth that follows is about how Lugh fulfilled his destiny to free his people.

One day Lugh traveled to the Land of the Living. He went to the castle at Tara of the Dannan king, Nuada of the Silver Hand. The keeper of the palace asked Lugh what service he had to offer the king.

"I am a carpenter," Lugh responded.

"We have a fine carpenter now. He is called Luchta, the son of Luchad," said the keeper of the castle.

"I am also a smith," said Lugh.

"We have a master smith," answered the castle keeper.

"I'm a warrior, too," said Lugh.

"Ogma is our warrior," responded the keeper of the palace.

Lugh then told the keeper he could do a host of things. One by one he listed all the occupations and arts he knew. He was a poet, a harper, a man of science, a physician, somebody who weighed measures of things, or a spencer, and on and on until he ran out of occupations. Each time Lugh offered a service to the king, the castle keeper responded as he had done the first time. That is, that the court of Nuada of the Silver Hand already had so and so by the name of such and such, who was a master of that particular service.

Lugh became frustrated. "Ask the king if he has one man in his service who is a master of all of these arts. If he does, then I will go away and no longer seek entrance to the castle," said Lugh proudly.

Lugh was then invited into the castle by the keeper. King Nuada of the Silver Hand granted him an audience. The king gave Lugh the surname of Ildanach, which meant "The All-Craftsman," Prince of all the Sciences. He was also given the name, Lugh Lamfada, or Lugh of the Long Arm.

When Lugh returned to the Land of the Dead, he transported many magical gifts. One was the Boat of Mananan, the son of Lir the Sea God. The boat could read a person's thoughts and could travel anywhere the person wanted to go. The second gift was the Horse of Mananan, which was able to travel to any location, by land or sea. The third object was a most

CREATION

# THE THREE
# CIRCLES OF LIFE

## *Wales*

 HIS IS THE MYTH OF HOW THE WORLD WAS CREATED, according to the beliefs of the Cymry. They lived in the British Isles in what is now Wales. They were Celtic people, who were of Cymric descent. Unlike the Celtic people that lived in Ireland, they were not Gaelic in origin.

Here is how the Cymric people believed the world was created. In the beginning there was nothing. All that existed were two primary forces. One force was God. The other force was Cythrawl. God ruled over all the energy that was associated with the creation of life and that produced love. Cythrawl ruled over all the energy that destroyed life and produced suffering and nothingness.

God pronounced His unspeakable Name. When He did, He created the Manred. The Manred was the substance that formed the universe. This substance was made of the tiniest particles of matter, which were atoms. Each particle of matter, or atom, was a microcosm, or a little world. God's force was present in each microcosm. At the same time as God was present in each microcosm, each tiny atom was also a part of God. That meant that each atom was part of the Whole.

Everything that God made belonged in three circles that had one common center. These were called concentric circles, and they held all that God made. The inner circle was called Abred. In Abred, all life had grown out of Annwn (pronounced "Annoon"). Annwn was the Cymric word for Hades, or the Fairyland. Because life in Annwn was created from Hades, everything that existed there was still in a struggle with Cythrawl, the destruction force of nothingness.

The middle circle of the three circles of life was called Gwynfyd, or Purity. All life in this circle existed as pure energy. Much rejoicing happened in Gwynfyd. Here life was victorious over evil. The struggle with Cythrawl that involved suffering and pain was over. Humans could live in Gwynfyd only after they had lived through all the lower life-forms of matter, like rocks and trees and animals. And only after they had felt all the different types of suffering. No one could experience the love and happiness of the middle circle until they understood the suffering of the innermost circle.

The outermost circle of the three was named Ceugant. The last circle was Infinity. Only God dwelled in the circle called Ceugant.

These ancient teachings of the Cymric people about creation were found in what was called "Barddas." "Barddas" was given to a Welsh bard, a poet-singer, in the sixteenth century. Here are some questions and answers from the teachings. The questions, marked by a Q, are those that would have been asked by the Cymric people of Wales. The answers, shown with an A, could be those spoken by a human who had nearly completed the struggle with the destruction power of Cythrawl. The human would next have moved to the innermost circle, called Gwynfyd.

Q. "Whence didst thou proceed?"

A. "I came from the Great World, having my beginning in Annwn."

Q. "Where art thou now? and how camest thou to what thou art?"

A. "I am in the Little World. I came having traversed the circle of Abred, and now I am a Man, at its extreme limits."

Q. "What wert thou before thou didst become a man, in the circle of Abred?"

A. "I was in Annwn, the least possible form of life, and the nearest to absolute death. I came through every form capable of a body and life. I came to the state of man along the circle of Abred. I was parted in Annwn from the dead by the gift of God and his unlimited and endless love."

Q. "Through how many different forms didst thou come, and what happened unto thee?"

A. "Through every form capable of life — in water, in earth, in air. There happened unto me every severe thing, every hardship, every evil and every suffering. Little was the goodness of Gwynfyd before I became a man. Gwynfyd cannot be obtained without seeing and knowing everything. But it is not possible to see or to know everything without suffering everything. And there can be no full and perfect love that does not produce the things necessary to lead to the knowledge that causes Gwynfyd."[4]

4 "Barddas," vol. i, pp.224. Reprinted in T.W. Rolleston, *Celtic Myths and Legends*, (New York: Dover Publications, Inc., 1990), pp. 334-335.

# HOW PWYLL BECAME LORD OF THE UNDERWORLD

## *Wales*

 WYLL WAS THE PRINCE OF DYFED. THIS IS THE STORY OF how Prince Pwyll came to merit the title, Pen Annwn. The Cymric words translated to Head of Hades, lord of the Underworld.

One day, Prince Pwyll was hunting in the woods of Glyn Cuch. He watched a strange pack of dogs in pursuit of a stag, an adult male red deer. The unfamiliar hounds had coats that were completely white. Their ears were red. Inexperienced in the ways of fairies, the prince did not recognize the significance of the color of the hounds' ears. Had he known, he would have realized that red-eared hounds, like red-eared men, belonged to the world of magic. So, Prince Pwyll chased away the dogs and set off hunting again with his own hound, whose ears were not red. Before long he came upon a nobleman riding through the woods.

"How discourteous of you to run off those hounds," challenged the nobleman on horseback.

"Might I make amends for my actions, sir?" offered Prince Pwyll, and he asked the nobleman his name.

The nobleman identified himself as Arawn, and he told Prince Pwyll he was a king in Annwn. A rival named Havgan was in close pursuit of Arawn, and the king told the young prince that for chasing away the hounds, he could indeed make amends.

"I beg you to confront Havgan one year from now in single combat," said Arawn.

Then Arawn told Prince Pwyll his plan. Pwyll would take on the appearance of Arawn and govern in the kingdom of Annwn until the day he was to meet Havgan one year hence. The king, likewise, would assume the prince's physical appearance and rule Dyfed in Pwyll's place. Arawn explained to Pwyll that there was only one way to confront Havgan.

"You must lay him low with but one single stroke. If you strike him more than once, Havgan will revive again, as strong as before," instructed Arawn.

The young prince honorably agreed to what Arawn suggested as his amends. Off to the land of Annwn, he went. He dutifully ruled in the land during the day in the disguise of Arawn. At night he shared a chamber with the wife of the king, but he treated her like a sister, turning his back to her and going to sleep. Finally the fateful day arrived when Prince Pwyll had to face Arawn's foe, Havgan.

At the ford of a river, Pwyll, in the appearance of Arawn, confronted Havgan. They faced off against each other on horseback, tilting at each other with their spears. At the first clash of metal, Pwyll pierced the rival of Arawn. So severe was the blow that Havgan flew from his horse and fell to the ground. He was mortally wounded.

"In the name of heaven, please finish the task and slay me," pleaded Havgan.

"Slay thee who may, I will not," retorted Prince Pwyll, in the disguise of Arawn.

Havgan recognized that his end was upon him, and he ordered his army to carry him elsewhere to die. Pwyll then united the two lands of Annwn, the one that belonged to Arawn and the one that had been governed by the defeated Havgan. The peoples of the land rejoiced when Pwyll as King Arawn proclaimed himself their master. The princes and lords of the land that had belonged to Havgan also declared their loyalty to Arawn.

As agreed, Prince Pwyll rode off to meet King Arawn in Glyn Cuch, the location of their encounter one year earlier. Arawn listened to Pwyll's account of the battle with Havgan. He thanked Pwyll for uniting his land.

"When you return to your own dominions, you will recognize what I have done for you to compensate," proclaimed Arawn.

Prince Pwyll assumed his own countenance, and King Arawn regained his. Each rode away in his own likeness to take possession of his rightful land. At the court in Annwn the feasting and merrymaking was still strong over the defeat of Havgan. Arawn joined the merrymakers upon his return. No one knew that he was a different king than Pwyll in his disguise.

When night fell, Arawn took his rightful place with the queen. He asked her why she was so silent.

"For a year you have not spoken this much in our chambers. Nor have you shown me tenderness," responded the queen.

"I now know a man as faithful in friendship as any I can call a friend," answered Arawn. And he told her what had happened between himself and Pwyll.

"You have indeed found a faithful friend," she said.

In his land of Dyfed, Pwyll assembled his lords to ask them to judge his manner of ruling during the past year.

"Lord, your wisdom was never so great as you showed it this year. You were never so kind or generous, and your justice was also great," they responded.

They listened intently while Pwyll recounted for them what had transpired during the year.

"Thank heaven that you have found such a friendship," said one lord.

Another lord asked Pwyll to render unto the kingdom of Dyfed the type of rule the people had enjoyed over the recent year. The other lords agreed wholeheartedly with the request. And Pwyll responded that in the eyes of heaven he would do so.

Afterward the two rulers exchanged rich gifts of horses, hounds, and jewels to celebrate their friendship. Henceforth, Pwyll also owned the title, lord of Annwn, in memory of the adventure.

# THE MAGIC CAULDRON

## *Wales*

 HIS MYTH IS A TALE ABOUT A MAGIC CAULDRON. THE cauldron originally came from Ireland. It resided in Wales for a time, but then it returned to Ireland. Not only did the cauldron possess certain powers, it also forged an understanding between the rulers of the two countries. Here is the story of the magic cauldron.

Bran the Blessed was king of the Isle of the Mighty, which was at the time the land of Britain, and that land included Wales. Bran had his court at Harlech. At Bran's court were also the members of the royal family. These included Bran's brother Manawyddan, the son of Llyr, and his sister, Branwen. Two sons whom Bran's mother bore to Eurosswyd were also at court. Nissyen was a gentle youth. Evnissyen, by contrast, was never so content as when he caused difficulty and strife.

One day Bran looked out from Harlech at sea, and he witnessed thirteen ships sailing with the help of a fair wind from Ireland. Bright flags flew from the ships' masts. In the front ship a man held up a triangular Norman shield pointed upward in the gesture of peace. Upon landing, the visitors greeted Bran and explained the reason for their coming.

Among them was Matholwch, the king of Ireland. He had come to request the hand of Branwen, Bran's sister, in marriage. It was Matholwch's intention that the marriage forge a union between Ireland and the Isle of the Mighty, making both countries more powerful because of it.

Gaiety spread throughout the land, because Branwen was a favorite of the people. The people sang, "Branwen is the fairest damsel in the world."

Bran took counsel with his lords, then he agreed to the marriage. In the place called Aberffraw, Branwen became the bride of the Irish king. Guests feasted and celebrated in tents for many days.

During the festivities the evil Evnissyen, half brother of Bran and Branwen, chanced upon some fine horses at rest.

"To whom do these belong?" he inquired.

"They are the horses of Matholwch, Branwen's new husband," responded the keeper of the animals.

"And how has it happened that such a fine maiden as she has been given in marriage without my consent? I could be offered no greater insult," proclaimed Evnissyen.

With his words of anger, Evnissyen rushed upon the horses. He cut off their lips to the teeth, he removed the ears of their fine heads, and he chopped off their tails! He even excised the eyes of some.

When Matholwch was informed of the evildoings, he ordered his countrymen to put out to sea immediately. Bran sent messengers after the Irish king, offering sound horses for every animal that Matholwch had lost, a staff of silver as tall as himself, and a plate of gold the size of his face. Bran told his messengers to arrange a meeting between himself and Matholwch. Matholwch reluctantly agreed.

When the two kings met, Bran offered Matholwch another treasure, the magic cauldron.

"I know this cauldron," said Matholwch. "It comes from a lake in Ireland that is near the Fairy Mounds. The lake is the Lake of the Cauldron."

Matholwch told Bran a story.

"I once met a tall, ill-looking fellow with a wife bigger than himself, and the cauldron was strapped on his back," began Matholwch.

Matholwch explained that he had hired the man to work for him. Six weeks later the strange man's wife gave birth to a son, who was born as a fully armed warrior. As if the event were not odd enough, it repeated itself every six weeks. By year's end the tall, ill-looking man and his wife had so many warrior sons they could have passed as a war god and war goddess. As for the warrior sons, they fought among themselves constantly. That is, when they were not causing turmoil in the land.

Finally Matholwch had a house of iron built. He enticed the father, mother, and all their children inside. Matholwch then barred the door. He heaped coals around the house and heated them until they turned white-hot. He hoped to roast them to death. As soon as the walls softened and took on the color of the coals, the man and his wife burst through them and fled. Their warrior children remained inside and burned to death.

Bran then spoke. "The man was called Llassar Llaesgyvnewid. His wife was Kymideu Kymeinvoll. They came next to Britain," he began.

Bran explained to Matholwch that he himself had taken pity on the couple and had housed them. They filled the land with their offspring, who prospered wherever they went. Their descendants lived in strong, fortified villages and they owned the finest weapons ever seen. To repay him for his kindness, the couple gave Bran the cauldron.

Bran told the Irish king that if a slain man were thrown into the cauldron, he would emerge physically sound, but be unable to speak. Matholwch accepted the gift of the magic cauldron from Bran. Matholwch forgave Bran for his half brother's evil deed, and he sailed back to Ireland with his new wife, Branwen. Thus, a strong union was formed between the two countries.

# THE MOON CALENDAR OF TREES

## *British Isles*

REES WERE SACRED TO THE CELTS. THEY WERE THE people who lived in the countries we now call England, Scotland, Ireland, and Wales. The Celtic people believed that trees joined the earth goddess with the sky god. The two halves of the world came together because of the way they grew. Their roots were grounded in the earth, and their branches reached up to the heavens.

Besides connecting the earth and the sky, trees were sacred because they served humans and animals. As charcoal they gave fuel for cooking and for keeping warm. As boards they provided ships and shelters. As leaves or bark, trees made medicine. And they offered a home for animals, who lived in their leaves, branches, trunks, and roots.

Trees possessed magic, too. Fairies called Dryads were found wherever there were trees. Gnomes were said to live in the roots of large oaks, from which they could keep watch over all woodland creatures.

The Celts kept time by the full moon. They named each of their moons for a different tree. In the Celtic year there were thirteen months, one for each full moon.

The full moon was called Esbat. Esbat came from the French word for frolic. The full moon was a time for joyful celebration. The mother goddess showed herself in the full moon. She shared her spirit with humans during Esbat. The Celts believed the energy of Esbat was felt for three days before, and three days after, the full moon.

The calendar began with the first full moon after Yule. In our time we use another name for Yule, the Winter Solstice. It is the shortest day of our current calendar, and the day we call December 21st. On Yule, the Celts celebrated with many of the same decorations and traditions that modern Western cultures use to celebrate Christmas. Evergreen trees, wreaths, holly, mistletoe, lots of delicious food, and dancing were how the Celtic people honored Yule. They believed that on the night of Yule, the Holly King, who was the god of the year that was nearly over, did battle with the Oak King, who was the god of the coming year. The Holly King was always the loser in the battle.

Each of the thirteen trees in the moon calendar of the Celtic people had their own special magic. Each tree was sacred to either the earth goddess or the sky god. If a tree was important to the earth goddess, the moon named for that tree was a feminine moon. It gave abundant female energy to humans until the next moon showed its face. When a moon was named for a tree that was important to the sky god, the moon was a masculine moon. It gave tremendous male energy to humans until the next moon.

The first moon was the Birch Moon, and it was a feminine moon. The birch tree was believed to protect children. It also was the tree of purity and creativity. The Birch Moon was nicknamed the Moon of Beginning.

The second moon was the Rowan Moon. It was a masculine moon. In Scotland, even today, the rowan tree is planted near the entrances to people's homes because it is believed to keep away evil spirits. Its red berries have been favorites for centuries among the birds that feed on them. The Rowan Moon was nicknamed the Spirit Moon.

The Ash Moon was the third moon. It was a feminine moon. The ash tree was believed to protect humans, to heal them, and to bring them prosperity. The Ash Moon was nicknamed the Moon of Waters.

The fourth moon was the Alder Moon, a masculine moon. The alder tree possessed weather magic. It helped humans with a sense of duty and mental ability. The Alder Moon was nicknamed the Moon of Self-Guidance.

The fifth moon, a feminine moon, was the Willow Moon. The willow tree was believed to have magic for women and to help bring romantic love. The Willow Moon was nicknamed the Witches' Moon or the Moon of Balance.

The Hawthorn Moon was the sixth moon, a masculine moon. The hawthorn tree could bring peace and prosperity. The Hawthorn Moon was nicknamed the Summer Moon.

The seventh moon, also a masculine moon, was the Oak Moon. The oak tree was believed to hold magic for men and to bring all positive things. The Oak Moon was nicknamed the Moon of Strength or the Bear Moon.

The eighth moon was the Holly Moon, a feminine moon. The holly tree was believed to be magical for animals and was capable of protection. The Holly Moon was nicknamed the Moon of Encirclement.

The Hazel Moon, also a feminine moon, was the ninth moon. The hazel tree was believed to help humans contact the spirit world. The Hazel Moon was nicknamed the Moon of the Wise.

The tenth moon was the Vine Moon. It was the only moon that was both feminine and masculine. Vines had different powers, depending on the type. Blackberry vines brought prosperity and protection. Blueberries brought dream magic. Grapes held inspiration, and thistles brought courage. The Vine Moon was nicknamed the Moon of Celebration.

The Ivy Moon was the eleventh moon, and it was masculine. Ivy brought healing, protection and cooperation. The Ivy Moon was nick-named the Moon of Resilience, or the moon to teach people to be more flexible in their beliefs and habits.

The Reed Moon was the twelfth moon, and it was feminine. The reed tree brought the gifts of love and family. The Reed Moon was nicknamed the Moon of the Home or the Winter Moon.

The thirteenth moon was the Elder Moon, and it was masculine. The elder tree had the powers of prosperity and of healing ills from evil spirits. The Elder Moon was nicknamed the Moon of Completeness.

# HOW CUCHULAIN GOT HIS NAME

## *Ireland*

 OME SAID CUCHULAIN WAS THE SON OF LUGH, "the shining one," the god of the sun, light, fire, and the grain harvest. When Cuchulain encountered trouble, he would often call upon Lugh to lend him the powers he needed to survive. He did not ask Lugh for help in this story.

Cuchulain's story begins when he was thirteen. At this time he was called Setanta.

"Setanta, wake up, you lazy boy. Why sleep outside when King Conor offers us the comfort of the castle?" said a lad two years Cuchulain's elder.

Rousing himself from the sweet nap he had been taking, Setanta rushed for the stable. He, like the companion who woke him, was a student at King Conor's court. His duty was to ride with the other young people of the court.

Astride his large roan horse, Setanta was quickly ready for the day's journey to Quelgny and the neighboring court of King Cullan. He encountered a host of people heading for the same feast—warriors, both male and female, nobles, peasants, children, and other court students like himself. Everyone's spirits were high. Some in the group carried the banners of their clans.

As he rode, Setanta thought about many things. He was the nephew of a great chieftain, yet he did not feel kinship with his very name. Why didn't he have the sense of loyalty to his clan that these others felt? He didn't even hold much store in the gold-and-green banner of King Conor that flew regally at the head of the procession. Then something strange happened. The saddle girth beneath Setanta snapped open in the middle. Setanta found himself disheveled on the ground. The other court students teased him, and he laughed along with them. When their teasing quieted, he told them he had to go back to the castle to repair the saddle girth. He would join them afterward.

Setanta walked his horse to the stable. He relaced the leather strap of the saddle and fitted it once more under his horse. He enjoyed setting out alone for Quelgny this time. He breathed in the spring air of the northern Irish countryside near Ulster. Flowers dotted the many knolls. His eyes warmed to the fresh green of the rolling hills surrounding him. But when he saw the sun was lower than he had realized, he urged his horse to go faster. He did not wish to miss the feast that awaited him. Nonetheless, he arrived after the feast had begun.

Setanta welcomed the sounds of bagpipes and the traditional goatskin drum. Singing and dancing feet accompanied the music. He rushed for the banquet hall, thinking of how hungry he was from the ride. But he stopped short when he heard a low growl behind him. The most tremendous hound dog he had ever seen stared at him, with red eyes, teeth bared, and raised hackles. The animal was ready to pounce. Setanta knew the stories of the renowned Irish wolfhound of King Cullan. Then he wondered why the animal was loose in the banquet hall.

Because he was good with animals, Setanta reached down to show the dog he meant no harm. But the hound jumped for his neck, and Setanta saw in that instant that the dog meant to kill him. The hound dug its teeth into Setanta's neck, and the boy did not have time to draw his sword. So he grabbed the beast by the neck and hurled it away from him with all the strength he had. The dog twisted in the air, landed headfirst against a stone post of the fortress gate, and died. Not one drop of blood spilled from the beast.

The other merrymakers in the banquet hall heard the crash and rushed to investigate. At the head of the group was King Cullan, who, when he saw what had happened, was not ashamed to cry for his beloved dog.

"Forgive me," said Setanta.

"The hound did what he had to do, son, and so did you," responded Cullan. "But how did you, such a young boy, kill him without spilling any blood?"

Then Cullan spoke to the dead animal. "Oh, my friend, what will I do without you?" he grieved.

"I am he who must do something. Give me a pup of this hound that I may train it as the equal of this one. I lay a geise, a magical and sacred bond, that if the pup is unable to take over the duties of its father, I will stand in its stead," promised Setanta.

Cullan accepted the geise. Then King Conor stepped forward. He reached into his snakeskin pouch and pulled from it a shiny stone with bands of red, white, and black. It was called an adder's egg.

"Take it," said King Conor to Setanta. "It is the stone of the blessed earth of Ulster. The bands represent our goddess. With it you are bound to her honor. You have earned this stone tonight."

King Conor spoke to the crowd in the hall. "Tonight Setanta has slain an enemy, made a geise, and earned the right to become an adult. He will no longer be called Setanta. He is now the Hound of Cullan, or Cuchulain. Let all who hear his name honor it."

And Setanta felt kinship with his name—Cuchulain—for the first time in his life.

# More Naming Lessons

## *Ireland*

UCHULAIN WONDERED WHERE HE WOULD GO NOW that his duty to Cullan was complete. It was the last night of the geise, his magical and sacred bond. The night was exactly one year from the night that Cuchulain killed Cullan's attacking wolfhound, and Cullan came to him.

"My friend, I regret that this is your last evening at Fortress Cullan. Great events rest on your horizon, however. King Conor sent a messenger today. He requests that you go to the great warrior Scathach in the Isles of Shadow," said Cullan.

"Please, inform King Conor that I will leave at daybreak," answered Cuchulain.

Cuchulain belonged to the court of King Conor, so he had no choice but to go to Scathach. Besides, it was a great honor to learn from Scathach, the warrior goddess who had taught the greatest Celt warriors for many lifetimes. Also, it was tradition that men learn the art of battle from women, and that women learn it from men.

He found passage over the Irish Sea. On the far shore, with monsters in close pursuit, he crossed the Otherworldly desert that belonged to the Land of the Dead. Pockets of intense cold and scorching heat sapped his strength. The mists of mystery hung about him, blocking any view of the Isles of Shadow.

At the Perilous Glen, Cuchulain knew the Isles were near. But a fearsome giant stood in his path. The more that he feared the giant, the greater it grew until it was tremendous in stature. He began to despair that he knew no magic to tame the giant, then he realized it was his own fear that required taming. He grabbed the monster by the neck and tossed him off the path like he had tossed the Hound of Cullan. The giant dissolved into Mother Earth.

A year and a day of travel later, Cuchulain came to the bog-covered Plain of Ill Fortune. Scathach's school was just beyond the Plain. To step into the unending mudhole would mean sinking to his certain death.

Suddenly, behind him, he heard strange hooves beating in the air. He turned to see a golden horse carrying a huge man in yellow clothing. The horse snorted fire, its orange hooves high above the ground. The man dismounted. Golden rays shone from his face, and his eyes were compassionate, yet powerful. He reached into his pack and handed Cuchulain a large golden wheel.

"Roll this wheel before you on the Plain and its heat will dry the earth so you can cross," said the man.

Cuchulain thanked the stranger, and the magnificent man and his horse rode away as they had come. As the man said, the wheel allowed Cuchulain to cross the Plain of Ill Fortune to his destination, the Isles of Shadow. Old friends from the court of King Conor were playing a game of hurling on a golden field. They invited Cuchulain to play and asked news of Ireland. Cuchulain answered their questions but refused the offer of the game. He explained he must go immediately to find Scathach. The friends warned that she came when she was ready, for there was no way anyone could cross the Bridge of the Leaps to get to her, certainly not until they had studied for at least three years.

Cuchulain ignored their warnings. He put one foot down upon the bridge, and he found himself hurled upon the shore where he had started. Still, he was determined to uncover the magic of the Bridge of the Leaps. He reminded himself that most magical secrets are hidden in very obvious places. Then he pondered the name of the bridge. Leap? Leap! He harnessed all the energy he possessed after the long journey, and he leaped!

"How did you get across my bridge, young Cuchulain?" said a timeless voice.

"I leaped, as it instructed me to do," he responded.

"Perhaps you are the warrior I have sought these many years, and who was foretold," said Scathach. Dark eyes inspected him from her ageless face. A red cape cloaked her formless body. A magnificent ruby-and-emerald-studded sword, the legendary magical sword called Gae Bolg, was in her grasp.

"Sleep well tonight, Cuchulain. Tomorrow will be the longest day of your life," said the warrior goddess.

For three years Cuchulain studied with her. His muscles grew strong, his mind sharpened, and he became a Celtic warrior without an equal at the school. Scathach honored him with the best seat at her table. One evening she invited him to speak with her privately.

"Cuchulain, you have been given the best that I have to offer. Gae Bolg, too, is yours if you can prove you are as wise as you are strong," she said.

Cuchulain doubted himself in matters of wit, but he desired the sword of which every Celtic warrior dreamed.

"You will return to Ulster when you leave here. King Conor has gone to war against the kingdom of Connacht. He needs you to form an elite squadron of warriors you are to call the Red Branch. Tell me why you would call them thus, and you will have Gae Bolg," challenged Scathach.

Cuchulain pondered the meaning of the title, and he responded. "I earned my name Cuchulain through valor. When I came to the Isles of Shadow, I permitted the bridge to teach me the secret of crossing. The answer is in the name itself once again. Red is for the blood that must spill to defend Ulster. And we warriors must grow strong and give birth to new warriors like the branches of the mighty oak tree."

Scathach raised Gae Bolg and handed it to Cuchulain, who gripped the mighty sword by its golden hilt. The young warrior knew that his lessons of naming were complete.

# Queen Maeve and the Wild Sow

## Ireland

 AEVE WAS QUEEN OF CONNACHT. SHE CAME TO LIFE as the goddess of supreme power, or sovereignty, and no king could rule Connacht without her as queen. Maeve's kingdom was at war with the kingdom of Ulster. Both kingdoms were in Ireland.

"Queen Maeve, a hunting party has formed in the courtyard as you requested," said her groom one morning.

The queen's golden hair was tied back in a ribbon to keep it out of her way. Stout leather boots covered her feet. Her knife rested inside one of the boots next to her muscular calf. The scabbard of her sword bore her crest of a crowned wheat sprig on a field of green, red, and purple. On her shoulder was a quiver of arrows. Her crossbow was in her hands.

"Geansai," she commanded the strongest horse in the kingdom, maybe even in Ireland. His name meant jumper. He was as white as milk, and he wore the red and purple plumage of royalty.

"Huntsman, sound the charge," said Maeve, in order to begin the hunt.

The queen had challenged her court many times to race her for the lead.

Though they had tried, not a horseman could overtake her and Geansai. Three leagues from the castle and still in the lead, Queen Maeve stopped at a crossroads. She dismounted quickly to pay respect to Flidais, goddess of the hunt. She also left an offering for Epona, the Horse Mother. Approaching hoofbeats told her the others had arrived.

"We go to the Forest of the Bottomless Cauldron today. I feel like tracking the Wild Sow of the Wilderness," she instructed the huntsman.

When the huntsman informed the rest of the court of the queen's intention, many of them asked to be excused from the hunt. The queen dismissed those that asked, because she had no use for anyone afraid of a mere pig. Only twelve warriors remained. In Maeve's eyes these were the ones worthy of the challenge. The huntsman again blew the call to the hunt, and the queen turned Geansai toward the northwest for the dense Forest of the Bottomless Cauldron.

The ground became rocky and very steep. They had to leap hedgerows on many occasions. At the crest of a tall hill, Queen Maeve paused to wait for the others. Below, the ground was lush and of the darkest green. A hint of moisture hung on the breeze. It was the Valley of the Vanished, beyond which lay the Forest of the Bottomless Cauldron. Few had survived the Forest, although Maeve had. She had gone to answer a dare once, even though the challenger had fled before entering.

"How do you wish to proceed, Queen Maeve?" asked the huntsman.

"We will go north near the stream. There we will tether the horses, as the Forest is too thick and treacherous for them," she responded.

The warriors made their way behind the queen through the density of the Forest. Silence surrounded them. The earth smelled wild. Suddenly the queen stopped in alarm. She unsheathed her sword, and the twelve warriors in her party did the same. They did not hear what she did, but they knew to trust her instincts.

A band of warriors from Ulster showed themselves in the small clearing. The boldest of them challenged Queen Maeve. He made to strike several blows, but she deflected every one of them. She assessed his battle skills and saw that before every blow he gave a hint of what his next movement would be. Thus, she was able to maneuver his back against a broad oak tree. She drew her sword, and he could not escape its thrust.

The twelve warriors in her party, meanwhile, were engaged in heavy battle with the enemy. The leader of the Ulstermen came forward.

"Who sent you? Ulster's cowardly king?" demanded Queen Maeve of the enemy leader.

When he told her no, she knew he was lying out of allegiance to the king.

"Two-thirds of your men are dead. Consider yourself lucky that I am going to allow the rest of you to escape. But you must make a geise upon yourself that, if ever you return to Connacht uninvited, you will be my servant for nine years, and your firstborn will follow as my servant after you," said Maeve.

The enemy leader agreed to the sacred and magical bond she proposed. When Maeve looked to her warriors, she saw that eleven had survived despite the overwhelming number of the enemy they had fought. She sent three warriors to disarm the Ulstermen and to escort them to the border. Then she continued with the remaining eight warriors in her quest of the Wild Sow of the Wilderness.

Soon Maeve and her party came to another clearing, this one in the mouth of a dark, rounded cave. The quarry she sought rested peacefully in the mouth of the cave. The sow lowered her head and bared her teeth. She stood two heads taller than any sow the warriors had ever seen. A ring of woven silver hung from her nose. Its value was enormous, although no one in the land knew exactly how it happened to get there.

The sow made ready to charge. Several of Maeve's warriors unleashed arrows at the animal, but the sow dodged every one. The giant pig positioned its charge directly at Queen Maeve. She released a great bellow against which Maeve unloaded an arrow with her finest aim. The point lodged between the fiery eyes of the sow. The pig stumbled, righted herself, then fell dead.

Because the honor of the kill was hers, Maeve reached into her boot for her knife. She deftly cut open the sow's chest and extracted the animal's still warm heart, and she offered the prize to Flidais, goddess of the hunt.

At the castle Maeve adorned herself with the silk robes of her royal office. She was the first to taste the sow at the banquet. Her warriors received the second portions. No one in the court entertained a question about the identity of the finest warrior in the land.

# Etain and Midir

## *Ireland*

ITH FIFTY MAIDENS TO ACCOMPANY HER, ETAIN MADE the short trip to a woodland pool to wash her hair. Her hair was in two golden braids. A small ball of gold hung from each. Etain sat upon the soft bank of the pool, and one of her maidens began to unfasten the long locks. Etain's reflection in the pool showed her loveliness. Her eyes were tender, and her nose and lips were perfectly sculpted. Her long neck was as delicate as a swan's.

King Eochaid of Ireland was passing through the same woods with a party of horsemen. The king and his court agreed that no one among them had ever seen such a fair maid.

"She looks to have come from the Fairy Mounds," said the king about Etain.

He began immediately to woo Etain. Shortly afterward he asked her father for Etain's hand in marriage. King Eochaid and Etain were married, and the king returned to Tara with his queen.

Strange circumstances started to show themselves. On one of the first mornings of his marriage, the king was out riding early. He was startled to find a young warrior beside him on the plain. The stranger wore a purple tunic and carried a pointed spear in one hand and a white shield speckled with gems of gold in the other. His golden hair hung to his shoulders, and his eyes were a rich gray. The king and the stranger did not exchange even a word before the warrior disappeared.

When the king returned to the castle, he informed no one in the court of what he had seen. He climbed instead to the highest tower and looked out on the plain. Upon the high ground he noticed a blossom that glowed in all the colors he had ever witnessed.

Then the king's brother Ailill fell ill. The sickness was so severe that no leech could cure it. The poor king had to leave Tara and his brother to tour his kingdom of Ireland. He begged Queen Etain to care for Ailill in his absence. He asked the queen to promise to do everything possible to cure his brother. And if Ailill were to die, the king entreated her to provide him the burial of a prince. Etain agreed to what her husband asked.

As soon as the king departed, the queen went to visit the sick Ailill to ask him what she could do to make him feel more comfortable. The prince told Etain that he was pining away out of love for her. If she did not meet him the following day outside the castle, he would surely die. Etain promised to meet Ailill because she had vowed to the king to care for his brother.

The next day Etain waited for Ailill at the meeting spot.

"You are one who has forgotten," said Ailill when he arrived. Then he left.

The following day Etain waited again.

"You are one who has forgotten," said Ailill once more before he left her alone.

On the third day Etain was also there waiting.

"O fair-haired woman, will you not come with me?" asked Ailill. And he chanted a song in her honor. When he finished, he spoke to Etain again.

"I am not Ailill. I cast him into a deep slumber, and I filled him with love for you. I am Midir the Proud, king among the Immortals. In the Land of the Immortals, I loved you. And you loved me."

Etain protested that she did not know this man who spoke to her.

He continued, nonetheless. "Fuamnach, my queen, was jealous of you. So she changed you into a butterfly. She blew a tempest, and she banished you. You flew into the palace of Oengus, the god of love, and my foster son. He made you a home of glass and put within it a garden of flowers. There he guarded you. But Fuamnach discovered your whereabouts. When you exited your glass home, she blew another tempest and drove you through the air. You traveled to the house of Etar. His wife held a drinking cup in which you landed. When she drank the ale in the cup, she swallowed you. She gave birth to you, and since that mortal birth you have forgotten me. I claim you now as my bride, queen in the Land of the Immortals."

"I am wife of the king of Ireland. I know not of your country. To me, you are a nameless man," said Etain.

"If King Eochaid gives me your hand, will you accompany me?" asked Midir.

"If he bids me, I will go," responded Etain.

When King Eochaid returned, he fleetingly saw the golden-haired stranger again on the plain. Upon entering Tara he found his brother fully cured and without any recollection of having pined for the queen. The stranger entered the castle gate after Eochaid and challenged him to a game of chess. The king accepted the challenge. They played two games, which the king won. After the first game, when the strange warrior asked the king what he desired for a prize, the king requested treasure. After the second the king asked for a great work. The stranger fulfilled both requests.

The third game began in earnest. This time around, the stranger won. For his prize he asked to hold Etain in his arms and kiss her. The king could not outrightly deny the request, as his requests had been honored. So he told the stranger to return in one month for his prize. Meanwhile, King Eochaid gathered a great army to protect the palace. At the end of the month, he hosted a marvelous feast for his nobles and his royal family. Suddenly, into the banquet hall, came Midir the Proud, whom all recognized in his true form.

"I claim my prize, King of Ireland," announced Midir.

When Midir held Etain in his arms, she remembered all the love she had felt for him in the Land of the Immortals. She rose with Midir into the air and out of the palace window. When the king and his guests hurried to look, they saw two swans in flight toward Slievenamon, Midir the Proud's fairy palace.

# THE SIX PROHIBITIONS

## *Ireland*

ING CONAIRE WAS THE MILDEST AND GENTLEST OF ALL the kings in the world. It was said that Conaire was the most noble and beautiful king to ever rule Ireland. So dear was his temperament and so handsome his countenance! During his reign not a cloud obscured the golden rays of the sun. Dew clung to the blades of grass until after noontime. The voices of every person in the whole of Ireland were as sweet as the harmonious strains of harps.

Conaire's mother was mortal, but his father was from the Land of the Immortals. The Dannan folk who lived on the plains of earth vowed vengeance on the bloodline from which Conaire came, because Conaire was related to King Eochaid. King Eochaid had burned the Dannan plains in retaliation upon King Midir, who had stolen his wife and had brought her to live in the Land of the Immortals.

Before he became the king of Ireland, Conaire was given six prohibitions, or geise, things he had to promise not to do. He had agreed, and he knew that if he broke the geise, he would bring the vengeance of the Dannans upon himself.

These were the prohibitions:

He could not permit plunder in the land.

He could not go out on a ninth night from Tara, his castle.

He could not go around Tara to the right, nor could he go around Bregia to the left.

He could not hunt the evil beasts of Cerna.

He could never let three Reds go ahead of him to the house of a Red.

He could not let a solitary woman enter a house where he was after sunset.

Conaire's foster brothers disturbed the peace in his kingdom by raiding the land. For three years they raided Ireland. The people of the land despaired that their peace was broken, and they implored the king to help.

"Let every father slay his own son. But my foster brothers must be spared," responded King Conaire, breaking the first prohibition.

The foster brothers did not relent, and they brought their destruction by sea to Britain. They banded with Ingcel the One-eyed, banished son of the king of Britain. Unknowingly, when the evildoers raided Britain, they destroyed the fortress where Ingcel's father and his seven brothers were staying. They killed every one of them. Ingcel insisted that they now raid Ireland in similar fashion.

Once they beached in Tara, the Britain asked about the lighted mansion he saw.

"It is a guest house, the guest house of Da Derga, and as sacred as every guest house is in every land. We cannot raid it," responded one of Conaire's foster brothers. Derga meant "Red" in his language.

Still, the Britain Ingcel demanded destruction for destruction. And the worst of the foster brothers agreed to the raid on the guest house. Meanwhile, King Conaire left Tara to settle a dispute between two of his serfs. He left on a ninth night. And another prohibition was broken.

On the king's return trip to Tara, he and his cavalcade saw the signs of the raiding by the party that he did not know included his foster brothers. He advised his cavalcade to go a different way home. They went to the right around Tara, and they rounded Bregia from the left. Strange beasts threatened them, but they did not recognize the animals as the evil beasts of Cerna. So they hunted them. Conaire broke two more prohibitions.

The king realized he would not reach the castle that evening because it had grown late. He instructed his party that they would stay at the guest house on the road to Tara. Just then, three men clad in red, seated upon red steeds, moved onto the road. The king ordered one of his men to ride ahead and offer a reward to one of the red-dressed men if he would turn aside and let Conaire pass. But the men in red continued to ride ahead of the king.

"Another of my geise has now been broken," lamented Conaire.

The king's party entered the guest house, and the king sat upon the couch while his best warriors guarded the entrance. A woman stopped by the doorposts of the house. Her cloak was filthy, smelling of damp earth.

"Please, let me enter," said the woman to the king.

"Allow her to enter. It is our duty," Conaire instructed his guards, breaking the last prohibition.

The raiding party of Conaire's foster brothers and the banished Britain prince laid waste of the hostel. They burned the ground outside and threw lighted torches into the guest house. King Conaire was extremely thirsty, and his strongest warrior went out into the blaze to find him something to drink. But the wells and the rivers and the lakes of Ireland hid themselves at the bidding of the Dannan folk. At Loch Gara, far from the guest house, the king's warrior dipped in the king's golden cup and filled it before the loch could hide itself. When the warrior returned to the hostel, he saw one of the raiders cut off Conaire's head. The warrior took his master's head into his hands and poured the drink into Conaire's mouth.

A piper, one of three bagpipers dressed in red, spoke to the warrior. "Now we ride back to the Land of the Immortals."

# Bran in the Land of the Immortals

## *Wales*

 PRINCE BRAN WAS THE SON OF LLYR, WHO WAS THE GOD of the sea, and the father of the sea god Manannan. In this myth Bran comes face-to-face with Manannan on his sea journey to an enchanted island.

One day Prince Bran hosted a feast in his castle. The nobles and important people from the countryside who had been invited to the event were in the banquet hall. Otherwise, the castle was barred shut. The ramparts were closed, and no one could enter.

There appeared out of nowhere a woman in the doorway of the banquet hall. She had not been invited, and not a person in the hall, including Prince Bran, had ever seen her before that day. She was fairer than any woman any of them had ever laid eyes upon. Her clothing, though also fine, was like no raiments they had ever witnessed. The woman held out a branch toward Bran, whose seat was raised above his guests. The branch had white blossoms with a sweet fragrance. The woman began to sing this chant:

"Crystal and silver
The branch that to you I show;
'Tis from a wondrous isle—
Distant seas close it...."[5]

The stranger sang many verses. When the song was finished, she disappeared.

The following day Prince Bran heard music wherever he went. He heard it when he stood still, and he heard it whenever he moved. He looked out across the plain for the source of the melody, but he saw no one singing or playing. He sat upon a mound and glanced toward the sea for the source, but he again found no one. So he lay upon the mound and fell asleep.

In his dream Bran saw the woman who had given him the branch. "Arise, be no longer unheeding. Launch your ship upon the sea and sail until you come to the island I sang to you about," she said to the prince.

Bran ordered his ship to be made ready for voyage. He gathered thrice nine companions for his crew. Over each of the groups of nine, he set one of his three foster brothers. They launched the ship from an inlet and set sail for the outer sea. For two and a half days, they saw only waves and the monsters of the deep. On the third day they saw something stranger than any of the monsters of the days before. Coming directly toward them was a chariot on the surface of the sea.

The driver of the chariot made a resplendent appearance. His magnificent horses moved as easily as if they were galloping over a plain. When the chariot neared the ship, the driver reined in his horses and spoke to Bran and his companions.

"I am Manannan MacLer, the lord of the sea. I am on a voyage to your land to seek a queen who will bear me a son. He will be named Mongan."

5 Padriac Colum, *Myths of the World*, (New York: Macmillan Company, 1930), p. 152.

Bran and his crew watched as the chariot withdrew for their country, then they sailed on. They came upon an island, where trees with white blossoms grew upon the shore. When they landed, they were greeted by the queen. She was the woman who had appeared twice to Bran.

"Welcome, Prince Bran," said the queen.

But Bran and his crew were fearful of landing, and they decided to sail away. The queen threw a ball of thread at their ship. When Bran caught it, the thread stuck to his palm. With the other end of the thread in her grasp, the queen wound Bran and his ship back to the island.

She informed them that this island was one of fifty in a chain, and that each island was larger than Ireland. It was named Emne. All who lived on the islands existed without fear of death, treachery, or the pain of parting. Bran and the mariners enjoyed the marvels of Emne for many days. But one day the first of Bran's foster brothers came to him with a concern.

"In Ireland the blossoms fall from the trees, and the leaves blow away. With the storms the ravens come. I have never seen a land as this, where nothing changes. You must bring us back home," said the foster brother.

When Bran told the queen, she was very sad, but she agreed to let them go on one condition. "Let no one, neither yourself nor any of your company, set foot upon the ground of your country. When you have looked upon the changing land, return to me here in the Land of the Everliving."

Bran accepted the condition, and he and his mariners set sail for home. When they had sailed a short distance, another island came into their view. Upon it was a multitude of people playing games and laughing. Bran sent one of his foster brothers to inspect the situation and to return with a report. But as soon as the brother set foot upon the island, which was called the Island of Merriment, he began to play with the others, and he did not return. So the others sailed on until they came upon the mist of Ireland.

A crowd of people was upon the shore, and the mariners shouted a greeting to them. "Bran, the prince of this territory is here," they cried.

"We know no one by that name," said the spokesman of the people. "But in our stories, Prince Bran is said to be one who made a voyage overseas."

Bran told the mariners to turn the ship away from the shore. But the foster brother who desired so deeply to see things change at home jumped overboard and swam to shore. The people ran to him, but even as they touched him, he fell dead upon the sand. To the people on shore, as well as to the mariners, the foster brother appeared to be like one who had been dead and buried for a lifetime.

Then Bran spoke to the crowd from the ship. He told them the wondrous story of what had happened since he set sail. When the story was finished, Prince Bran and his companions sailed back over the sea to the Land of the Immortals and the queen. From that day onward, there were no further tidings of Prince Bran in the land.

# MATH, THE SON OF MATHONWY, AND HIS NEPHEWS

## *Wales*

 HE KING OF ANNWFN SENT TWO GIFTS. TO PRYDERI, the son of Pwyll, the king gave a drove of swine. Pryderi ruled in the South. To Math, who ruled in the North and was the son of Mathonwy, the king sent Gwydion, who was the son of Math's sister.

"Lord, I have heard the animals that were given to the South are of a type formerly unknown on this island," said Gwydion to his uncle.

"What are these animals called," inquired Math.

"Pigs, Lord," answered Gwydion.

"What kind of animals are they?" asked Math, his interest growing.

"Small animals, whose flesh is better than that of oxen," reported Gwydion.

"Who owns them? And by what means can they be obtained?" demanded Math.

"Pryderi, the son of Pwyll, is the owner. And I know a way to obtain them," said Gwydion, slyly.

He told his uncle that he would go in disguise as one of twelve bards to obtain the swine from Pryderi. Math gave his blessing to his sister's son. Little did he know that it was really Gwydion's intention to wrong his uncle. Gwydion's brother Gilvaethwy had taken very ill, and Gwydion blamed Math for his brother's condition. You see, Gilvaethwy had fallen desperately in love with the maiden Goewin. Since his infatuation with Goewin, Gilvaethwy's hue, his aspect, and his very spirits had dimmed.

Gwydion had asked his brother the cause of his illness one day recently. At the time Gilvaethwy had rebuffed Gwydion's questions because of something that all in the North knew. Yet, Gwydion had persisted in the questioning.

Finally Gilvaethwy gave a hint of the problem. "About what ails me, I cannot speak to anyone. Everyone knows that, even if people speak in the lowest tone possible and the wind meets the message, Math, the son of Mathonwy, will know what was said."

"Hold your peace, I know your intention," Gwydion had said.

He had understood at that moment that his brother was sick over his love for Goewin. She was currently involved with Math, who was unable to exist unless he could place his feet upon the lap of a maiden. Goewin was that maiden. The only thing that could take the place of the foot habit for Math was war. Thus, Gwydion designed a plan to create a war so that his brother could take Goewin away from Math, and he confided the plan to his brother. Gilvaethwy decided to disguise himself, too, as a bard.

Presently Gwydion and Gilvaethwy and the ten other pretend bards departed for the land to the South that was ruled by Pryderi. They were invited to a banquet upon their arrival, and Pryderi placed Gwydion alongside himself at the table. When Prince Pryderi requested a tale from the visiting bards, Gwydion said that he himself was the chief of song. According to custom he should recite first. All evening long Gwydion entertained the prince and his court with tales, and he charmed everyone. At the end of the evening, Pryderi asked Gwydion what he would choose as his reward.

"I crave the animals that were sent to you from Annwfn," answered Gwydion.

"Were it not for the covenant between myself and my land over these animals, your request would be most easy to grant. The covenant states that the swine will not go from me until they have produced double their number in this land," said Pryderi.

"Lord, give me not the swine tonight. But neither refuse them to me," answered Gwydion.

It was agreed according to Gwydion's wishes. For his part Gwydion immediately began to work a magic charm. When he reappeared before Pryderi, he brought with him twelve steeds, followed by twelve black greyhounds, each with a white breast. Upon the greyhounds were collars and leashes of gold. The steeds were outfitted with saddles and bridles of gold.

"Here is your release from the covenant, Prince. Surely, you may exchange the swine for something better," offered Gwydion.

Pryderi and his court accepted the offer. They had no idea that the animals that Gwydion produced were actually made of fungus. Gwydion and his party departed in haste, because the illusion was to last only twenty-four hours. No sooner had they returned to the court of Math, but the trumpets of war sounded. Math and his army made ready to meet the advancing forces of Pryderi, who had discovered the trick.

Gwydion and Gilvaethwy fought alongside Math during the day. That night Math and his advisors planned for the next morning's battle. Gilvaethwy sat upon the couch where his uncle usually met Goewin, and he wooed her.

The following day the battle was fierce. Math's forces were overpowered. Pryderi challenged Gwydion in individual combat. Gwydion again worked his charms, and he slew Pryderi. When Math returned to his court, he found that his nephews had fled. Uncovering their deception, Math decreed that no one in the land could give them food nor drink. After a short time the scheming nephews returned to Math's court. They discovered that Math had married Goewin. They also agreed to receive the punishment for their trickery.

# THE MAIDEN MADE OF FLOWERS

## *Wales*

LEU WAS THE SON OF THE EVIL ARIANRHOD. THOUGH Gwydion hid Lleu in a chest when he was a baby to spare his life, the young Lleu did not escape his mother's curse.

"This son will never have a wife from any race of people that inhabits the earth," Arianrhod had vowed when she discovered her son was alive.

When Lleu had grown to the age of marriage, Gwydion brought him to the court of his uncle Math, son of Mathonwy. Gwydion complained bitterly to Math about the curse of Arianrhod. Math admired Lleu's handsomeness, and he understood his good character.

He spoke to Gwydion. "Surely, this youth has attained a man's stature, and he is the comeliest youth I've ever seen. You and I will form a wife for him of flowers."

They took blossoms from the oak, blossoms from the broom, and blossoms from the meadowsweet. With these they produced the fairest, most graceful maiden either of them could imagine. They baptized the maiden, and they gave her the name of Blodeuwedd, which meant "flower face."

Blodeuwedd and Lleu were married, and Math hosted a great feast in their honor. At the dinner Gwydion hinted to his uncle that it would be very difficult for the newlyweds without any possessions. Math gave Lleu a parcel of land, and upon it Lleu built a palace for himself and Blodeuwedd. In the land Lleu was loved for the goodness of his rule.

One day it was necessary for Lleu to pay a visit to Math at his court. After he set out, Blodeuwedd heard the sound of a horn as she walked the palace grounds. A tired stag passed before her, followed by hounds and huntsmen and a crowd of people on foot. Blodeuwedd sent a page to inquire the name of the chief of these strangers.

"Gronw, lord of Penllyn, is the chieftain," reported the page.

Gronw overtook the stag by the river and killed it. By that time night was falling. As was fitting toward strangers, Blodeuwedd invited Gronw to stay the night in the castle. No sooner did she look upon Gronw, then she was filled with love for him. Gronw felt the same sentiment toward Blodeuwedd. They talked of their affection that evening before the fire. The next morning Gronw decided to take his leave.

"I pray you not to go from me today," entreated Blodeuwedd.

Gronw acquiesced. That evening they discussed how they might be together forever.

"You must learn from Lleu how he will meet his death," counseled Gronw.

The following morning when he again intended to leave, Blodeuwedd begged him to stay. The next morning the same thing happened. But on the fourth day, Gronw left for his home. That evening Lleu returned to the palace. He found Blodeuwedd very quiet, and inquired about it.

"I was feeling sorrow about your dying before myself. For the sake of heaven, tell me how you might be slain," responded Blodeuwedd.

"I can only be slain by a wound from a spear that has been one year in the forming. The slaying cannot happen in a house or outside, not on horseback nor on foot. Only in a bath by the side of a river, with a roof over the cauldron, thatched tightly. A deer must be brought and put outside the cauldron. I must place one foot on the deer's back and the other on the edge of the cauldron. Only under these conditions can I be slain," explained Lleu.

Blodeuwedd feigned relief over her husband's words. But the next day she sent the details in a message to Gronw. He began to work at once on the spear. One year hence, when the weapon was formed, Gronw dispatched a messenger to inform Blodeuwedd that he and the spear were ready. On receiving the message Blodeuwedd asked Lleu to please show her exactly how the bath would happen on the day of his slaying. Lleu was glad to comply with his wife's request, because he believed that it would soothe her worry over his death.

When Lleu rose out of the thatch-covered cauldron and put one foot on its edge and the other on the back of a deer, Gronw hurled his spear. Lleu screamed, then flew up in the form of an eagle. That night Blodeuwedd and Gronw went together to the palace. The following day Gronw took possession of Lleu's rule.

The tidings reached Math, who reported what had happened to his nephew Gwydion. Vowing to avenge Lleu, Gwydion searched in many places, and for a long time, for the young man. He was invited into a house one night. A man and his family and their swineherd were present. The man asked the swineherd whether the sow had come back to the sty. When the swineherd answered yes, the man inquired if the swineherd knew yet where the sow went every day. And the boy said no. Gwydion asked the boy if he could open the sty with him the next day in order to follow the sow to wherever it was that she spent the daytime hours. The boy agreed.

Gwydion tracked the sow at great speed across a river and a brook. She stopped under a tree and began to feed on putrid flesh. When Gwydion glanced into the tree, he saw an eagle shake himself. From the eagle's body dropped vermin and decayed flesh. Gwydion began to sing to the eagle.

The eagle sat upon his knee, and Gwydion struck the bird with his magic wand. Lleu returned to his own body, but he was nothing but skin and bone. For one year Lleu healed himself. At the end of the year, Math assembled his entire court and they made for the palace of Blodeuwedd. Blodeuwedd attempted to flee, but Gwydion overtook her.

"I will not slay you, but I will do worse than that. I will turn you into a bird. You will never show your face in the light of day, and the other birds will attack you and chase you away. You will keep your name, and the owl you are to become will always be called Blodeuwedd," declared Gwydion.

From that moment Blodeuwedd was an owl, hateful to all other birds.

# Branwen's Starling, Bran's Head

## *Wales*

Branwen was the beloved sister of Bran the Blessed, king of the Isle of the Mighty, which included the land of Britain and the land of Wales. Branwen was married to Matholwch, the king of Ireland. Since her marriage Branwen lived on the island of Ireland. At the time of the marriage on the Isle of the Mighty, however, an unfortunate event took place. Bran's evil half brother destroyed the Irish king's horses. Despite the amends that were made at that time between the two kings, Bran and Matholwch, the insult remained an open wound to the Irish. The foster brothers of Matholwch fed the wound with their continued hatred of Bran. Their hatred found its way to the new Irish queen, Branwen.

On the island of Ireland, the foster brothers poisoned Matholwch's love for Branwen. The brothers influenced the king to banish his queen from the royal quarters. They made her cook for the court. They ordered the butcher to come to Branwen every day after he cut the meat and to give her a blow on the ear. Finally their hatred persuaded Matholwch to bar any passage by ship between Ireland and the Isle of the Mighty.

Poor Branwen reared a starling under cover in her kitchen. She taught the bird to speak. She told the starling how kind her brother was and of the life she used to have on the Isle of the Mighty as the good king's sister. Each day the bird grew in strength. One day Branwen attached a letter she wrote about her woes in Ireland to the bird's wing. Then she sent the starling to her brother. The loyal bird found Bran and lighted upon his shoulder, ruffling its feathers so the king could see the letter.

After he read it, the grieving Bran called together sevenscore and four of his chiefmen, a total of 144 loyal followers. They met together in council and decided to rescue Branwen. They set sail immediately.

Some swineherds were upon the beach in Matholwch's kingdom. "Lord, we have marvelous news," they told their king. "A wood we have seen upon the sea. Beside the wood was a vast mountain that moved. A lofty ridge was at the top of the mountain, and a lake was on either side of the ridge. And the wood and the mountain, and the ridge and the lake, all these things moved," they exclaimed.

"There is none who can know anything concerning this but Branwen," responded King Matholwch.

When asked to explain, Branwen's heart jumped. "The trees of the forest are the yards and masts of the sea. The mountain is Bran, my brother. The ridge is his nose that pulsates with wrath. His two eyes are the lakes on either side of the ridge."

The men of the island of Ireland entered Matholwch's palace from one side. The men of the Isle of the Mighty came by the other direction. They sat together in council, and there was peace between them. King Bran called the boy Nissyen, son of Branwen, and the future king of Ireland, to himself. Nissyen then went forward to Bran's evil half brother, the same half brother who had destroyed the horses that belonged to Matholwch. At that instant the half brother cried out, knowing the unthinkable deed he was about to do. He took hold of Nissyen and threw him into the fire, where he burned to death.

Bran grasped his sister with one hand and his shield with his other. He supported Branwen between the shield and his shoulder during the terrible fight that followed. Only seven of the warriors from the Isle of the Mighty survived. King Bran himself was wounded in the foot with a poison dart. He commanded his warriors to cut off his head and carry it to the White Tower in London, under which they were to bury it with his face toward France.

Branwen cried out, "Woe is me that I was ever born. Two islands have been destroyed because of me."

She uttered a piercing moan, and her heart broke. Her countrymen buried her on the island of Ireland upon the banks of the Alaw. The evil half brother of Bran threw himself into the fire where the prince had burned. And his heart burst open, too.

The seven survivors from the Isle of the Mighty set sail, bearing Bran's mighty head. They buried it as he had directed them. Bran intended the head to lie under the White Tower as a charm against invasion.

Caradoc, Bran's son, when told of his father's death, also died of a broken heart. Caswallawn, a son of Beli, had grabbed the throne of Bran and the other sons of Llyr while Bran was on the island of Ireland. He began to rule as king of the Isle of the Mighty.

# HOW EVERYTHING DISAPPEARED AND REAPPEARED

## *Wales*

ANAWYDDAN WAS THE SECOND HUSBAND OF RHIANNON, the goddess of fertility and the Otherworld. Pryderi was Rhiannon's son, and he was married to Kicva. The four of them lived in Rhiannon's castle at Narberth.

One day after finishing the first course of a feast, the two men, Manawyddan and Pryderi, rose from the table to take a walk on the castle grounds. A peal of thunder and a mist so thick that it obscured all light surrounded them and continued for some time. When the thunder stopped and the mist lifted, the men looked about them. Neither cattle nor other herds nor any of their attendants could they see. In fact, when they returned to the castle, they found only Rhiannon and Kicva. The rest of the court had disappeared, as well.

"In the name of heaven," said Manawyddan to Pryderi, "what has happened? Let us go and investigate."

Some of their dogs mysteriously returned and ran to a nearby bush, then drew back with their hair bristled. When Manawyddan and Pryderi approached the bush, they saw a wild boar, pure white in color. The boar observed the men and fell back a short distance from them. Then the boar took off running, with the dogs and men in pursuit. The chase led to a castle. The lofty structure occupied a setting where there had never been a building. The boar charged into the castle, followed by the dogs.

Manawyddan and Pryderi did not enter, because there was a strangeness about the place. Not a sound flowed from inside, despite the pack of hounds that had entered.

"I cannot give up my dogs," said Pryderi. Nothing that Manawyddan said could deter him from going into the castle. Manawyddan did not follow his stepson.

Inside the castle Pryderi could find no trace of the dogs nor the boar. There was not a sign of humans nor their provisions. But in the center of the castle, Pryderi saw a marble fountain. Near it was a golden bowl upon a marble slab, which was suspended from chains hung from some indistinguishable site in the air. The beauty of the gold and the rich workmanship captivated Pryderi, and he reached out to touch the bowl. His hands adhered to it, his feet stuck to the slab, and he could not speak a word.

Manawyddan waited until the sun was low in the sky, yet neither Pryderi nor the animals exited the castle. So he returned to his home at Narberth and told Rhiannon of the curious tidings. She rushed after her son and found him just as her husband had reported. But when she grabbed to release his hold of the bowl, she, too, was attached, right behind him. Her feet had stuck to the slab, and she could not utter a word.

Manawyddan, husband of Rhiannon, and Kicva, wife of Pryderi, ate what provisions were stored at Narberth. When the food was gone, they traveled to Britain and worked at making shoes until they had saved enough money to return to Narberth with a burden of wheat. In the spring they sowed three crofts, which prospered and produced wheat. The crop was so fruitful that neither of them had ever seen the likes of it. When the time to harvest came, they marveled at what they had grown.

"I will reap this tomorrow," Manawyddan said of the first croft.

But when he went the next morning to reap the wheat, nothing but bare straw remained. He traveled to the second croft, deciding to reap that wheat the following day. But the following morning he witnessed the same devastation he had seen at the first croft. Manawyddan determined to watch the third croft all night.

To his amazement, the mightiest host of mice in the world made their way into the croft and carried away every bit of his crop. They moved rapidly and efficiently. Only one mouse was slow enough for Manawyddan to catch. So great was his anger that he drew two forks and was about to suspend the mouse from them to hang it, when he saw a scholar passing by.

"I will give you a pound if you let the mouse go," offered the scholar.

"I will not let it go free," answered Manawyddan.

"As you will," said the scholar, and he moved on.

Manawyddan was about to hang the mouse a second time, when a priest walked by.

"I will give you three pounds if you let the mouse go," pleaded the priest.

"I will not," protested Manawyddan.

"As you will," answered the priest, and he moved on.

A third time Manawyddan set out to hang the mouse. This time a bishop happened by with a large retinue.

"I will give you four-and-twenty pounds, all the horses you see in this party, and seven loads of baggage if you let the mouse go," said the bishop.

"I will not," protested Manawyddan.

"I am Lloyd, son of Kilwed. I cast a charm over this land to avenge

Gawl, son of Clud. Upon Pryderi did I avenge Gawl. My wife and the ladies of my court were the mice who attacked your crop, but my wife has not been well. For this reason you caught her. I will restore to you Pryderi and Rhiannon if you set her free," said the bishop.

"I will not," answered Manawyddan. "That is, until I see before me Pryderi and Rhiannon."

"Behold, here they come," said the bishop, and he produced Manawyddan's wife and stepson.

"Now give my wife her liberty," demanded the bishop.

"I will not set her free until you vow that there will be no more charms against any of us and that our land and our crops will be forever plentiful," persisted Manawyddan.

"You were wise in asking this," said the bishop.

Manawyddan witnessed Rhiannon's lands. They were tilled and full of herds, and the attendants of the court reappeared. Only then did he rejoice in life as they had known it before, and he released the mouse to the bishop in the form of his wife.

LOVE

# KILWICH AND OLWEN

## *Wales*

 HIS IS A MYTH ABOUT HOW KILWICH SEARCHED FOR the maiden Olwen to propose marriage to her. Kilwich was not quite old enough to marry, but one day his stepmother told him it was his destiny to wed Olwen. From that moment Kilwich was filled with a hopeless love for the maiden, whom he did not know, and whose whereabouts were also unknown to him.

Like the characters in many myths, the stepmother was seeking revenge. She had been stolen from her husband after he was slain by Kilwich's father and his party of warriors. The stepmother's brother was Yspadaden Penkawr, the father of Olwen. Yspadaden Penkawr had spent his lifetime doing evil deeds. Through revenge the stepmother enticed Kilwich into the world of Yspadaden Penkawr.

Kilwich bid good-bye to his father. "Arthur, king of the Isle of the Mighty, is your cousin," said his father.

Kilwich set off in haste for the court of King Arthur. At the gate he asked for the porter. Arthur and his guests were dining in the great hall, and the porter told Kilwich that none could enter but the son of a king of a privileged country, or a craftsperson bringing a craft. Kilwich said he was Arthur's cousin. The porter answered that a cousin did not satisfy either of the two conditions he had mentioned. Thereupon Kilwich raised a com-motion so great over the porter's injustice that the porter was forced to go against regulations. He reported the arrival of a guest to the king, and Arthur asked to have the persistent guest admitted.

"Greeting be unto you, sovereign ruler of this island," said Kilwich respectfully.

Arthur invited Kilwich to sit among the guests and to partake in the feast before them. But Kilwich answered that he did not wish to eat nor drink. It was a boon from the king that he desired.

"Whatever your tongue may name, I will give you," King Arthur answered his cousin.

When Kilwich explained his quest, Arthur said he would dispatch mes-sengers to accompany Kilwich to every land within his dominions to seek the whereabouts of the maiden. Arthur sent Kay, Bedwyr, Kyndelig, Gurhyr, Gwalstat, Gawain, and Menue. They journeyed until they came to a vast open plain, where they saw the fairest castle in the world. A herds-man was tending a tremendous flock of sheep.

"We are an embassy from Arthur, come to seek Olwen, the daughter of Yspadaden Penkawr," spoke Kay.

"Oh, men! The mercy of heaven be upon you. None who ever came hither on this quest has returned alive," answered the herdsman.

The men followed the herdsman to his dwelling, where they met his wife. When the woman learned of the men's purpose, she opened a stone chest before the chimney and drew from it a youth with curly yellow hair.

"Why do you hide this youth?" demanded Gurhyr.

"He is but a remnant of my three-and-twenty sons, all slain by Yspadaden Penkawr. I pray you, return from where you came," she responded.

The messengers requested that the youth be allowed to join them and promised to protect him. So Arthur's men, Kilwich, and the youth made

And the fragments all grew lovely.
From the cracked egg's lower fragment,
Rose the lofty arch of heaven,
From the yolk, the upper portion,
Now became the sun's bright lustre;
From the white, the upper portion,
Rose the moon that shines so brightly;
Whatso in the egg was mottled,
Now became the stars in heaven,
Whatso in the egg was blackish,
In the air as cloudlets floated.[6]

As you've heard, maybe even sung, the mother teal sat brooding for three days on the nest that the Water-Mother made possible. But still the eggs did not hatch, the seven eggs, six golden and one of iron. Each day the Mother of Waters grew hotter. The skin of her knee upon which the teal sat was so hot, it burned. The veins of her knee felt on the verge of melting. What could the Mother of Waters do? She jerked her knee to relieve the heat and the throbbing.

But the very eggs for which the mother teal tried so hard to find a safe place to hatch, fell into the water anyway. Yet the epic tells us the eggs were not wasted. They became wondrous things: heaven, the sun, the moon, the stars, and the clouds! Surely, the mother teal's efforts were worthwhile.

6 W.F. Kirby (trans.) *Kalevala: The Land of the Heroes.* Vol. 1, (London: J.M. Dent, 1907,) pp.5-7. Reprinted in Barbara C. Sproul, *Primal Myths, Creating the World,* (New York: Harper & Row, Publishers, 1979), pp.176-178.

# Fire and Ice: The Beginning of the World

N THE BEGINNING OF TIME, NOTHING EXISTED EXCEPT for Allfather. Allfather was a powerful entity that was unseen and unheard. There was no light, no earth, no seas, no birds or animals, no humans. There was darkness everywhere.

In the great void of the universe, there was a chasm so deep and dark that it was impossible to guess how far down it descended. It was called the chasm of yawning, or Ginnungagap. To the north of the chasm was Niflheim, a great area of mist that rose above the flowing streams of the Elivagar. The streams and mist eventually found their way to the yawning chasm, where they delivered their waters to the hungry mouth of rock. When the cold air of the chasm touched the water, it caused it to turn to ice. Soon the chasm was covered with a glistening frozen waterfall.

To the south of this region was the land of Muspellheim. It was here that the element of fire existed, jealously guarded by Surtr, the flame giant. Surtr possessed a magnificent light sword that flashed through the darkness of the universe, and sent sparks flying everywhere. Several embers fell into the chasm of ice, melting some of the frozen waters.

Great clouds of steam rose above the abyss, then cooled. Layer upon layer of frost appeared as the heat and the cold came together. From this union, through the will of Allfather, Ymir, an ice giant, was created.

Ymir stumbled through the rocky landscape. He was hungry. Eventually he found a giant cow whose udder was dripping with sweet milk. Ymir knew that this creature, called Audhumla, was fashioned from the same forces that had created him. He approached the cow and asked permission to drink her milk. The cow consented.

While Ymir was busy drinking Audhumla's milk, the great cow began to lick an ice block with her tongue in hopes of finding salt. Over and over her large cow's tongue stripped away layers of the ice; until at last a figure began to appear in the transparent block.

The creature was known as the god Buri.

Meanwhile, Ymir, who was now greatly satisfied by his meal of cow's milk, fell asleep on the ground. While he slept, two children appeared from under his arm. One was a girl and the other a boy. A giant with six heads sprang from his immense feet. The giant was called Thrudgelmir, and he immediately had a son, whom he called Bergelmir.

Buri, who had come from the ice, also had children. His children had children and thus, an entire race of gods and goddesses was created. The giants felt threatened by these creatures and decided to attack them. A war began that would last many, many years. It was the war between the ice, or frost, giants and the gods and goddesses.

Finally Buri's son Bor married the giantess Bestla. Together they had three children: Odin, or "spirit," Vili, or "will," and Ve, or "holy." The three sons of Buri and Bestla joined in the war against the frost giants. They killed the great giant Ymir. Ymir was so big that his blood flooded the world, drowning all the other giants except for his grandson, Bergelmir. Bergelmir and his wife managed to escape from the deluge of blood and retreated to a place known as the home of the giants or Jotunheim. Here they existed for many, many years and produced numerous offspring, who would begin a new race of frost giants.

The gods and goddesses, meanwhile, decided to use the enormous corpse of the giant Ymir. From his flesh they created the earth, or Midgard. From his blood and sweat, they created the oceans, rivers, and streams. His teeth became cliffs and mountains; his hair became the trees, bushes, and vegetation.

Ymir's great skull was raised high above the newly created earth and formed the foundation for heaven. His brains drifted through the expanse of sky and became clouds. Four dwarfs were positioned beneath the skull to hold it in place. They were called North, South, East, and West. Inside the skull the gods and goddesses trapped bits of sparks from the sword of Surtr, which became stars and comets. From the larger embers they fashioned the sun and moon.

The sun, Sol, and moon, Mani, traveled through the sky in glorious chariots drawn by powerful horses. They were surrounded by beings known as Dawn, Day, Noon, Afternoon, Night, and the Four Seasons. Thus, the new world became logical and organized.

The chariots of Sol and Mani were chased through the sky by two fierce wolves called Skoll, or "repulsion," and Hati, "hatred." The wolves hoped to capture the two celestial beings and eat them so that the earth could return to perpetual darkness once more. The inhabitants of the earth, however, carefully watched the skies for the presence of the wolves, and when they saw them, they made such noise that they scared them away.

Other creatures sprang from the decaying corpse of Ymir. These beings were known as dwarfs, trolls, or gnomes. The gods and goddesses endowed these creatures with great intelligence, but soon discovered that they had a very mischievous nature. Eventually the dwarfs were banished to the underworld, where they were forced to remain during the day. There they mined for precious metals like gold and silver.

Some of the small creatures that came from Ymir were not evil. They were known as fairies or elves, and were permitted to live in the skies.

The god Odin, who had been the leader of all the other gods and goddesses, found a special place for them to dwell, known as Asgard. It was here that the twelve gods and twenty-four goddesses lived and ruled over the universe.

# The Tree of Life

 N THE CENTER OF THE UNIVERSE, THERE WAS A GREAT AND mighty ash tree that grew from the bowels of the earth to the very vault of heaven. It was called Yggdrasil.

Yggdrasil possessed three enormous roots that anchored the giant ash into the ground. One root descended into the depths of Niflheim, the world of the dead. Another dug into the Jotunheim, or the abode of the frost giants. The third was anchored in the realm of Asgard, where the Norse gods and goddesses lived.

Beneath the root of Niflheim lived a serpent named Nidhogg. Nidhogg enjoyed biting the root of Yggdrasil with his sharp teeth in hopes of weakening the tree. High above him an eagle was perched in the uppermost branches of Yggdrasil. The eagle could see far and wide over the landscape of the world. On the eagle's beak, there sat a hawk, whose keen eyesight could see even farther than that of the eagle.

The serpent, coiled in the depths of Niflheim, was afraid of the eagle, and the eagle was annoyed by the presence of the snake at the bottom of the tree. Each day the squirrel Ratatosk ran up and down the trunk of Yggdrasil, instigating trouble between the cunning serpent and the powerful eagle. He would spread rumors of the eagle's desire to destroy the serpent, and the serpent's desire to crush the eagle. Thus, the eagle and the serpent were constantly at odds with each other.

At the root of Jotunheim, in the land of the frost giants, there was a sacred well. Anyone who drank from this well would gain all the knowledge of the world. The well was guarded by the giant Mimir.

The root of Asgard was also protected. The three Norns—Urd ("Past"), Verdandi ("Present"), and Skuld ("Future")—watered the root of the sacred tree of the Norse gods and goddesses with sweet water to keep it green and growing. The world of Asgard was composed of many great halls, where the gods and goddesses gathered and held council. It was in the hall of Gladsheim that the most powerful god, Odin, resided. Odin would sit on his throne, dressed in a robe of royal blue. Beside him were his two wolves, Geri and Freki.

It was important for Odin to know all that occurred in Yggdrasil. He kept two pet ravens, Huginn ("thought") and Muninn ("memory"), who flew from their perch every morning and traveled throughout the world. They returned to Odin at night to tell him everything they had seen and heard.

Odin's constant desire for knowledge could only be quenched by drinking from the well of Niflheim. To accomplish this, Odin knew that he had to make a great sacrifice to the giant Mimir. In return for allowing him to drink from the well, Mimir demanded that Odin pluck out one of his eyes. Partially blinded, Odin returned to his kingdom in Asgard, with the satisfaction of knowing he possessed the ability to predict the future.

On another occasion Odin wished to own the secret of the Runes. The Runes were a set of symbols that could interpret the meaning of life. Odin allowed himself to be impaled by a spear to the center of Yggdrasil, where he hung for nine days and nights. Taking no food or drink, Odin became weak and delirious, until in this mystical state, he obtained the secret of the Runes.

The middle section of Yggdrasil was called Midgard, or "middle garden."

It was here that the first man and woman lived. Odin had created them from a pair of logs he had found while walking along the seashore. They were known as Ask and Embla. While Odin had breathed life into them, it was his brothers who bestowed them with other useful gifts. From the god Vili they received intelligence and emotion, and from Ve they obtained the senses of sight and hearing. They dwelled in Midgard in relative peace, producing many offspring.

The people of Midgard were protected by the gods and goddesses of Asgard. Between the two worlds was a beautiful bridge called Bifrost, or rainbow. The rainbow bridge was guarded by Heimdal. It was his job to keep a lighted fire at one end of the bridge to discourage the frost giants from crossing it and destroying the earth and the home of the gods.

From the gnarled roots of Yggdrasil, where the hissing serpent lay in his lair, and the gods and goddesses feasted in their golden halls; to the middle section of the great tree where the humans lived; to the very top where the giant eagle wrapped his talons around the highest branch, all activity that shaped the universe took place. Heaven, earth, and the underworld existed together in a great drama that unfolded over time and is repeated in many, many stories.

# ODIN AND THE WALL

 DIN WAS THE MOST POWERFUL AND REVERED OF ALL the Norse gods and goddesses. He was the son of Bor and Bestla, who also produced two other sons, Vili and Ve. It was Odin who organized the Norse deities in the great kingdom of Asgard, dispensing his wisdom, judgment, and passion for battle. Odin sat upon his throne wearing a blue mantle, or cloak, around his shoulders. He held the spear Gungnir at his side while he was at court. Gungnir was so powerful that anyone who took an oath before it could never break his promise. On his finger he wore the powerful ring known as Draupnir. It was made of gold and covered with precious stones.

Odin was known to wander the earth of Midgard in disguise. He dressed as an old man with a cane, a floppy, brimmed hat, and gray hair. He only had one eye, for he had sacrificed the other in order to gain all of the wisdom contained in the well of Mimir, the giant. Odin was greatly interested in the events of Midgard. He had two ravens, Huginn ("thought") and Muninn ("memory"), who flew around the earth by day, and returned to tell Odin all they had seen and heard each night.

Odin was constantly aware of the danger of the frost giants, fierce-looking creatures who lived in the land of Jutunheim. The gods and goddesses of Asgard had been battling with the giants for many years. One day a stranger approached Odin with a suggestion of how to protect Asgard from an attack.

"Great Odin," the stranger began, "I can build a wall that can go around the land of the gods and goddesses. This wall will be so high and so thick that no one will be able to penetrate it."

Odin was intrigued by the stranger's plan. But he was wise enough to know that such a project would cost a great deal. He asked the stranger what payment he expected in return for such a wall.

"I will tell you, soon," the stranger told Odin. "There is much work to do. I will have your wall built within a year."

Odin thought for a moment. A wall to keep out the frost giants would be worth any cost, providing that the stranger would complete the wall in one year's time. He decided that he would allow the stranger to begin.

The stranger left Asgard and returned the following morning. He brought with him a strong, large horse. Everyone expected that the horse would be used to pull stones to the site of the wall. Amazingly, it was the horse who lifted the stones to their respective positions, and then applied mortar to them to keep them in place. The horse worked both day and night without stopping for food or water.

The gods and goddesses of Asgard watched in wonder as the wall took shape. It grew higher and higher with every passing day. Odin was also awed at this achievement. Yet, in his heart, he was fearful of the price the stranger might extract for such a feat.

Odin approached the stranger again.

"We are grateful for your hard work," he told him. "But, we are anxious to know what it is that you expect for payment."

The stranger answered Odin.

"When I have completed the wall, as I have agreed, you must give me the sun, the moon, and the goddess Freyja."

Odin was horrified when he heard the stranger's request.

"I cannot give you these things!" he replied. "No one can own the sun and the moon, for the world will die without them. And, I am not willing to give you the goddess Freyja."

"Then, I cannot continue my work," the stranger told him.

The stranger and his horse left Asgard. The wall was unfinished. Odin was in despair until the figure of Loki appeared before him. Loki was a being who was half god, half creature, for his father was the wind giant.

"I can help you," Loki told Odin. "Let the stranger continue to build the wall. I promise you that he will not finish in the time he has promised. Then, you do not have to give him what he asks for."

Odin summoned the stranger back to Asgard and told him to continue his work. He promised him that if he did complete the wall within a year, that he would give him the sun and the moon and the goddess Freyja.

The stranger and the horse resumed their frantic pace and continued to build the wall. Again, day after day, the stones rose higher and higher around Asgard.

One evening, shortly before the year's deadline would arrive, Loki turned himself into a white female horse. In this form he approached the wall. He pranced in the moonlight before the stranger's horse, Svadilfari. Svadilfari had never seen such a beautiful creature. With little coaxing he forgot what he had been doing and followed the mare into the woods.

The next morning the stranger arrived at the work site to find that his helper, the horse, was missing. He searched for Svadilfari high and low, but he could not find him. Angered and shamed, he knew that he could not complete the wall in time. He left Asgard.

The rest of the gods and goddesses completed the unfinished section of the wall. They were happy in knowing that they were protected from the frost giants. Odin, however, was not as pleased. He was saddened that he had tricked the stranger. In his heart he knew that one day the stranger would seek revenge and side with the frost giants in a terrible war.

# THE DEATH OF BALDR

ALDR WAS THE SON OF THE GREAT, POWERFUL GOD ODIN and his wife Frigg. His parents loved him very much, as did all the inhabitants of Asgard, the land of the gods and goddesses. Baldr's hair was as yellow as spun gold. His eyes were as blue and bright as the Northern Lights. He was nimble and resourceful, gentle and kind to all he met.

One day Odin instructed his two pet ravens to fly over Midgard, the world of humans, and bring him news of recent events. When the pair returned to Odin that evening, they told him a terrible prophecy.

"The queen of Hel, the underworld, has prepared a bed for your son Baldr," they told him.

Odin told the dark news to Frigg. Then he mounted his loyal horse, Sleipnir, who had eight legs, and prepared to descend into the underworld. The world of Hel was dark and foreboding. Sleipnir traveled quickly over the molten, rocky landscape, careful to avoid the wolves and monsters that attempted to bite his forelegs. At last, Odin and Sleipnir arrived before the palace of the queen of Hel.

Several corpses lay scattered before the palace walls. Odin evoked a special spell to rouse them from their eternal sleep. An old woman, wrapped in a burial shroud, sat up and addressed the mighty god of Asgard.

"Our noble queen desires a god to sit with her on her throne of ice and fire," she told him. "This god is to be your son Baldr."

"I am the powerful, all-knowing god Odin. Is there nothing that I can do to prevent the queen from taking my son?" Odin asked the corpse.

"There is nothing you can do," the old woman spoke. "Now let me return to my eternal sleep. It is not right that you have brought me out of death."

Odin sadly rode out of the depths of Hel and returned to his wife. When Frigg heard what he had to report of his journey, she began to cry.

"There must be something we can do to save our Baldr!"

Frigg went out into the world and instructed every living and inanimate object to pledge allegiance to her.

"No one is to hurt my son," she said. "You, the rivers and trees, the wind and rain; you, the people of earth, and the dwarfs and fairies and elves; none of you must harm my Baldr."

Everything Frigg had spoken to, took a vow not to hurt Baldr. When she was finished with her task, Frigg returned to Odin and told him what she had done.

Loki, the half god, who was known for his love of tricks and foolery, had heard what the world had promised to Odin's wife. He wondered if there was one animal or plant or rock that had not promised to obey Frigg's wishes. He disguised himself as an old woman and approached Frigg.

"Goddess," he spoke to her in an old hag's voice. "How resourceful you are to protect your beloved Baldr. I have heard that nothing in the sea or sky or on land will harm him."

"This is true," Frigg admitted happily.

"Is there nothing, nothing at all that will harm him?"

Frigg thought for a moment, then answered.

"There is nothing, old woman, except for the small white plant that grows on the mighty oak trees. This flower did not make a promise to me, for I was too busy with all the other things of earth, and did not stop to talk to it. Yet, I have no fear of this plant. Soon I will go to it, and make it promise me the same as I have received from all other things in this world."

Loki, who now knew a very dangerous secret, left Frigg and traveled to earth. He observed the dwarfs and elves playing a game with Baldr. They were throwing projectiles and stones at him. Yet, the stones and objects bounced off his skin, because everything in the world had vowed to Frigg not to harm him.

Loki climbed to the top of an old oak and removed a sprig of mistletoe, the white flower that grows there. He gave the flower to one of the elves and said, "Here, take this and throw it at Baldr."

The elf looked at the tiny flower and laughed. "Surely, this will not hurt him," he said and then flung the mistletoe at Baldr.

When the flower touched Baldr, it caused him to tremble and seize with pain. He fell to the ground, gasping for air. No one could help him. Several dwarfs ran from the place to tell Odin and Frigg what had happened.

Baldr died in his mother's arms several moments later. Frigg was in deep despair, when she realized that the tiny mistletoe had killed her son.

Nanna, Baldr's wife, was also by his side. She wept for her dead husband, who was loved by all the inhabitants of the world.

On a gray and cold day, Odin ordered a great ship, *Hringhorni*, to be launched into the sea with Baldr's body. The ship was set on fire as it floated away from the land. Dwarfs and elves, mortals, and the gods and goddesses of Asgard all bid farewell to Baldr.

Odin climbed upon a black cliff that hung over the waters. He watched the flaming ship sail into the outline of the golden sun. Then he whispered to his son.

"Sleep well, Baldr. Someday the world will be a good place in which to live. There will be no war and no death. It is on that day that I will find you again."

# Loki, Prince of Trouble and Tricks

N MOST CULTURES OF THE WORLD, THERE ARE STORIES of "tricksters," colorful characters who enjoy having fun by fooling people. Sometimes the games the tricksters play are harmless. Sometimes, however, their antics can cause dire consequences in the world of humans and immortals.

Loki was a trickster in Norse mythology. He appeared in many, many forms. His ability to change shape and personality allowed him to assume different identities and to become involved in world events on all levels.

Loki was born to a goddess and a wind giant. He could provide protection in times of trouble. When Odin was unable to pay the price for the construction of a wall to protect the kingdom of Asgard, Loki changed himself into a beautiful mare and tricked the magical horse Svadilfari into running away with him. Thus, the horse was unable to complete his work on the wall, and Odin was not obliged to pay his owner his costly fee.

Sometimes Loki's tricks were harmful. When the queen of Hel, the underworld, desired to have Odin's son Baldr as her mate, Odin's wife Frigg made everyone and everything promise not to harm Baldr. This way, Baldr would never be mortally wounded. Loki, disguised as an old woman, gained Frigg's confidence, and got her to admit that the mistletoe had not vowed to protect Baldr. Loki used this information to destroy Baldr.

Loki had three children, who were mothered by a witch. His first child was Fenrir the wolf. The second child, an evil serpent, was called Midgardsorm. The third was a woman whose form was so dreadful that the gods feared her the most. She was to become the queen of Hel—a woman with two faces, one of a living person and the other a corpse. The gods and goddesses decided to throw her into the depths of Niflheim, or the underworld.

The immortals of Asgard flung the serpent into the ocean. It was not as easy to subdue the wolf Fenrir. The gods and goddesses tried to capture him, but he was too swift, being the son of Loki, for them to catch him.

They approached the clever dwarfs to see if they could bind Fenrir. The dwarfs agreed to perform the task. They asked for six magical ingredients: the roots of stones, the breath of a fish, the beards of women, the noise made by the footfalls of a cat, the sinews of bears, and the spittle of a bird. From the collected objects they made a slender rope that was so smooth and thin, no one believed it could hold Fenrir.

The god Tyr, who was a great fighter, decided to tie the rope around Fenrir's neck. He was able to tie the wolf to a stone, but not before Fenrir bit off his hand. Fenrir tried and tried to break free from the rope, but he could not. He was subdued until the great battle at the end of the world.

Loki also tried to escape. He turned himself into a salmon and swam away from his pursuers. The gods attempted to catch him in nets, but he was too slippery. When they tried to trap him in between some river rocks, Loki jumped through the air and got away. Finally one of the gods was able to hold Loki by his tail. He brought him to the riverbank and forced him to return to his normal form.

Loki was tied up inside a cave, where a mixture of poison was poured upon his head, drop by drop. Loki suffered a very slow and lingering torture, but he did not die. Loki, like his son Fenrir, would exist until the great battle at the end of the world.

# FREYJA, GODDESS OF LOVE

 REYJA WAS THE MOST BEAUTIFUL AND THE MOST LOVED goddess in Norse mythology. She had pale skin, golden hair, and large blue eyes. Strong, compassionate, kind, and wise, Freyja entertained a multitude of guests in her beautiful palace called Sessrumnir, in the realm of the immortals, Asgard. Everyone enjoyed her laughter and gaiety.

Freyja was the subject of many stories and love songs. Lovers prayed to her to answer their requests. She traveled the realms of the heavens and earth in a chariot that was drawn by two gray cats. At times she was known as the goddess of fertility and fruitfulness, accompanying her brother Frey through the sky in his chariot that was filled with fruits, vegetables, and flowers. Freyja also possessed the plumage of a falcon woven into a wondrous cape that gave her the ability to fly through the air like a great bird.

When it was necessary, Freyja could be found on the battlefield, dressed in the garments of a warrior. She would carry a spear and shield, leading combatants to fight. Following a battle she would claim the souls of slain soldiers to accompany her to Folkvang, where she provided entertainment for them. Freyja was also certain to reunite lovers, and husbands and wives, in the halls of Folkvang so that they might find each other again after death.

Many gods desired the beautiful Freyja. She had many husbands, some of whom were Odin, god of the sky, Frey, god of the rain, and Odur, god of the sunshine.

It was Odur, however, that Freyja loved best. With him she had two daughters, Hnoss and Gersemi. The girls were very beautiful and were treated with the same respect and admiration that was given to their mother. Odur and Freyja traveled everywhere together. They were very content until Odur grew weary of Freyja one day and decided to set off on his own.

Odur's absence greatly saddened Freyja. She cried for days and months, covering fields and hills with her tears. Some of her tears penetrated the hard surface of the earth and turned to gold. Even the tiny fairies that Freyja befriended with great affection, could not make her smile.

Finally Freyja decided to set out to find her husband. She traveled through many lands. To those who met her on her sad journey she was known by many different names: Mardel, Horn, Gefn, Syr, Skjalf, and Thrungva. Everywhere she went, a trail of golden tears could be found beneath the dark soil of the earth.

One day Freyja came upon a myrtle tree in the land of the South. Beneath the tree she found her beloved husband Odur. Odur had missed his beautiful wife, as well, and was happy to be reunited with her. In honor of their reunion, Norse brides began to wear a sprig of myrtle flowers in their hair. The earth was also happy that the pair had found each other. Brightly colored blossoms, in deep green carpets of grass, began to spring up everywhere.

One of the most popular stories about Freyja involved a magnificent necklace. Freyja loved jewelry and loved to wear golden rings and bracelets. While wandering in the land of Svartalfaheim, which is located in the underworld, Freyja came upon some dwarfs who were fashioning a piece of jewelry. They were creating the most beautiful necklace she had ever seen. With their keen eyesight and tiny hands, they had made a golden rope that was covered with glittering diamonds that twinkled as brightly as the stars in the sky. The dwarfs had named the necklace Brisingamen. Brisingamen represented the bounty of the earth and the grandeur of the heavens. Freyja wanted the necklace for her own.

The dwarfs, however, were reluctant to give it to her.

"You must grant us a special favor," they told the goddess.

"What is it that you want?" Freyja asked, unable to take her eyes from their creation.

"You must promise to be our sponsor, and to protect us."

Freyja agreed to protect the dwarfs. They finished the necklace and placed it around the goddess's neck. It gleamed and glistened against Freyja's pale skin. She became so fond of the necklace that she wore it night and day. When the other gods and goddesses saw it, they asked Freyja if they might borrow it. She was reluctant to lend her necklace to anyone. She did allow the god Thor to wear it once or twice.

It is believed that when the people of earth looked up into the skies on special evenings, they could see the goddess Freyja crossing the heavens in her chariot. The diamonds that made up the necklace Brisingamen were so bright that they appeared to be stars. Thus, the people of the Northern lands believed that the Milky Way was really Freyja's necklace.

# THE HAMMER OF THOR

HEN GREAT DARK CLOUDS APPEAR OVER THE LANDS in the North, and the rumbling of thunder can be heard on distant hills, the people sometimes remark that the clamor they hear is the approaching sound of the god Thor.

The Norsemen revered and worshipped Thor for his many powers and attributes. The red-haired son of the god Odin and his wife Erda was tall and strong and muscular. He was an imposing figure in the face of his enemies.

Thor lived in Asgard, the home of the gods and goddesses in the great palace called Bilskirnir, or lightning. His association with lightning probably came from the time he spent with the gods Vingnir and Hlora, who represented "wings" and "heat." Thor's palace contained 540 rooms, where he entertained his guests with lavish entertainment and wonderful food.

Thor possessed the mighty hammer Miolnir, or "the crusher." He would throw his hammer at the frost giants in battle and send them running in fear. No matter how far Thor threw his hammer, it would always return to his hand. Miolnir blazed with sparks of fire. It was said that Thor was not permitted to cross the rainbow into Asgard with the hammer in his hand, for fear it would melt the beautiful ice bridge.

"I am the Thunderer! Here in my Northland,

My fastness and fortress, Reign I forever,

Here amid icebergs, rule I the nations;
This is my hammer, Miolnir the mighty;
Giants and sorcerers cannot withstand it."
          SAGA OF KING OLAF (Longfellow)

The Norse considered Miolnir a sacred object, not only of battle, but of blessing. Just as Christians make the sign of the cross, the ancient Norse would cross themselves to make the sign of the "hammer." This symbolic gesture was also used to bless a newborn infant or a newly married couple, and to bid a final farewell to a corpse on a funeral pyre.

The countries of the North portrayed Thor in different ways. In Sweden he was depicted wearing a broad-rimmed, floppy hat. Some believed that the roar of thunder during a storm was the sound of his chariot wheels rolling across the firmament of heaven. Others, like the German people, believed the noise came from the pots and pans and kettles he tied to the sides of the chariot.

Thor often traveled to Jotunheim, the land of the giants. The frost giants were badly behaved and thought nothing of provoking the gods and goddesses by sending frozen blasts of air into the world and destroying all vegetation and crops. During one journey to subdue the giants, Thor and Loki came upon a valley shrouded in mist. It was difficult to see anything around them. Stepping carefully through the fog, they found a peculiar dwelling that resembled a cave. Tired from their long journey, they decided to rest inside the mouth of the cave until morning.

Imagine their surprise when they woke up the next morning and discovered that they had been sleeping in a frost giant's glove! Fortunately, the giant was not malicious and agreed to guide Thor and Loki to the great palatial fort in the land of the giants.

When they arrived at the fort, Thor addressed the king of the frost giants, who was Utgard-Loki. He told the king that he had come to do battle with the giants, if necessary, to prevent them from troubling the gods and goddesses of Asgard.

Utgard-Loki was slightly amused at Thor's speech.

"I propose a contest," he told Thor. "Then, we can avoid battle with the mighty Thor and his hammer."

Thor thought for a moment, and then agreed.

"The first contest will be to see who can eat the most—a god or a giant," Utgard-Loki said.

Loki eagerly stepped up to the challenge.

"I'm so hungry," he declared. "There is no one who can eat more than I can."

The king called for a table to be piled with all kinds of meat. Then he summoned his cook from the kitchen and told him to sit at one end of the table, while Loki sat at the other. He gave them the signal to begin eating.

Loki devoured the meat in no time. But to his dismay, the cook had not only eaten the meat, but the wooden table, as well!

The next contest involved drinking. Utgard-Loki filled an enormous ram's horn with broth and brought it before Thor.

"If you can drink the entire contents of this horn in less than three gulps, you will win," he told him.

Thor placed the horn to his lips and drank as much as he could. However, no matter how hard he tried, he could not empty the horn. Reluctantly he conceded defeat.

Loki was instructed to run a race with a giant named Hugi. Hugi beat Loki without making any effort.

Thor was next challenged to lift Utgard-Loki's cat, who weighed a great deal. Thor felt confident that he could perform this deed with little problem. After struggling for many minutes, however, he was only able to raise the cat's paw off the ground.

Utgard-Loki smiled at the pair of gods.

"It seems to me that you have lost the contest," he told them.

"Apparently, we have," Thor said angrily.

Then Utgard-Loki shook his head and laughed out loud.

"Mighty Thor," he began. "I was warned of your arrival by one of the giants. Knowing that you were coming, and that you were a fierce warrior, I created these challenges to be unfair. Loki's challenger in the eating contest was none other than Logi, or wild fire. He ran his race with Thialfi, the fastest runner in the universe. When you attempted to drink from the horn, you were unaware that the bottom of the vessel was connected to the sea, and would be replenished with liquid after every swallow. Even the cat you attempted to lift was none other than the serpent who circles Midgard and is anchored deep into the soil of the earth. So, you see, no one could have won these contests!"

Thor was deeply angered by the frost giant's deception. He took out his hammer and attempted to throw it at the walls of the king's palace, but a great fog covered everything and made it impossible to see.

Thor and Loki left the world of the frost giants, knowing they had not completed their mission. They knew, however, that many more occasions would arise to do battle with the cunning giants in the future.

# THE MANY FACES OF ODIN

O THE PEOPLE IN THE COUNTRIES OF THE NORTH, Odin was considered one of the oldest and most powerful gods. Odin had many names, and unlike some of the gods and goddesses who lived in Asgard, he was associated with many things. Some of his nicknames were Alfodr ("father of the gods"), Valfodr ("father of the slain"), Veratyr ("lord of men"), Fjolsvidr ("wide in wisdom"), and Sidfodr ("father of victories"). The name "Odin" was also called Voden, Woden, Wotan, or Wuotan, and is believed to mean, "wild or furious." Our name for the day of the week, Wednesday, comes from "Woden's Day."

Odin was one of three sons born to Bor and the giantess Bestla. As the master of the universe, he had many wives and children. Erda, who was the goddess of the night, bore him a son called Thor, the god of thunder. Frigg, the most popular of his wives, was the goddess of the civilized world. Together Odin and Frigg had two sons, Baldr and Hermod. Odin also married the goddess Rinda, who represented the frozen earth. Their child, Vali, was the god of vegetation and growth.

It was Odin and his brothers Vili and Ve who killed the frost giant Ymir in the beginning of the universe and fashioned the world from his corpse. Odin is also credited with creating the first man and the first woman out of a pair of logs that he found along the seashore.

Odin's gifts of prophecy were legendary in Norse mythology. His ability to "see all" and "know all" allowed him to intervene with justice in the lives of mortals. He was also able, by virtue of his gifts, to battle the frost giants, who were the enemies of the Norse gods and goddesses known as the "Aesir."

Odin was portrayed in many ways. Worshipped and adored, his image was often one of a powerful, bearded god with a muscular body. Sometimes he was depicted on his throne, holding his magical spear, Gungnir. Two dark ravens were perched on either of his shoulders. At his feet were his pet wolves, Geri and Freki. Many of the ancient wooden carvings of him have not survived the harsh climate of the North, and there are very few of them left for us to see.

Odin liked to travel the earth, or Midgard, as an old beggar, or as "Gangrad the Wanderer." Few recognized the almighty god in his floppy hat, graying beard, and tattered clothing. The brim of his hat fell low on his forehead, making it difficult for anyone to see that he had only one eye. Odin had sacrificed one of his eyes to the giant Mimir, in order to be able to drink from the well of knowledge.

In this disguise Odin could easily walk among mortals without being detected as anything but an old man. He gained much knowledge in this way. Sometimes his true identity was discovered. The giant Vafthrudnir, believing the old man to be nothing more than a troublesome intruder, challenged him to a contest. He asked him many questions about the meaning of life, the life of the gods and goddesses, and the creation of the universe. The old man answered Vafthrudnir with no hesitation. When Vafthrudnir had no questions left, the old man began to question him. The giant tried his best to respond each time. Finally the old man asked Vafthrudnir what were the last words that the god Odin had spoken to his dead son Baldr. The giant looked at the old hermit in astonishment, then answered, "Who but Odin himself would know what these words of farewell were?"

Then Odin removed his disguise, and the giant trembled when he saw who it was that he had been questioning. Odin's trick was a way of showing that he could be everywhere in the universe, and that he knew all the secrets of the world.

Odin's fame as a powerful god lasted for many centuries. He is believed to be the Pied Piper in the famous medieval poem, "The Pied Piper of Hamelin." This legendary figure came to the town of Hamelin one day to help the people rid themselves of the rats that were overtaking their buildings and crops. He succeeded in luring the rats into the ocean by leading them out of hiding with a melody from his flute. But when he asked the people of Hamelin for payment, they declined to give it to him. In retribution the Pied Piper played another tune on his pipe, this time attracting all the children of Hamelin to follow him. They disappeared into the mountains and were never seen again. Odin's association with this poem comes from legendary stories of how he ushered the souls of the dead to their final resting place in the underworld.

There are some people who believe that Odin was actually an ancient, historical leader who lived in Asia Minor and was the king of a people known as the Aesir. The Aesir were eventually driven from their homelands by Roman troops and resettled in sections of Northern Europe. King Odin gave his people a system of writing, from his knowledge of a set of symbols called Runes. He also gave them a system or code of laws known as the "Havamal," or the High Song. This code of laws exists in poetic form. The laws speak of the proper way to bury the dead, the necessity for charity, hospitality, and truthfulness, and the importance of courage and patience.

An all-knowing god, a legendary hunter, a grieving father, a guide for the dead, a real man who walked the face of the earth—all these are images of Odin. Yet, there is no doubt that Odin, the powerful god of the immortal Aesir, influenced the lives of thousands and thousands of people in many Northern lands by way of the ancient mythological stories that were handed down from one generation to another.

# Seven Hundred Rings—Volund and the Valkyries

 OUNG, BEAUTIFUL, COURAGEOUS, AND KIND—THESE were some of the attributes of the Valkyries, the personal attendants of Odin. These battle maidens, who were the children of mortal kings or gods, served the all-powerful Odin by guiding the worthy souls of soldiers from the fields of combat into the afterlife of Valhalla.

The young women rode on magnificent white steeds that resembled clouds at sunrise. Garbed in helmets of silver and gold, with shields and spears flashing, they rode into battle and bestowed upon the wounded a gentle kiss that signified the beginning of the warrior's journey to heaven. Once they were in the kingdom of Valhalla, the soldiers were comforted by the Valkyries, who fed them nourishing food and filled their vessels with thirst-quenching mead, or ale.

Occasionally the maidens of Odin liked to travel to the earth to enjoy themselves and rest. To make such a journey, they donned the plumage of swans—brilliant, white feathers that covered their bodies. Once on earth they searched for a cool stream or small river in which to bathe. They left their swans' plumage on the banks of the water, and delighted in swimming in the warm sunshine.

It was not uncommon for mortals to spot the Valkyries while they were bathing. If one so desired, it was possible to prevent the maidens from leaving the earth by stealing their swan costumes. This happened one day to three Valkyries, Olrun, Alvit, and Svanhvit. Three young and handsome brothers were walking through the woods when they spied the women in a stream. Quietly they approached them through the bushes and took their swans' feathers. The maidens had no choice but to remain with the brothers. Thus, they stayed on the earth for many years and behaved as mortal wives. The story even claims that the women fell deeply in love with the brothers.

After a time, however, the maidens longed to return to Odin. They found their swans' plumage, which had been hidden in the woods, and took off from the land. When the brothers discovered what had happened, they were heartbroken. Two of the brothers decided to venture out to find their wives. The third brother, Volund, decided to remain behind, believing that one day his wife would remember their love and return to him. As a master craftsman, he enjoyed creating remarkable ornaments. Out of sorrow he spent his days re-creating the ring his beloved bride had given to him. Volund made seven hundred copies of the ring. He never tired of the work.

When he returned home from a day in the village, he sat and admired his rings. One day, to his surprise, he discovered that one ring was missing. His heart was full of hope that perhaps his wife had left him a sign that one day she would return.

That night, while he was sleeping, the soldiers of King Nidud of Sweden came upon Volund and took him as a captive. They took away his rings and the magical sword that he had forged. Knowing that Volund was a master smith, King Nidud forced him to create weapons and ornaments for his palace. Thus, Volund worked like a slave for many, many years.

Volund dreamed of being reunited with his wife. In hopes of escaping from the cruel king, he fashioned a pair of wings that resembled the ones his wife possessed. He kept them hidden from the watch guards in the palace as he continued his work.

A perfect opportunity for Volund to obtain his freedom finally presented itself. The king wished to have Volund's magical sword repaired. He took it to the imprisoned smith. Volund cleverly replaced his sword with another sword he had created. Taking his long-lost weapon in his hands, he was able to slay the prison guards. Before leaving the palace, however, he made the guards' skulls and teeth into jewelry, which he sent to the royal family as a tribute. Volund strapped on the wings he had created and flew past the window of the king. He called out to King Nidud and taunted him.

The king dispatched an archer to try and shoot Volund out of the sky. But the archer's arrow only managed to pierce a small sack of blood that Volund carried beneath his wing. Thinking that Volund was mortally wounded, the king praised his archer.

Volund flew far away from the king's palace and back to his small cottage. There, much to his surprise, he found his wife asleep in a chair. On her finger was the ring she had taken from his workshop. Filled with joy and happiness, Volund picked up the sleeping woman in his arms and flew with her to Alfheim, where they lived together in peace and harmony with the gods and goddesses.

# RAGNAROK—WINTER OF THE WORLD

 HE END OF THE WORLD THAT THE NORSE GOD ODIN had predicted would come was called Ragnarok. It was the great battle between the gods and goddesses and their enemies, the frost giants.

For three long years the season of winter fell over the sacred tree of the world, Yggdrasil. The first year, a heavy blanket of snow covered the lands and seas. A cruel, cold wind blew constantly, day and night, without ceasing. It was difficult for humans to keep warm. There was no spring for the planting of crops, and no autumn for harvesting them.

During the second year, the winter of the sword, there was much fighting in the world. The battlefields were filled with corpses; families fought against each other for food and supplies. Human blood stained the ever-drifting white snow.

The third year of winter was known as the winter of the wolf. An evil witch fed the great wolf Managarm on the bodies of those who were slain in battle. Managarm's appetite was insatiable. The more flesh he tasted, the more he wanted. The gods and goddesses of Asgard trembled as they thought of the prophecy they knew would come true. One day a ferocious wolf would spring from the bowels of the earth and eat the sun and moon, and the world would be no more.

In the depths of Hel, the underworld, a red rooster crowed. It woke the sleeping frost giants and stirred them to action. In the realm of the gods and goddesses, a golden cock announced the arrival of the greatest battle of all: Ragnarok.

Meanwhile, another wolf, Fenrir, pulled on the magic cord that bound him to the icy side of a mountain. He hungered for the opportunity to join the forces of Hel and the frost giants and to fight against the Aesir, the immortal gods. It was common knowledge that Fenrir could crush the universe with his jaws.

The armies of the Aesir mounted their horses and began the journey to combat the forces of the evil frost giants. Their numbers were so great that the world shook from the vibrations of the horses' hooves on the icy paths of the earth.

The venomous serpent Midgardsorm, who had been sleeping at the bottom of the seas, rose from the waves in a terrible rush of water. Great waves sprung into the air, bringing tidal waves and destruction to the earth. All living mortals were washed away. As the waters of the sea covered everything in sight, the frost giants climbed aboard their ship *Naglfar*, and joined the ships from the underworld.

Two mighty armies were about to converge in the middle of the universe. Before the cave of Gnipa, a hound howled in the winter winds. His wails announced the terrible event about to occur.

The god Odin retreated to the well of Mimir, to consult with the head of the giant. He dipped his hands into the well of wisdom and asked Mimir what he should do as the leader of all the gods and goddesses.

Mimir advised Odin to take the Aesir to Vigrith, crossing over the rainbow bridge, Bifrost, that separated the world of the gods from the world of the frost giants. There, a decisive battle for control of the universe would be fought.

The frost giants had already reached the bridge. They attempted to cross it, in their great numbers, but the bridge could not support them. It gave way, spilling the giants into the valley below.

When the forces of gods and goddesses reached Bifrost, they saw that it had been destroyed, and they led their horses down the steep slopes of the valley to the bottom.

By now all the armies were gathered. The battleships of Hel with their gleaming bloodred sails joined the dark ship of the frost giants. The wolf Fenrir had broken free of his bonds and leaped into the fray. Down the ragged sides of the valley rode Odin and Thor, Freyja and Frey, and all the other gods and goddesses. They were joined by the fallen heroes of Valhalla.

Odin turned toward the legions behind him and spoke. "It is here that we must fight for control of the world. If we must die, let us die so that the forces of Hel and the frost giants are destroyed forever, and the world will know peace once more."

With that, he rode into battle. The wolf Fenrir spotted him, and opened his mighty jaws wide enough to devour Odin. The mighty god was no more.

Thor rushed to seek revenge for Odin's death but was stopped by the serpent Midgardsorm. Midgardsorm opened his mouth, about to spray the world with a film of deadly poison. But Thor took his hammer, Miolnir, and struck the huge snake nine times. Midgardsorm reared his ugly head one last time before he exhaled enough venom to kill Thor.

One by one the gods and goddesses of the Aesir fell to the deadly forces that surrounded them. The trickster Loki killed the guardian of the rainbow bridge, Heimdall. The god Tyr managed to defend himself valiantly through the battle, until the hound of Hel caught him by surprise and fatally attacked him.

Fires blazed everywhere, consuming the trunk and branches of Yggdrasil. The great eagle, perched in the highest branches of the tree, screeched before flying away in the heavens. Finally Sol and Mani, the sun and earth, were devoured by wolves, and the universe fell into darkness once more.

When the battle of Ragnarok was over, a calm silence fell over the smoking remains of the world. From the ashes of the destruction, the sons of Odin, Vidar and Vali, and the sons of Thor, Modi and Magni, rose up and climbed to the top of a mountain. There they found the hammer of the slain god Thor and used its magical powers to destroy the remaining forces of the frost giants.

In time, as Odin had claimed, the world returned to its former beauty. The four seasons returned; a new sun and a new moon were born. Lif and Lifthrasir, a man and a woman, who had survived the great flood of the deadly serpent, walked along the face of the earth and began a new race of people that survive to this day.

# THE SWORD OF TYR

HE DAY OF THE WEEK WE CALL TUESDAY IS NAMED after the Norse god Tyr, or Tiu, and means Tiu's day. Tyr was the god of war. His father was the mighty god Odin, and his mother was believed to be either Frigg, the queen of the gods, or a giantess who was the mistress of the sea. It was Tyr who had captured the wolf Fenrir, the evil offspring of the trickster Loki. Although Fenrir bit off Tyr's hand in combat, the god managed to tie the fierce animal to a boulder where he remained until the great battle between the gods and the frost giants.

Tyr's symbol was the sword. In many Northern countries great ceremonies were held to honor Tyr. With polished swords flashing, men would gather in two rows and raise their weapons until the tip of each man's sword touched that of the person directly across from him. Then they would challenge someone to jump over the two columns of men. Sometimes warriors would hold their swords together until they formed a circle or wheel. The chief of the warriors would stand in the center of the steel circle and address his troops.

Tyr's name or symbol was often engraved on a soldier's sword. It was believed that Tyr and Odin would bring victory to those who fought in their names.

The sword of Tyr is the subject of many legends. Its blade was believed to shine as brightly as the rays of the sun. It was created by the sons of the dwarf Ivald, who were also credited with making the spear that Odin carried with him. It is believed that Tyr entrusted his sacred sword to the Norse people who kept it hidden in a cave, where it hung for many years until it was found missing one day. No one knew who had taken the sword. A prophetess announced that the person who now possessed it would be a powerful leader who would die by the same sword that secured him victory.

The sword turned up in the city of Cologne, Germany, where the Roman prefect Vitellius was visiting his troops. It was presented to him by a strange, young man who predicted that Vitellius would become emperor. Vitellius accepted the gift and was declared emperor by the assembled Roman soldiers who occupied Cologne.

The tale of Tyr's sword did not end there, however. Vitellius carelessly left his sword in his tent one evening when he went out for a walk. When he returned, he found that it had been stolen.

The next day, much to Vitellius's surprise, an angry mob of Germans took him captive. They tied him to a tree, and out of the crowd stepped a young soldier who held up the missing sword. In one strong swing, he cut off Vitellius's head.

The German soldier kept the sword and won many battles with it. Finally, as an old man, he returned to his homeland near the Danube River. He buried the sword beneath his house for safekeeping. Even as he lay dying, he refused to tell anyone the whereabouts of the weapon. It was his belief that it would be found by the one person destined to conquer the world.

The German lands were eventually conquered by the barbarian Huns, with Attila as their leader. One day as Attila was reviewing his troops in the countryside, he stepped on a sharp object in the grass. He instructed one of his men to unearth it and discovered that it was a beautiful sword. He looked closely at the markings engraved on it, and declared that it was the sword of Tyr. Attila was very pleased with his find and used the weapon in much of his fighting.

However, as the Norse prophetess had predicted, the leader of the Huns suffered the same fate as the former owner of the sword. After many years of fighting, Attila desired to return to Hungary. He married the Burgundian princess Ildico, whose father he had killed. Ildico wanted revenge on her new husband. On their wedding night, she waited for Attila to become very drunk. Once he fell into their bed, Ildico took his sword from his belt and killed him with it.

The sword does not reappear in stories until many, many years later, when it turned up in the possession of the Duke of Alva, a general in the Frankish army of Charles V. The duke believed in the power of the sword, but because his people were Christians, he could not tell them that it was the powerful sword of the Norse god Tyr. Instead, the duke declared that the sword was the weapon of the Archangel St. Michael. Forever after, it was known by that name.

# IMMORTALITY

# VALHALLA AND HEL

HE AFTERLIFE WAS OF GREAT IMPORTANCE TO THE Norse people. They believed that the great god Odin, or Valfodr ("father of the slain"), had created a special place for warriors to go after they had died valiantly in battle. Odin's personal attendants, the Valkyries ("choosers of the slain"), would descend upon the earth's battlefields and collect one half of all the dead. Then they would guide their souls to a special world. This place was called Valhalla, or the "hall of the chosen slain." It was situated in Asgard, the home of the gods and goddesses, in the middle of a beautiful forest called Glasir.

Odin himself might greet the fallen warriors at the gates of Valhalla and welcome them to their new life. The dead soldiers, or Einherjar, were housed in a magnificent palace that contained 540 doors. Through these great portals the souls of the dead could come and go, eight hundred abreast. The palace itself was constructed of armaments and weapons. The halls were lined with spears, the ceilings were covered with gleaming gold shields.

In each of the halls there were long wooden tables where the Einherjar could sit and feast. They were waited upon by the Valkyries, who were dressed in long, white, flowing gowns.

The Valkyries would replenish the warriors rams' horns with mead.

They would bring them platter after platter of delicious meat, cooked to perfection. The meat came from a magical boar called Saehrimnir. Each day Saehrimnir was killed and roasted. Each evening he came back to life so that the cook could kill and prepare him again for the next meal. Thus, the kitchen was always filled with enough food to eat.

For entertainment the warriors would collect in the palace's courtyard, where they would don their armor and weapons. They would conduct mock battles, similar to the ones they had fought on earth. It would not matter if they wounded each other, for the Valkyries attended to them, and their wounds would heal instantly. Their battles pleased and amused Odin, who knew that they had all given their lives in his name.

For the mortal soldier, dying was not something to fear. He knew that in the life to come, the rewards of Valhalla awaited his valiant sacrifice in war.

Far below the earth, however, was a place to be feared. This was the kingdom of Hel in Niflheim. Hel was the goddess of death, and the daughter of the mischievous trickster Loki. Loki's other offspring were Fenrir, the wolf, and a giant serpent. When Odin realized the evil powers that Loki's three children possessed, he banished them from his kingdom in Asgard. The wolf was tied to a giant boulder by the god Tyr. The serpent was cast into the bottom of the sea, and Hel was flung into a chasm in the earth, the entrance to Niflheim, where she dwelled in the shadowy depths of her new kingdom.

One could only reach Hel's kingdom by traveling to the farthest regions in the North, and traversing terrible, rough roads. The Norse often buried their dead with shoes that had thick soles so that the journey was not so difficult.

The bridge to the underworld was maintained by a skeleton called Modgud, who extracted a payment in blood for the right to cross over the bridge and into Hel's realm. After crossing the bridge, the dead soul would

come upon a huge iron gate, the Hel-gate, which was guarded by a ferocious hound, Garm, by the mouth of the Gnipa cave. The only way to
silence the dog of Hel was to offer him a special piece of bread called a Hel-
cake.

Hel greeted newcomers to her kingdom while seated upon her black
throne in the hall of misery called Eljudnir. Some of the people who came
to her were thieves, murderers, and common criminals. Others had died of
disease and hunger. Some did not have the honor of shedding their blood
in the name of Odin before dying.

Despite the eerie atmosphere of Hel's kingdom, it was not a place of
doom, unless one had committed a crime. For those who needed to be punished, there was the land of Nastrond. In this dark and terrible abode, the
dead would wander eternally through cold water up to their waist, or be
made to climb through a cavern filled with deadly snakes.

Hel was credited with visiting the earth in order to bring plague, pestilence, and famine to humans. Some of the Northern races believe that it
was Hel who brought the deadly Black Plague to Europe.

Most people preferred to imagine being reunited with those they loved
in the afterlife. They strove to live a good life, to die a valiant death, and
to have their souls rise to the land of the gods and goddesses, where they
would live in tranquility.

# THE SALT OF THE SEA

N MANY MYTHS AND LEGENDS THERE ARE EXPLANA-TIONS for natural phenomena. Some are fantastic and improbable. Others are clever and must have provided comfort to those who passed the tales from one generation to the other. The oceans and waterways of Northern Europe were very important to the people, who were avid fishermen, explorers, and conquerors. Here is the Norse explanation for why the seas of the world are filled with salt.

Frodi was the King of Denmark. He was the son of the god Frey, who came to earth many times and ruled in Sweden as Ingvi-Frey, and in Denmark as Fridleef. Frodi's mother was the beautiful Freygerda, whom Frey had rescued from a deadly dragon.

Frodi was also known as "Peace Frodi," for his people lived in relative peace for many years. Frodi had acquired two giant millstones—round stones that were used to grind grain. These stones were so large and heavy that it was very difficult for Frodi's servants to turn them.

King Frodi visited Sweden, where he purchased two giantesses, Menja and Fenja, who were very large and very muscular. The two women were capable of lifting heavy weights and of working for long hours. Frodi was pleased with his servants and brought them back to Denmark, where he instructed them to turn the millstones. According to the legend, he did not want them to grind wheat, but to produce gold, peace, and prosperity.

The task was a simple one for the giantesses. Day and night they turned the great millstones and filled the king's palace with gold, peace, and prosperity until these items overflowed throughout the kingdom. The people of Denmark were very happy with the bounty they had received in the name of the king.

Even though there were no more storage areas to keep the products of the women's labor, King Frodi did not allow the giantesses to rest. He wanted more and more of the magical products they ground for him. He only allowed them to stop long enough to sing a special song, which assisted them in grinding.

After several months the women grew weak from their labor. Their arms ached and were quite sore. They knew they had to find a way to escape from their bondage.

One evening, while King Frodi was asleep, they decided to cast a spell over Denmark. They sang a new song as they turned the millstones. This song was one of revenge and murder. The song drifted out into the air until it reached the Viking Mysinger. He was moved by the meaning of the lyrics and felt sorry for the slaves. Mysinger arrived in Denmark while its king and his subjects were sleeping, and proceeded to kill them all.

Menja and Fenja were happy that King Frodi had been destroyed. At last they could take a well-deserved rest from their hard work. But it would not be for long. The Viking Mysinger was intrigued by the massive millstones and wished to load them onto his ship. Only Menja and Fenja could lift the stones. He asked them to join him on his voyage. Believing his intentions to be kind, they did.

However, once the women were aboard the Viking vessel, Mysinger made them grind again. This time they were grinding salt, which was very valuable, and was used to preserve meat and food during long sea voyages.

At first the women thought the Viking's request was reasonable. After some time they soon realized that he was as cruel and unfeeling as their former owner, Frodi.

Out upon the sea, the giantesses had no one to turn to for help. They knew they could not escape from the Viking's control, so they devised a plan. They began to grind the salt in such quantities that the ship began to list to one side and then to another. The Viking sailors began to shout at the women and asked them to stop grinding so much. But Menja and Fenja kept at their work. Soon the ship was overflowing with salt. It poured out over the deck and into the quarters below. Still the women kept grinding.

Finally the Viking vessel could no longer bear the weight of the two giant millstones and all the salt. It foundered and sank into the cold gray sea, killing all on board.

It is believed that the ship sank in the Pentland Firth, or off of the northwestern coast of Norway. As it descended into the sea, its weight caused a huge hole, or vortex, in the water. The vortex spiraled toward the ocean floor in a deadly whirlpool, known as a maelstrom. All of the salt slid from the ship and was carried away by the ocean's currents. And that is how the ancient Norse believed that the waters of the seas became filled with salt.

# The Norns, Goddesses of Fate

 HE NORNS WERE THREE SISTERS, URD, VERDANDI, and Skuld. These spirits or goddesses lived under the great ash tree Yggdrasil, where they were chosen to warn the gods and goddesses of Asgard of coming danger, and to teach them lessons from their past.

Urd was very old and wrinkled. She always looked backward, preoccupied with events that had occurred in the past. Verdandi was young and vibrant. She looked straight ahead, concerned with the present moment and all of its potential. Skuld always looked in the opposite direction of where Urd was gazing, for she was in charge of seeing the future. In her hands she held an unopened book, a symbol of things that had not yet passed in time.

Besides instructing the immortals, the Norns were responsible for watering Yggdrasil and keeping its soil fertile. They guarded the golden apples that hung on the tree, and made certain that no one picked these fruits, for they were believed to contain the secrets of great knowledge and experience.

The three sisters were in charge of the great birds of the Urdar fountain. This pair of birds was believed to be the first swans. Sometimes the Norns collected the birds' feathers and dressed in them to visit the earth.

When they were not busy with these tasks, the Norns spun a magnificent web, called the web of fate. The web of fate was tremendous, indeed, and could stretch from the top of a tall mountain, across the sea, and to the crest of another mountain many miles away.

Odin was very interested in learning about his destiny. He often called upon the Norns to hear their predictions. Once he called them to the Urdar fountain and asked them what would happen to him and the world of the Asgard.

The sisters answered him in a riddle:

"Early begun, Further spun,

One day done, With joy once more won."

Odin did not know the meaning of their verse. The Norns were trying to tell him that although he would be defeated in a great battle at the end of the world, his son would rise out of the ashes of that war and lead the universe in peace once more.

It was not only the gods and goddesses of Asgard who sought the powers of the Norns. Many humans also wished to interpret their past, improve their present condition, or see what would occur in the future.

Once, when the three sisters were visiting Denmark, they went to the home of a nobleman whose wife was about to give birth. When the tiny baby was born, the sisters gathered around him. The people of the town had heard that the Norns were in the nobleman's house, and dropped their chores and work to crowd inside the home and listen to the sisters. Urd proclaimed that the child would be very handsome and brave. Verdandi announced that the child would be prosperous and rich. But before Skuld could say anything, she was dumped from her chair by the crowd of townspeople, anxious to hear the predictions of the Norns.

Skuld was insulted by what had happened. She stood up and walked over to the mother of the new infant.

"See that candle, there on your night table? When its flame goes out, your baby will die," Skuld pronounced.

The other Norns were appalled by Skuld's behavior. They knew, however, that they could not undo what she had said. The flame of the candle was burning lower and lower. The baby's mother began to cry as she watched the wax melt.

Finally Urd approached the candle. She snuffed it out with her fingers and handed it to the mother.

"Be certain that your child carries this candle with him, wherever he goes. He will live a long life. When he is tired of living, he has only to light this candle again, and when it burns out, his life will be over as my sister has predicted."

The mother was grateful for Urd's actions. In her honor she named her baby, Nornagesta. In time, Nornagesta grew up to be handsome and brave. He was very successful in life and traveled to many places. He lived for hundreds and hundreds of years and saw many changes take place on earth. After living a long life, however, he grew weary. His old religion had been replaced by a new one called Christianity. Nornagesta no longer wished to be alive. Silently he lit the candle he had carried with him throughout his life. As the candle burned, he remembered all the things he had done, and places he had visited. At last, the flame flickered out, and as the Norn Skuld had predicted, Nornagesta fell over and died.

# THE GIANTS, MAKERS OF MOUNTAINS

HO WERE THE GIANTS IN NORSE MYTHOLOGY? Most believe they were the first creatures to exist from the beginning of time. From the body of the frost giant Ymir, who emerged from the abyss of Ginnungagap, the whole world was fashioned.

Sometimes Ymir, the first frost giant, is referred to as Fornjotnr. Fornjotnr was an ancient being who was identified with snow, ice, and fire. He had three sons: Hler, the sea, Kari, the air, and Loki, fire. From these three came other giants such as the giants who ruled the seas—Gymir, Grendel, and Mimir; the storm giants; Thiassi, Thrym, and Beli—and Fenrir and Hel, who were the gods of death and hell.

The giants were creatures of tremendous size and weight. They had incredible appetites and consumed enormous amounts of food and drink. The giants did not care for sunlight and often traveled at night or in the fog. They were not as intelligent as the gods and goddesses of Asgard, though it was believed that they possessed much knowledge about the natural world and knew the secrets of the past. Even the great god Odin traveled to the giant Mimir to drink from his well of knowledge.

In Iceland, Switzerland, Germany, and many of the Scandinavian countries, the giants were credited with creating the mountains and hills of the
world. It was said that their footsteps were so heavy when they walked,
they left deep impressions in the soil, and drove great cones of rock up from
the earth. An avalanche in the Alps might be interpreted by some as a
giant sneezing or walking about in the snow.

Once, a giant called Senjemand fell in love with a Scandinavian maid-
en named Juterna-jesta. He proposed to her, but she refused him because
he was so ugly. Senjemand vowed revenge against the beautiful, young
woman. While she was walking in the fields, he shot an arrow at her.
Fortunately for Juterna-jesta, another giant happened to be nearby and saw
the arrow flying through the air. He was also infatuated with the woman
and threw his large hat in the path of the arrow. The arrow missed its mark,
but hit the ground. It left a hole in the side of a mountain that is still
referred to as the place where Senjemand's arrow scarred the earth.

The giants possessed a great ship called *Mannigfual*. The ship journeyed
throughout the waters of the Atlantic Ocean. *Mannigfual* was a very large,
imposing sight on the ocean. It was so big that the giants could ride their
horses around its deck. One day, after drinking too much mead, the pilot
of the ship got lost and directed *Mannigfual* to the North Sea. When he
realized what he had done, he attempted to return to the ocean by way of
the English Channel. Unfortunately, *Mannigfual* was too large for such a
slim body of water. The giants appeared to be stuck, until someone came
up with the idea of rubbing soap along the sides of the ship to make it eas-
ier for it to pass through the Channel. The idea worked and the great vessel slipped through, but not without leaving a white film of soap along the
rocks. This is the story of how the "white cliffs of Dover" in England came
to look like they do.

The giants dwelled in the land of Jotunheim. "Jotun" means "great eater." They were the traditional enemies of the gods and goddesses. Many battles were fought by the Aesir against the giants in order to protect the earth from their ravages. The frost giants of the North could destroy crops by blowing cold air through the farmlands of Scandinavia. The Norse gods Odin and Thor visited Jotunheim many times to subdue the reckless giants and return the world to order.

The final battle between the giants and the gods was called Ragnarok. It was an important fight that would decide the fate of the world. The giants joined forces with the powers of the underworld to fight against the Aesir. They rode their horses to the rainbow bridge that separated their world from the world of the gods and goddesses. With the evil wolf Fenrir on their side, they managed to kill many gods. Odin and Thor were destroyed in the fighting. The giants did not win, however. The sons of Odin and Thor managed to survive and eventually killed the race of frost giants, allowing the earth to flourish once more.

# LITTLE FOLK:
# THE ELVES AND DWARFS

F YOU HAPPEN TO VISIT THE MOUNTAIN REGIONS OF Scandinavia, you might hear the voices of the dwarfs, or little people, who are believed to live there. Dressed in red hats, or "Tarnkappe," that make them invisible to humans, the dwarfs are known for repeating the last words spoken by humans. Some people consider these sounds to be echoes bouncing off the mountain peaks. To others, the sounds are the voices of mischievous dwarfs.

The first dwarfs came from the slain body of the frost giant, Ymir. They were also known as trolls, goblins, kobolds, brownies, or pucks. Tiny and deformed, with wrinkled faces and little eyes, the gods considered them harmless. Despite their size, they possessed great knowledge of the future and were often consulted by the immortals.

The dwarfs lived underground, beneath the rocks and among the roots. They were cunning, jumping swiftly from one place to another in an instant.

The king of the dwarfs was called Andvari, or sometimes Oberon. He lived in a magnificent palace, far below the earth. The palace was decorated with ornaments and finery crafted by the dwarfs. Occasionally Andvari instructed the dwarfs to make a weapon for a mortal or a god, such as the famous sword Angantyr, which could cut through anything in the world—

even iron or stone. The dwarfs created the beautiful diamond necklace Brisingamen, which was eventually owned by the goddess Freyja.

The dwarfs were known for getting along well with humans when they wished to be kind. They would perform household tasks, or assist a farmer in his labors. If the humans were ungrateful, the dwarfs would never return.

Eventually the people of the Northern lands lost their belief in the gods and goddesses and the dwarfs decided to leave their homeland. No one is certain where they went, but it is believed that their remains can still be sighted in places like the Peak of the Trolls in the mountains of Norway. It is believed that the dwarfs fought a battle here with each other, and were turned to stone when they failed to seek shelter from the rising sun.

Other magical creatures of Norse mythology are the elves and fairies. These were tiny, winged beings that danced in the spaces between the earth and the skies. They flew among flowers and danced under the moonlight. The elves' special day was Midsummer's night, when they gathered to celebrate their king, Oberon, who was also the king of the dwarfs.

It is believed that the fairies created a magical circle in the grass called a fairy circle. If one stood inside the circle, he or she might be able to see the fairies. The Norse believed that the person who was able to do this would be doomed.

The elves or fairies were also mischievous and liked to play tricks on humans. They would tie the tails of horses into knots, which the farmers referred to as "elf-knots." Still, the people of Scandinavia revered the tiny beings, and carved their images into the doorposts of their houses. They offered them bowls of honey or milk, known as "alfablot."

It is believed that some of the fairies or elves lived as long as the plants or trees that they attended. They were called wood nymphs or tree maidens.

The stories of dwarfs, elves, and fairies are found in almost every culture in Europe, from Ireland and England to Russia, Scandinavia, and the countries of the Mediterranean.

# SIGURD, HERO OF THE NORTH

HE STORY OF SIGURD COMES FROM A VERY OLD NORSE story called the *Volsunga Saga*. The story has been passed on to us in many forms such as opera, poems, and books. Sigurd is just one of numerous characters in the great epic. He was the son of Sigmund, the great Norse hero, and the princess Hiordis. When Sigmund was slain, Sigurd was raised by the Viking elf Helfrat, who took Sigurd's mother as his wife.

Sigurd learned many things under the tutelage of Helfrat and Regin, a wise, old man who had knowledge of all things. Sigurd could read and write, speak different languages, carve intricate runes or symbols in wood, ride a swift horse, and fight as a capable soldier.

Regin knew all of these things about young Sigurd and decided to use his talents. One evening he sat before a fire and asked Sigurd to sit with him and listen to a story.

Regin told the story of the elf king's treasure. Once, there was an elf king named Hreidmar, who had three sons. The elf king was fond of all of his sons. Fafnir was the eldest and was a fierce warrior. Otter, the second son, could change his form at will, and Regin, the youngest, loved to decorate his father's house with golden objects.

One day the gods of the Aesir, Odin, Hoenir, and Loki came to the land where the elf king reigned. As they walked along, Loki, the trickster, saw an otter basking in the sunlight. He killed the sleeping animal and threw his pelt over his shoulder without thinking that he had done anything wrong. However, when the three gods reached Hreidmar's palace, and the elf king saw what Loki was carrying, he flew into a rage.

"You have killed my son Otter," Hreidmar shouted at the three. "For this you will remain imprisoned with me until one of you has collected enough gold to cover Otter's skin and fill his body."

The three gods decided that Loki, the clever one, should go out and see if he could collect enough gold for the task. Loki knew that the otter's skin would stretch, so he had to collect an enormous supply of the precious metal. He traveled to the elf Andvari and made him surrender his great treasure. Andvari was not pleased, but knew he was no match for the mischievous Loki.

Loki returned with the treasure and dumped it at the feet of Hreidmar. Hreidmar and his sons were so busy admiring all the gold and treasure that they did not pay attention when the three gods got away.

The sons of the elf king began to fight, and finally Fafnir killed his father and kept the treasure for himself. Regin went out into the world to become a teacher, and Fafnir turned into a fire-breathing dragon because he was so mean and greedy.

When Regin had finished his story, he asked Sigurd if he would consider killing Fafnir the dragon in revenge for the death of his father. Sigurd agreed and asked his teacher to make him a sword that was invincible. Regin made a powerful weapon for Sigurd and sent him to the land where Fafnir was living.

When Sigurd arrived, he searched for the dragon. An old man appeared before him; a man with a floppy-rimmed hat and one eye. Sigurd did not recognize the man as the god Odin. Disguised, Odin offered Sigurd a way to slay the dragon. He told him to build a trench in the earth that would lead from the river up a hill. This was the path that the dragon took every day when he returned from drinking water at the river's edge. Sigurd did as Odin told him, and hid in the deep trench until he saw an enormous shadow pass over him. He could feel the dragon's hot breath and saw clouds of steam rising in the air from the monster's nostrils.

Sigurd waited until the dragon was directly over him and then took his sword and thrust it into the dragon's chest. The animal screamed and roared in pain, then fell over dead. Sigurd climbed out of the trench.

Regin watched what Sigurd had done, and when the dragon was dead, he approached the young warrior. Regin was afraid that Sigurd, having slain the dragon, would ask for a large reward. Thus, Regin pretended to be sorrowful that Sigurd had actually killed his brother.

"I will not ask for your life in exchange," he told Sigurd, "but will ask you to cut out the dragon's heart from his chest and roast it for me."

Sigurd agreed. While the heart of the dragon was roasting over a fire, Sigurd reached out to see if it was sufficiently cooked. The heart was hot to the touch, and Sigurd brought his burnt fingertips to his mouth. When the dragon's blood touched Sigurd's mouth, he received a magic gift. He was able to hear the language of the trees and the birds and all living things.

A flock of birds flying overhead called down to Sigurd with a warning.

"Don't trust the elf Regin, for he means to destroy you!"

Sigurd heeded the birds' warning and killed Regin. He gathered the gold that the dragon had been hoarding and loaded it onto his horse. Sigurd rode away, having slain the mighty dragon and receiving the power to communicate with the creatures of the world.

# OTHER MYTHS

# HOW THE SUN AND THE WORLD WERE CREATED

## *Egypt*

N THE BEGINNING THE WORLD WAS A WASTE OF WATER where the Great Father lived. Nu was the name of the water and of the Great Father, because the water and the god were deep. The sun god appeared as a shining egg that floated upon Nu's breast.

Ra is the name by which the sun god is best known. Ra was greater than Nu. He became the divine father and ruler of all the gods. The first gods he created were Shu, the god of wind and air, who wore an ostrich feather on his head, and his twin sister, Tefnut, who had the head of a lioness. Tefnut was the goddess of the dew and the rain. Their children were Geb and Nut.

Ra had commanded Geb and Nut not to have children. They were to remain childless every month of the year. But the god Thoth, who was guardian of the moon, took pity on the pair. Thoth added a seventy-second part of the moon's light to the normal cycle of the moon. This created five new days, which, before then, had not belonged to the Egyptian calendar of three hundred days. On the five new days Geb and Nut gave birth to five children, including Osiris, Isis, and Nephthys.

Upon Ra's orders Shu forever separated Geb, the earth god, from Nut, the goddess of the sky. Shu elevated Nut into the air and held her belly in the sky with his arms. Only her toes and fingertips touched the earth. Across Nut's belly became the stars and the constellations, which formed the arch of the heavens in Shu's arms and which lighted the earth.

Ra had a secret name, which neither the gods nor men knew. The goddess Isis, daughter of the earth and the sky, and great-granddaughter of Ra, wanted to know the name. But Ra hid his name in his heart and would not reveal it through speech.

Ra had grown very old, and he drooled when he spoke. One day Isis followed the sun god as he walked on the earth. Looking closely at the ground, she found saliva that had dripped from Ra's mouth. With her power of enchantment Isis baked the saliva along with some particles of the earth upon which it lay. She shaped the mixture into an invisible, venomous serpent. When Ra came near the serpent, it stung him. The sun god was stricken with pain so unbearable that the cry that broke from his lips was heard in highest heaven.

His body trembled and his teeth clattered. The venom overflowed his flesh like the Nile River when it flooded the land of Egypt. Finally the great, ancient god calmed his great affliction enough to speak.

"Gather about me, you who are my children, so that I may make known the grievous thing that has befallen me. I am stricken with great pain, so great that never before has such sorrow and pain been mine. Lo! I have not the power to make known who has stricken me thus," said Ra.

All of Ra's children grieved with the sun god except Isis, who spoke, "Reveal your secret name, divine Father, for its power must surely deliver you from your pain and distress."

But Ra cried out once more only in pain. Poison burned his flesh. His body trembled. He appeared on the verge of death.

Again Isis spoke to him. "If you will reveal your name of power to me, I will have the strength to heal you."

In his pain Ra raged, "It is my will that Isis be given my secret name, that it leave my heart and enter hers."

When he had spoken these words, Ra vanished for a short time from the eyes of the other gods. Thick darkness covered the earth. Isis waited anxiously for the secret name of Ra. Then she felt it in her heart.

"Depart, O venom, from Ra. Come forth from his heart and his flesh, flow out from his mouth. Let Ra live, for the secret name has been given to me," said Isis.

The words of Isis healed the sun god, who was made whole again. Yet, Ra was indeed old, and in a short time other gods would question his rule as Isis did. The ingratitude of humans finally drove Ra far into the heavens beyond reach. At that time Nut, the goddess of the sky, took the form of a cow and carried Ra on her back into the vault of heaven.

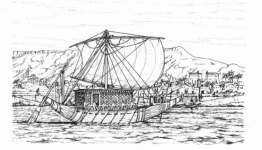

# DESTRUCTION

# ISIS AND OSIRIS

## *Egypt*

 SIS AND OSIRIS WERE THE DAUGHTER AND SON OF Geb, the earth god, and Nut, the goddess of the sky. Set was their younger brother, who was very jealous of Osiris. The struggle between Osiris and Set is one of the best-known myths of ancient Egypt. Out of their struggle, Osiris became known for all things related to creation, the water of life, and blessing. Set became the symbol of destruction, drought, and evil.

When Osiris was born, a voice from within the heavens proclaimed, "Now has come the lord of all things."

The prophecy was true. When the sun god and creator, Ra, ascended into heaven on the back of Nut, who had taken the form of a cow, Osiris took Ra's place. He became king of the gods and the land of Egypt. Under the rule of Osiris, peace prevailed over all of Egypt.

Osiris was king, and Isis was queen. Isis possessed great wisdom. When humankind required food to eat, Isis gathered wild barley and wheat. With the gift from Isis, Osiris taught humans to till the soil, which had been flooded, to sow seed, and to reap the harvest. Osiris saw that peace and prosperity thrived in Egypt, so he set out to teach this wisdom to all humans. Isis reigned over Egypt in the absence of Osiris.

But in the absence of Osiris, Set determined to stir up rebellion in Egypt. At his every turn, however, Isis was stronger, and she thwarted Set's efforts. Set then plotted outright against Osiris. In his camp were seventy-two men and the queen of Ethiopia.

A great feast was held in Egypt upon the return of Osiris. Set attended with his fellow conspirators. He also brought a decorated chest made in the measurements of the body of Osiris, the king of the land. Amid the joyous celebration of the feast, Set announced that he would bestow the chest upon the person whose body fit the box's exact proportions. One after another, the guests tried to enter the chest, but to no avail. Then, to wondrous applause, Osiris came forward. He lay down and filled the box in its every dimension. When he went to raise himself in triumph, the evil conspirators sprang forward and shut the lid. They nailed it fast and sealed it with lead.

Within the rampant confusion that followed, Set commanded his evil followers to secretly dispose of the chest in the Nile River. When morning came, Osiris, still inside the chest, was carried out to the ocean. The chest and its occupant tossed hopelessly upon the waves.

Grief-stricken, Isis donned the garments of mourning and wandered the land of Egypt, searching for the body of Osiris. She roamed long days in vain until she came upon some children by the shore. They told her how the chest had entered the sea at the mouth of the Nile. Meanwhile, the traitor Set ascended the throne of Osiris.

Isis became a fugitive in the kingdom, where she sought protection from her enemies and those of the former king. Seven scorpions served as her protectors. Watching from heaven, Ra witnessed her distress, and he took pity.

One day Isis came to the house of a poor woman. But upon seeing the scorpions, the woman slammed the door. One scorpion found entry into the house. The scorpion bit the woman's child, and the unfortunate child died. The poor mother shrieked with sorrow, which touched the heart of Isis. The queen uttered some magical words, and the dead child came back to life. Accepting the woman's invitation, Isis remained in the house, where she gave birth to her son, Horus.

Word of the birth of Horus reached Set, who became determined to put the infant to death. Out of heaven, to the rescue of the rightful heir to the throne of Osiris, came the god Thoth. Thoth warned Isis of the danger, and she fled with Horus into the night.

Thoth, the moon guardian, had the head of an ibis, a bird like a heron except with a long, downwardly curved bill. Above the ibis was a moon disc. Thoth possessed complete wisdom. He invented the arts and the sciences. He measured time and was charged with all the calculations. At times Thoth was as powerful as Ra, the sun god and creator.

Because of Thoth, Horus would grow into manhood, and one day he would slay the murderer of his father.

# RA AND THE TWO BROTHERS

## *Egypt*

HE SUN GOD RA OFTEN WALKED ON EARTH AND TOOK human form. In this myth the god answered the plea of a young man against the evil doings of his older brother.

Anpu was Bata's older brother. Anpu had a house and a wife. Bata lived with Anpu and his wife like a son. Bata tended his brother's oxen, plowed the land, and harvested the grain. At the end of each long day, Bata slept with the cattle. Bata's spirit was the spirit of a god.

One day Anpu grew furious at his younger brother. When he returned to his house, Anpu's wife had told her husband a lie about how Bata had hurt her. She did this because she was angry that Bata did not return the affections she showed him. She was captivated by the younger brother's beauty and strength. The younger brother had told Anpu's wife that he considered her as dear as his own mother. Besides, she was his brother's wife.

Believing his wife's false words, Anpu sharpened his dagger. He set out to slay Bata when he returned with the cattle. But the oxen understood what Anpu had in mind to do, and they warned the kind Bata.

"Beware! Your elder brother is hiding behind the door, hoping to slay you with a dagger. Do not move in his direction," said the first ox.

The second ox spoke. "Take speedy flight," the ox said to Bata.

Bata looked through the door of the barn and saw that what the oxen said was true. He took flight like the second ox suggested. Anju, with his dagger drawn, pursued him closely.

Bata cried out to Ra, the sun god. "O blessed lord! Help me, because you are he who distinguishes between falsehood and truth."

Walking through Egypt in human form, Ra heard the cry. He created a wide stream to flow between Anpu, on the right and Bata on the left. Crocodiles filled the stream with a great gnashing of jaws.

Bata cried, "When Ra, the sun god, makes the earth bright again, I will reveal in his presence all that I know. He shall judge between us."

At sunrise the following day, when Ra appeared in his glory, the brothers faced each other over the stream and the crocodiles. Bata explained to his brother what had happened with Anpu's wife. Anpu was anguished, and he wished to join Bata on the opposite bank of the stream.

Bata said, "Go to your home, Anpu, and tend your oxen. I can no longer dwell with you. I must depart into the land of the flowering acacia tree. My soul will leave my body and dwell in the highest blossom. When the tree is cut down, my soul will fall. Seek it if you so desire."

Before Anpu could respond, Bata continued, "You must place my soul in a vessel of water. When you do, I will come back to life and mend all that has happened. Behold! When the hour comes for the quest, the beer you are given will bubble, and the wine will have a foul smell."

One day the acacia, where Bata's soul dwelled, was chopped down. When the tree fell, the petals scattered. Among them was Bata's soul. Anpu's beer bubbled and the wine in his goblet had a foul smell. Anpu reached for his staff and with set out for his journey.

For three years Anpu searched for his brother's soul. At the beginning of the fourth year, he yearned to return to the land of Egypt. At the dawn of the new day, when he decided to see Egypt once more, Anpu found a seed from the acacia. He dropped the seed into a vessel filled with water, and Bata came to life.

When night came, the brothers embraced. Their wounds were healed.

# THE LANGUAGE OF THE CREATOR

## *Benin (Fon)*

HE FON PEOPLE IN THE PRESENT COUNTRY OF BENIN believed that the creator god was female and male. One side of the god's body was female and was called Mawu. The male side was called Lisa. The eyes of Mawu formed the moon, while Lisa's eyes made the sun. Mawu ruled the night, and Lisa was ruler of the day. Because the god was named for both its halves, the Creator was called Mawu-Lisa.

Mawu-Lisa had seven children. Six of them ruled the six domains of heaven and earth. The seventh was called Legba. Mawu chose Legba to represent her everywhere in the world of men and gods. Legba knew the language of Mawu-Lisa, which was called Fa. He also spoke the languages of all the other gods in all the places they ruled.

This is the story about Legba and Fa, the language of the Creator, who were his parents.

After the world was created, two men named Koda and Chada came down from the sky. Koda and Chada were numodato, or prophets. The numodato assembled the people and told them they had a message for them from Mawu.

"It is necessary that every person has his or her Fa," said Koda and Chada.

The people were confused about the message. "What is this thing called Fa?" they asked.

"Fa is the writing that Mawu uses to create each person. Mawu gave the writing to Legba, and only Legba can assist Mawu in her work," said the numodato, who had come from heaven.

"Tell us more about the Fa of Mawu and Legba," the people begged.

Koda and Chada explained, "Mawu is always seated, and Legba is forever before her. Mawu's orders for humans, which she has given to Legba, are called Fa. Therefore, all humans who have been created have their Fa, which exists in the house of Legba. The place where humans were created is called by the name of Fe. Mawu has charged Legba to bring to each individual his or her Fa, which is the writing that Mawu used to create the individual. Humans must know their Fa so they may know what to eat and what not to eat, what to do and what not to do."

The humans tried to understand the words they had heard about Fa. They listened carefully as the numodato told them the rest of Mawu's message. The Fa that Legba gave to each human would tell that individual which god to worship. But without Fa each individual would never know his or her god.

"If you fail to worship Legba first, Legba will never reveal your destiny. And Legba will never identify the god you are to worship," said Koda and Chada.

The humans learned that Mawu wrote their destiny every day. She gave what she wrote to Legba every day. The writings told Legba who would die, who would be born, the dangers individuals would encounter, and the fortune other individuals would enjoy. Only Legba, and then only if he wishes, can change the fate that awaits every human.

"We understand that Fa is necessary for us," said the people.

But time passed. The people remembered that Fa was necessary and the will of Mawu. However, they forgot about Legba.

It happened that three other men descended to earth. They came to Gisa, in the country of Nigeria near a river called Anya. Their names were Adjaka, Oka, and Ogbena.

"You cannot forget that Mawu told you it is important to worship Legba, too," said the three men, reminding the people of the message from Koda and Chada.

The people heard the words and waited for more instruction.

Adjaka, Oka and Ogbena, the messengers of the gods, chose a man called Alaundje. They taught Alaundje about Fa. Alaundje traveled across the land, and he instructed others in the message of Fa. In his travels, he taught Djisa. Djisa learned the message, and he taught Fa and Legba to the people of Dahomey.

The people who listened to the teaching of Fa and Legba learned from Djisa how to read the writing of Mawu. They were called bokono, or priests. They were bokono, because in the sky Legba is called bokono.

# IMMORTALITY

# THE JOURNEY OF GILGAMESH

## *Sumer-Babylon*

ILGAMESH WAS THE PROUD AND BEAUTIFUL KING OF Uruk. He was ambitious and smart and loved to learn all there was to know about life. Gilgamesh's curiosity troubled his mother, Ninsunna.

"Why do you desire to know so much, my son?" she asked him.

"It is important to me," Gilgamesh replied, "to experience everything in the world—to taste every type of food, smell every fragrance, journey to every land, enjoy every dance. Can't you understand that?"

Ninsunna shook her head.

"Gilgamesh, although you come from the gods, part of you is still mortal. You cannot know and experience everything. One day you will die, as all mortals die."

When Gilgamesh heard what his mother had told him, he flew into a rage.

"I do not wish to die!" he exclaimed angrily. "My great friend Enkidu died. I miss him terribly, and I do not wish to follow him into the land of the dead. I will learn the secret of living forever."

Gilgamesh's mother tried to comfort her son.

"I only know of one person who has managed to escape death. His name is Uta-Napishtim, or Uta-Napishtim, the Remote. He survived a mighty ordeal and was granted everlasting life. He lives beyond Mount Mashu, which is very far away."

Gilgamesh made up his mind to find Uta-Napishtim, the Remote. He traveled toward Mount Mashu. It was a long journey filled with many perils. He was pursued by the fierce lions of the forest. The Scorpion Men, who hid behind the boulders of the mountains, jumped out at him and tried to frighten him.

Gilgamesh continued on his way. Sometimes it was so dark he could barely see in front of himself. Finally, in the distance, Gilgamesh saw a great, glowing light. He had reached the home of Uta-Napishtim.

The old man greeted Gilgamesh and asked him why he had come so far from his home.

"Tell me how you have earned the right to live forever, Uta-Napishtim," Gilgamesh asked him. "This is what I wish to learn."

Uta-Napishtim invited Gilgamesh to sit beside him on the ground.

"Here is my story. I lived in Shurippak, the city of the sun. One day the god Ea came to me and told me that the gods were displeased with humans and wished to destroy the earth. They were going to send a great flood to cover the world.

"Ea instructed me to build a very large ship and to prepare for the deluge. Then he told me to bring my family into the ship, as well as many animals, and to wait for the rains to fall. I did this. A great storm came and the skies were filled with black clouds. Thunder shook the ground and bolts of lightning raced through the heavens with hot, white light. For many days it rained and rained without stopping. We almost forgot what it was like to see the sun or to walk on dry land.

"We were very afraid, but I trusted that Ea had told me the truth, and that I would be saved. After a long while, the rains stopped falling and I sent a bird out from my ship to seek land. The bird returned to me, exhausted after failing to find a place to land. In time I sent another bird, a raven, to fly from the ship. I was overjoyed when the raven did not return to me, for it had found a dry patch of earth on which to live. This was a very good sign.

"Eventually the great flood waters receded and our ship rested upon a cliff. We left the ship with all of the creatures we had carried with us, and gave thanks to Ea and Ishtar, the goddess of heaven."

"But how did you come to be immortal?" Gilgamesh asked.

"The gods saw that I obeyed Ea, and as a reward they granted me immortality."

Gilgamesh jumped to his feet. "That does not help me, Uta-Napishtim, for I have not been tested as you have. Is there no way I can live forever?"

"Everything in this world lives and dies, Gilgamesh," Uta-Napishtim told him. "Yet, there may be a way for you to get your wish. Here is a special plant. Take this plant with you, back to your home. When you are there, you may eat it, and perhaps it will give you eternal youth."

Gilgamesh did as he was told and began the long journey home again. On the way he stopped to rest near a clear pool of water. He was so thirsty that he put the magic plant on the ground, and stepped into the pool to drink from it. Gilgamesh did not notice the snake that crawled in the grass, not far from the water. The snake saw the plant and ate it.

Gilgamesh had lost his chance for immortality. Finally he realized that even though he was a rich and powerful man, he could not escape death.

Legend tells us that the snake, after eating the plant intended for Gilgamesh, was able to shed his skin and regain his youth. Therefore, all snakes have kept this unique ability to this very day.

# THE EBONY HORSE

## *Arabia*

HE EBONY HORSE IS ONE STORY FROM A GREAT collection of tales known as *The Thousand and One Nights*, or *The Arabian Nights*. These stories may have originated in North Africa, though some have been traced to Persia and ancient India. They were told in the marketplaces of the Moslem world during the Middle Ages.

The story begins with the king of the Persians, Sabur, who was a wealthy, powerful man. Sabur was respected by those he ruled, for he was kind, compassionate, and fair. He had three beautiful daughters who were compared to the stars in the heavens and the fragrant blossoms of the garden. Sabur also had a son, the prince Kamar al-Akmar, or Moon of Moons.

One day three men came to Sabur's kingdom with the intent of offering him gifts. The first man was Hindi, or Indian; the second was a Greek; and the third was a Farsi, or Persian.

The Hindi presented Sabur with a golden horn.

The king then asked the man what was the purpose of his gift.

"This horn shall warn you, Sire, if enemies approach your city."

The king was pleased with the gift and took it gratefully.

The Greek offered Sabur a basin of silver in which rested a peacock of gold and twenty-four chicks.

"How can I use this gift?" the king asked.

"The golden peacock will peck one of each of its chicks on the hour, for twenty-four hours, thus allowing you to tell what time it is."

The king was also delighted with this present.

Next the Persian approached the king. He brought before him a magnificent wooden horse carved of fine ebony.

"This is a beautiful statue, my friend," the king declared. "How does it work?"

"Sire," the Persian replied, "this horse has the ability to fly through the air and to take you wherever you wish to go. Let me demonstrate."

With that, the man climbed upon the wooden horse and turned a key in the horse's neck. Magically, the animal's hooves left the ground and it glided with its rider throughout the palace hall. The king was overcome with awe.

"I am so pleased with my gifts," the king announced. "I wish to give to you three something in return. Is there anything that you wish for?"

The three consulted with each other and then spoke.

"We would like the hands of your fair daughters in marriage," they told him.

"Consider it done," the king replied.

The king's daughters were in hiding while this conversation was taking place and had heard what was about to transpire. The two older princesses were not entirely displeased with the arrangement, but the youngest princess knew that she was the most beautiful, and that her father would give her to the man who had presented him with the most fascinating gift. This would be the Persian, and his ugliness and old age caused the young girl to shudder.

She retreated to her room and began to cry. Meanwhile, her brother, the prince, was passing by and heard her wailing.

"What is the matter, dear Sister?" he asked her.

"Our father has promised me in marriage to an old, dirty, ugly man. I do not wish to spend my life with this Persian."

"Don't fear," the prince assured his sister. "Let me handle this situation."

Kamar al-Akmar went to his father and told him that he was not impressed with the Persian's flying horse, and less impressed with the idea that the princess should marry such a man.

"Don't judge him, yet" the king advised his son. "Take a ride on the ebony horse, and perhaps you will change your mind."

The prince agreed to do this and mounted the wooden steed. The Persian, fearing that the prince's opinion would influence the king, decided to play a trick on him.

"Here is the key to make the horse climb into the sky," he told the prince. "Happy journeys to you, Your Majesty."

The prince turned the key, and the horse rose from the palace floor. It rose higher and higher until the ceiling could not contain it. It broke through one of the skylights and continued to climb into the air.

The prince, however, was wise enough to know what the Persian had done. "This man is trying to get rid of me so that he may have my sister. If there is a key to make this animal climb into the air, then there must be a key to make it descend, as well."

The prince felt along the horse's neck, and sure enough, he found another key, which he turned. The horse began to descend. Thrilled by his discovery, the prince took the horse over many lands, rising and diving at will to see the wonders of the world.

He happened upon a great palace, like the palace of his father. He guided the ebony horse to the roof and looked inside one of the windows. There, to his surprise, he found a woman sleeping alone. She was the most beautiful woman he had ever seen. He walked over to her, but not before the guards of the palace were upon him.

"You will die, intruder," they told him. "Come with us before this lady's father and state your case."

The prince went before the sultan of the palace and tried to explain that he was of royalty, as well, and wished to marry the sleeping princess.

"If this is true," the sultan declared, "you must demonstrate your worthiness to all of us. You must enter into battle with my army."

The prince thought for a moment, then answered that he would do such a thing.

In the early morning, the great armies of the sultan gathered in a battlefield. They were amazed when the single figure of the prince arrived on horseback. "We will slaughter him, for sure," they thought.

The prince, however, turned the key in the neck of the ebony horse and rose above the charging soldiers. They were so afraid, that they dropped their weapons and ran. The sultan, having seen what had happened, knew that the prince was a powerful figure. He agreed to allow him to marry his daughter.

Kamar al-Akmar returned to his father and his sisters with his new bride. He accused the Persian of playing a trick on him by not divulging where the second key was located on the ebony horse. The king, hearing this, and knowing that his son could have been carried away for good, banished the Persian from his court.

Then the king ordered the flying horse to be broken into a thousand pieces and discarded. The youngest princess rejoiced at her brother's saving actions. A great festival was held in honor of the prince and the bride he had found while flying on the ebony horse.

# ALADDIN, OR THE WONDERFUL LAMP

## *Arabia*

HE STORY OF ALADDIN'S LAMP HAS BEEN TRANSLATED into many languages throughout the world and is one of the most popular stories from the collection of *Arabian Nights*.

There once was a poor Chinese tailor who had a lazy, rude son named Aladdin. Despite the tailor's efforts to try and teach his son a trade, the boy preferred to daydream and idle the hours away playing in the streets of the city.

When Aladdin's father passed away, it became his mother's burden alone to feed and clothe Aladdin.

One day an old man appeared in Aladdin's home, identifying himself as the brother of Aladdin's dead father. He told Aladdin's mother that he had come to see her, upon learning of his brother's death, and would try and teach her son a respectable trade so that he might have a good livelihood. Aladdin's mother was overjoyed at the news.

The uncle proposed that he open a shop for Aladdin. He gave him gold and new clothing. He took Aladdin to many different lands to do business with merchants. On one such journey the two stopped in the desert to rest from their travels. Aladdin's uncle built a fire for warmth. Then he did something quite strange. He threw a handful of dust into the fire and recited bizarre words that Aladdin could not understand.

The earth began to shake and tremble. With a mighty jolt a crevice appeared in the sand, like a long, narrow tunnel. The uncle instructed Aladdin to crawl into the tunnel.

"In this tunnel are riches galore, Aladdin," his uncle told him. "Climb in and secure them for me. Please be careful not to touch anything else you see." Then the man added, "Take this lamp with you so that you can see what you are doing. When you have gone deep into the tunnel, empty the oil from the lamp and blow out the light. Tuck the lamp into your belt. Be certain to bring the lamp back to me."

Aladdin was confused, but did as the man asked. He crawled down into the crevice in the sand. To his amazement, he saw enormous trees bearing jewels and precious gemstones in every color of the rainbow. Some of the stones were the size of his fist. Aladdin gathered as many as he could, blew out the light of the lamp, emptied the oil from it, and returned to the surface. He reached out his hand to his uncle for assistance in climbing out of the tunnel, but his uncle refused.

"Give me the lamp first, and then I will help you," he told Aladdin.

As his arms were full of gems, Aladdin could not give the lamp to his uncle. "I will give it to you as soon as I am out!" he told the man.

But Aladdin's uncle did not listen. He grabbed several stones from Aladdin's arms, then pronounced more strange words. The tunnel began to close around Aladdin. He fell helplessly to the bottom.

Aladdin now knew that his uncle was not his uncle at all, but really an evil magician. He rubbed the old lamp in his belt, in hopes of coaxing a bit more oil from its sides so that he could light another fire, but it was hopeless. Or nearly hopeless.

From the spout of the lamp, a stream of unearthly gas appeared. It rose over Aladdin's head and collected itself into the shape of an odd-looking man.

"I am the genie of the lamp," the figure said to Aladdin. "Until you emptied the oil of this lamp in the presence of the treasure buried here, I was doomed to remain inside the lamp forever. Now I am free. What is it that you desire, O Master?"

Aladdin rubbed his eyes. He could not believe what he was seeing.

"Anything that I want?"

"Yes," answered the genie.

"Please, return me to my mother," Aladdin asked him. No sooner had he said the words, then the genie blinked his eyes, and Aladdin was transported to his mother's home. She was overjoyed to see her son, safe and sound.

"We must never share this lamp with your uncle, or let him know that you are alive," she told Aladdin when he related to her what had happened that day.

The genie granted Aladdin and his mother many wishes. No longer did his mother have to work hard to earn money for food. They had all they could hope for.

Years passed and Aladdin and his mother were very happy, until one day when Aladdin expressed his desire to marry the sultan's daughter.

"You cannot do this," his mother told him. "You are the poor son of a tailor!"

"Yes," Aladdin replied, "but I am the poor son of a tailor who has a magic lamp. With the genie's help I can wear fine clothes and present many wondrous things to this princess."

"Even so," his mother answered him, "the princess you wish to marry is promised to the grand wezir's son. They are to be married this very evening."

Aladdin panicked. Perhaps it was too late to make his dream come true.

He rubbed the lamp and asked the genie for help. Together they devised a special plan.

On the night that the grand wezir's son married the princess, the genie placed a spell on him. Instead of sleeping in the bedroom of his new bride, the bridegroom decided to sleep outdoors under some orange trees. The bride was greatly distressed and asked her father what she should do.

"Perhaps he is just tired from a long day of festivity," the sultan told her. "Give him another chance to be with you this evening."

On that evening, though, the wezir's son slept in the horse stables. The princess was very distraught. "I believe he does not love me," she told her father. "Is there no one who loves me enough to be my husband?"

Before the sultan could answer his daughter, a young man stepped from the courtyard. He was dressed in fine clothing and carried a magnificent sword of gold.

"I am Aladdin," he told the sultan, "a man of means and wealth. I have admired your daughter from afar. But, now, I believe the time is right to present myself to you, and ask for her hand in marriage."

The sultan looked at his daughter. He would have no trouble finding another suitor for her, for she was intelligent and beautiful, and the sultan's kingdom was worth a great deal. However, he saw something in his daughter's eyes that told him that she had found true love with the young man before her.

"Take my daughter and treat her well," he told Aladdin. "If you are kind and good to her, I will bestow on you my kingdom and all my riches."

Aladdin promised he would love and cherish the princess. They were married in a wonderful ceremony, which was attended by his mother. And although Aladdin's evil uncle returned again to trick Aladdin into giving up the magic lamp, Aladdin was able to foil him, and keep it to the end of his days.

# INDRA AND THE DEMON VRITRA

## *India*

NDRA WAS A GREAT WARRIOR GOD. HE WAS ONE OF THE four gods present at the signing of the treaty that brought peace to ancient India. A very important god, Indra was also the god of Nature and the lord of heaven. He held a thunderbolt in one arm and a bow in the other. His steed was the elephant Airavata, who was born from the sea of milk. At the time of Indra's birth, humans begged the gods to protect them. They cried out against the demon Vritra, who imprisoned their cattle and threatened to starve them. Indra was born in order to fight his first battle against Vritra. In response to the cry he heard from humankind, he overcame the demon with his thunderbolt.

The story that follows is about another battle.

A powerful priest, or Brahman, named Tvashtri, did not like Indra. The Brahman created a son with three heads and gave him great power like his own. With his first head, the son read the *Vedas*, the sacred teachings. He ate with the second. He could see every speck along the horizon with the third head. The Brahman wished to give his son Indra's throne. To protect the throne, Indra killed the Brahman's son with his thunderbolt.

The body of the young, dead Brahman radiated glorious light, and Indra saw that the danger to his power still existed. A woodcutter passed by, and Indra ordered him to cut off the young Brahman's three heads. Great flocks of doves and other birds flew forth from where he chopped. Indra had still not escaped the Brahman's threat.

Now the Brahman, who created the son, brought to life a huge demon named Vritra to avenge his son's death. The demon's very head touched the sky. When Indra tried to battle Vritra, the demon seized the god, put him into his maw, and swallowed him. The other gods were horrified at the spectacle, and they gagged Vritra. Indra contracted his body tightly. As soon as Vritra opened his mouth, the captive god jumped through the demon's ugly jaws and flew to safety.

Indra paid a visit to the Rishis, the seven sages or wise men that formed the constellation of the Great Bear. Many people believed that Indra's thunderbolt possessed its strength because it was formed from the bones of a Rishi. Indra and the Rishis together visited Vishnu, the supreme god that preserved the universe. Vishnu advised that Indra make peace with the demon through the negotiations of the Rishis. At the same time, Vishnu hinted that one day he himself might materialize into a weapon powerful enough to kill Vritra.

"Give me your solemn promise," said Vritra the demon to the Rishis, "that Indra will never attack me with any weapon of wood, stone, or iron, nor with anything dry, nor with anything wet. Promise, too, that he will never attack me by day nor by night."

The Rishis agreed to the demon's demands. Yet, Indra silently vowed revenge. One evening while he was at the seashore, he saw his enemy Vritra at a distance.

Indra reasoned out loud to himself. "The sun is setting on the horizon, and darkness is coming up. But it is not yet night and it is not altogether day. If I kill the demon now, between day and night, I will not break my promise."

At that moment a vast column of foam rose from the sea. Indra consoled himself that the structure was neither dry nor wet, nor stone, nor iron, nor wood. Seizing the foam, he hurled it at Vritra the demon and killed him. The strange foam column was none other than Vishnu, and nothing and nobody could resist the power of the preserver. With the defeat of Vritra, the other gods rejoiced. As a soft breeze blew over the land, even the beasts of the field were glad. In spite of the victory, the god of Nature, Indra, felt the burden of the great sin of slaying a Brahman.

Alas, this was not the last time that Indra would battle Vritra. Vritra would return to life again as the leader of the Danavas, demons that upset the balance of Nature. Vritra would cause drought, and Indra would bring rain to the land. In battle after battle Indra overcame the demon. As he did in this story, Indra repeatedly forced Vritra to retreat to the darkness of the ocean waters.

# How the World Was Created, Destroyed, and Created Again

## *India*

HE EARTH WAS SHAPED LIKE A WHEEL. IN THE CENTER of the world was Brahma's heaven. The heaven was called Mount Meru, and the mountain was 84,000 leagues high at its peak, or summit. The heaven was encircled by the River Ganges. The cities of Indra and the other gods surrounded it. The lower mountains, or the foothills, that scaled below Mount Meru were home to the Gandharvas, the good or benevolent spirits. The demons lived in the valleys.

The hood of the great serpent Shesha supported the whole world. When a great flood covered the universe, Shesha coiled up on the back of a tortoise. The world had many floods. At the end of each deluge, the world was born again.

Once, a golden cosmic egg glowed like fire and floated on the waters that buried the world. For a thousand years the lord of the universe brooded over the egg. Finally a lotus flower, as bright as a thousand suns, grew from his navel. The lotus spread and flourished until it contained the whole world. Brahma sprang from the lotus with the powers of the lord of the universe. He created the world from the parts of his body.

But, Brahma made some mistakes, and he had to learn from them. At first he created ignorance, and he tossed it away. But ignorance survived and became Night. From Night, the Beings of Darkness were born, and they set out to devour their creator.

"How can you eat your own father?" asked Brahma.

Some of the Beings of Darkness relented, but others did not soften in their desire to destroy Brahma. They became the Rakshasas, the enemies of men. Brahma learned from the experience, and he resolved to create immortal and heavenly beings. He brought to life four sages to finish his work. But the sages lost interest in the creation, and Brahma became angry. From his anger, Rudra sprang forth to complete the work.

When another flood covered the world, the world spirit threw a seed called Nara into the the waters. Called Narayana after Nara, the first dwelling, the spirit grew inside the egg as Brahma. After one year, Brahma made his body into two parts. One half was male, and the other half was female.

Viraj, a male, grew inside the female half, and Viraj created Manu. Manu was a sage, called a Rishi. Manu lived ten thousand years in the worship of Brahma. He survived other floods, and he became equal to Brahma in his glory.

One day Manu was meditating beside a stream. A fish spoke to him from the water.

"Please, protect me from this fish that is chasing me," the fish begged Manu.

Manu put the fish into a pond. After some time, the fish grew too big for the pond.

"Please, place me into the River Ganges," requested the fish.

Manu did as the fish asked. But time passed, and the fish grew too large for the river.

"Please, take me to the ocean," implored the fish.

At last the fish was content. Manu learned that he had rescued none other than Brahma himself. Brahma warned Manu of the coming destruction of the world by a great flood.

"Build an ark and place in it the seven Rishis and the seeds of everything," Brahma instructed.

No sooner did Manu do as Brahma asked,when the deluge began. Everything in the world was blanketed by water once more. The ark tossed about upon the surface, and cables tied to the horns of the fish moved it along. Finally, Manu's ark rested upon the highest peak of the Himalayas, where Manu moored it to a tree.

The waters receded after many years, and Manu and the ark descended into the valleys. To prepare for the creation of the next age, Manu performed many sacrifices.

Manu offered up milk, clarified butter, curds, and whey to Brahma. He repeated the gesture every day. A year passed, and Manu's offering grew into a beautiful woman.

"I am your daughter," said the beautiful woman to Manu. "Together, we will perform other sacrifices to Brahma. As a result you will become rich in children and cattle. You will obtain any blessing you desire."

Manu did as his daughter said. They were true in their devotion to Brahma. In return, Manu fathered the human race, and he received many blessings.

# SIVA AND THE CHURNING OF THE SEA

## *India*

HE GOD SIVA WAS KNOWN AS THE DESTROYER OF illusions. He was also merciful. His wisdom allowed him to dance to life with all his heart. Siva was sometimes called the god of dancing. In paintings he was shown with four arms. In his two upper hands he held a drum and doe. He used his two lower hands in gestures of giving and reassuring. His forehead had three horizontal stripes and a third eye in the center.

He dressed in tiger skin. One snake adorned his blue throat, and he wore another as a sacred cord at his waist. Others were coiled as bracelets on his arms. A trident, a three-pronged fish spear, and a crescent moon were in his knotted hair. Sometimes he also had the fifth head of Brahma, the Creator, or the goddess Ganga (of the River Ganges) in his hair. Siva rode on the bull Nandi.

Many stories have been told about Siva and why the god was painted as he was. One story surrounded Siva's visit to ten thousand Rishis, wise men who had become heretics. That is, they decided to follow their own beliefs and turned their backs on the truth. The Rishis cursed Siva when they saw him. When the god did not back off from the curses, they conjured a fierce tiger to devour Siva. With the nail of his little finger, the smiling god skinned the tiger and made himself a shawl with the animal's hide.

Next the heretics called forth a horrible snake to sting Siva. With the snake Siva made a garland for his neck. A demon black dwarf armed with a spiked club, called a mace, appeared out of nowhere. Siva lay the demon on its back and danced upon it. The dazzling rhythm of the god's dance stunned the Rishis. To convince them further of Siva's godliness, the heavens opened up so the other deities could watch the dance. Witnessing the event, the heretics threw themselves at Siva's feet, and they worshipped him.

In another story Siva again helped set things right in the world. It was long ago, and the god Indra had been cursed by a great Rishi named Durvasas. The curse caused the power of Indra and the three worlds to weaken. Vishnu, the preserver of the world, appeared to Indra.

"I will give you back your power. This is what you must do. Take Mount Mandara and the snake Vasuki. Use the mountain as a stick and the snake as a rope and churn the sea of milk. You will see that this creates the liquid of immortality and other wondrous gifts," said Vishnu.

Then Vishnu gave Indra a complication. "But you'll need the help of the demons. Forge an alliance with them and say that you will share the fruits of your common labor. I will personally make sure that they do not get their share."

The demons were called the Asuras. Indra and the gods of Mount Mandara and the snake Vasuki began their labor with the help of the demons. As a violently churning stick, the mountain greatly damaged the ocean. The heat of the mountain's rotation destroyed the animals and birds that had lived on its slopes. The mountain would have indeed perished if Indra had not drenched it with heavy rains from heaven. Still, the weight of the mountain bored into the earth and was about to break thorough the earth's crust.

Luckily, Vishnu was able to assume a great number of forms. This time the god became a gigantic turtle that supported the churning mountain. Though invisible, Vishnu was present at the same time among the gods and the demons hauling the rope. But the poor snake suffered greatly as the rope. Fountains of venom escaped his jaws and became a wide river that threatened to destroy gods, demons, men, and animals.

The distress caused Vishnu to call upon Siva with the trident hair. Siva heard the call, and the god drank the poison to save the world from destruction. The bitter poison burned Siva's throat, and it left its mark of a blue band. The moon appeared, and Siva grasped it to wear on his forehead. This same day a miraculous flying horse appeared out of the sea of milk as one of its gifts.

# ESU'S TRICK ON THE TWO FRIENDS

## *Brazil, Cuba, Nigeria (Yoruba)*

SU WAS THE GODS' MESSENGER. AS MESSENGER HE brought the will of the gods down to humans. Because he was partly in the world of the gods and as much in the world of humans, his legs were of different lengths. This caused Esu to limp. In his arms he carried a clabash, or gourd, inside of which was the ase. The ase was the word of Olodumare, the Creator, when he made the universe.

Sometimes Esu played tricks on humans. This is the myth of the two friends and the trick Esu played on them. The two friends took a vow of eternal friendship. Esu heard them telling each other they would be friends forever, and he decided to do something about it. His plan was to test their friendship.

Esu made a cloth cap. The cap's right side was black. Its left side was white. He found the two friends tilling their land. One friend was hoeing on the right side of the field. The other friend was clearing bushes on the left side. Into the middle of the field, riding between the men, was Esu, and on his head he wore the cap. The man on the right saw the black side of

Esu's cap. Of course, the man who was clearing bushes saw the white side of the messenger's cap.

When it was time for lunch, the friends took a break from their labors in the field. They met in the cool shade of some trees as they always did.

"Did you see the man with the white cap who greeted us this morning while we worked? He was quite pleasant, don't you think?" said the friend who worked on the left side of the field.

"Yes, he was rather pleasant," answered the second friend. "But I recall him as a man in a black cap, not a white one."

"It was certainly a white cap. And the man rode a magnificently caparisoned horse."

"His horse was wonderfully decorated. It must be the same man. But I tell you, his cap was dark, and it was black," insisted the friend who had been hoeing on the right side of the field.

"Clearly, you are fatigued. Or the hot sun has blinded you. How else would you mistake a white cap for a black cap?" questioned the first friend.

"I tell you, it was black, and I am not mistaken. I can still see him," answered the second friend.

With that, the two men began to fight. So severe was their fighting that their neighbors came running from every direction to intervene. But they could do nothing to stop the fight. Into the middle of the uproar, Esu appeared. He was very calm, and he pretended not to know anything about what was happening.

Esu spoke harshly. "What is the meaning of this uproar?"

"Two close friends are fighting," said someone.

"They are about to kill each other," said someone else.

"And neither will tell us the cause of the fight," said a third person.

"Please, stop them," pleaded a fourth.

Esu scolded, "Why do you two lifelong friends make such a public spectacle of yourselves?"

The second friend tried to explain to Esu what had happened. "A man rode through the field and greeted us. He wore a black cap on his head. But my friend said it was a white cap and that I must have been tired or blind or both to think it was black."

"It was white," insisted the first friend.

"Both of you are right," offered Esu.

"How can that be possible?" demanded both friends at the same time.

"I am the man who paid the visit over which you both quarrel. And here is the cap that caused the commotion," said Esu. Out of his pocket he pulled the two-colored cap.

"As you can see," Esu continued, "one side is white, and the other side is black. You each saw one side. Therefore, you each are right in what you saw. Are you not the two friends who vowed to be friends forever?"

The friends shook their heads at what they saw and heard.

"When you vowed eternal friendship, you did not reckon with Esu," said the god. "Don't you know that he who does not put Esu first has himself to blame if things backfire?"

# CREATION OF HEAVEN, EARTH, AND HUMANS AND THE NAMES OF THE SUN

## *China*

 NCIENT CHINA IN THE FOURTH CENTURY B.C., ABOUT 2,400 years ago, delighted to the "Questions of Heaven." There are said to be at least 160 questions in all about the beginnings of heaven, earth, and humans. You will soon know the meaning of a few of the questions.

When were brightness and gloom created? ... Where are the ends of the Nine Skies situated and where do they join up? ... How are the sun and moon connected? ... How was Nu Kua's body made? How did she ascend when she rose on high and became empress?

Before heaven and earth formed, only a shapeless, dark expanse existed. There were no forms, and all was dark and obscure. The gaping mass of darkness was called the Great Glory.

Two gods, Yin and Yang, were born out of the chaos. They wove the skies, and they designed the earth. The sky was a serene, peaceful light, and it was called Yang. The heavy darkness became the solid earth. It was called Yin. Yin and Yang separated into the Eight Poles, or pillars, that were fastened by cords to the dome that was the sky. The dome sky was vaulted. It was nine layers deep with nine celestial, or heavenly, gates. The eight pillars rested on a square area of land that was the earth.

Yang and Yin continued to share their energy, which became the four seasons. The four seasons scattered their force, which brought about the ten thousand things in nature. The hot breath of Yang, the sky, gave birth to fire. The energy of the fire became the sun.

The cold breath of Yin became water. The energy of the water became the moon. The energy that the sun and the moon did not need became the stars. Yang welcomed the sun, moon, and stars. Yin celebrated the rivers and rainwater, the dust and silt that emerged.

When Yin and Yang rose from the void, humankind did not exist. Nu Kua, the creator goddess, came into being and changed her form seventy times, so powerful was she. When she was ready, she kneaded yellow earth, and she made human beings. Nu Kua worked feverishly in her creation of humans. Though she worked hard, the goddess did not possess enough strength to complete her task.

So, Nu Kua took her cord, which was the type that builders used, a rope with a weight, or a plumb, at one end. She drew her cord through the mud, which made a furrow. When she lifted the cord from the furrow, she had created human beings from the mud.

The ancient Chinese showed Nu Kua with her builder's cord and a builder's compass. They believed that the rich aristocrats were the human beings whom Nu Kua fashioned by hand from the yellow earth. The ordinary folk were those whom the goddess made by running her cord through the mud.

***

Here is a myth about the sun's names. To the ancient Chinese there were fifteen stages in the sun's journey each day. Of the stages, five described the sun's light, and four related to the sun's position in the sky. Three stages referred to human mealtimes. Two stages described pestles, club-shaped tools to pound and grind. One stage told of the chariot driven by dragons.

The sun rose from Yang, or Sunny, Valley, where it bathed in Hsien Pool. After bathing, the sun brushed past the world tree, Leaning Mulberry. When it did so, it was called daybreak. The sun reached Winding Riverbank, and it was called daylight. When it came upon Ts'eng-ch'uan, its name was breakfast. At Mulberry Wilds, the sun was named supper, or the midday meal. When the sun reached Pivot Sunshine, it was called angle center. At K'un-wu, the sun was named perfect center.

At Mount Niao-tz'u, the sun was called small return. When it reached Sad Valley, it was called evening meal. At Nu-chi, the sun's name was great return. At Yuan Yu, the sun was high pestle. At Lan-shih, it was low pestle.

When the sun reached Sad Springs, it stopped the Woman, the charioteer, and she rested her six dragons. Here the sun was called tethered carriage. When the sun traveled on to Yu Yuan, it was called yellow gloaming. At Meng Valley, it was named fixed dusk. When the sun at last rose from Yu Yuan's riverbank and brightened the slopes of Meng Valley, it had covered 517,309 leagues. (A league measured somewhere between two-and-a-half and four-and-a-half miles.)

# SOME UGLY GODS WHO REWARDED HUMANS

## *China*

 EI-KUNG WAS CALLED MY LORD THUNDER. HE WAS repulsively ugly! Not only was he shown with a blue body, but he had wings and claws, too. He dressed only in a loin-cloth. At his side he carried one or more drums. He carried a mallet and a chisel in his hands. He used the chisel to punish the guilty. Some say he used the mallet to create a drumroll of thunder. Others say he drove in the chisel with his mallet.

Lei-kung had orders from heaven to punish those humans who had committed a crime unpunishable by human laws. He often required the aid of humans to enact the punishment. Here is a myth about My Lord Thunder.

One day a hunter was eagerly in pursuit of game. A violent storm took him by surprise in the thick of the forest. The storm was punctuated by lightning and thunder so fierce in intensity that the hunter was terrified. The outbursts seemed to be at their strongest directly over a tree with uplifted branches. The strange tree was not far from where the frightened man stood.

When the hunter lifted his eyes, he saw something even stranger. In the tree was a child holding a coarse flag. The flag was nothing more than a piece of filthy cloth tied to a splinter of wood.

My Lord Thunder also noticed the child. Just as the god was about to let loose a loud clap, the child waved the flag. Lei-kung suddenly stopped the outburst cold and retreated.

The hunter knew well that Lei-kung, like all gods, deplored things that were unclean. Such things were usually the work of an evil spirit. The man loaded his gun, raised it, and shot down the flag. Then Thunder struck the tree at once. The hunter was very close to the tree when Thunder struck, and he fainted.

When the man revived, he found a small roll of paper in his grasp. The message on the paper read: "Life prolonged for twelve years for helping with the work of heaven." The hunter then saw next to the shattered tree the grotesque corpse of an oversized lizard. He realized this to be the true form of the child he had seen with the filthy flag.

The god of Examination, named K'uei-hsing, was also one of the ugliest divinities in existence! He wore a constant grimace on his face. Bending forward, he held his left leg raised in a running posture while he propped on the head of a turtle called Ao. He carried a bushel basket in his left hand and a paintbrush in his right. With the paintbrush K'uei-hsing put a mark next to the names of the humans lucky enough to be chosen by the August Personage of Jade, Father-Heaven. In his bushel he measured the talents of all candidates. The god of Examination is a follower of the god of Literature, called Wen Ch'ang.

When the Chinese emperor gave an audience to scholars who passed their doctoral examinations, the emperor said, "May you alone stand on the head of Ao, the turtle that supported the god of Examination." What follows is a story about the student who took an examination.

The young student had worked hard in his preparation for the examination. The student, however, was not satisfied with his performance when he returned to his home. He knew that Wen Ch'ang and K'uei-hsing rewarded the efforts of hard work.

The student begged the gods to help him obtain good results from the examination. When the student slept, Wen Ch'ang appeared to him. In his dreams the student saw the god throw a bundle of examinations into a stove. The student saw his own test in the bundle. When the god removed the tests, they were entirely changed. Wen Ch'ang handed the student his examination, and the student knew to study the changed material very carefully.

Upon waking, the student learned that a great fire had destroyed the examination building during the night, and all the tests were burned. Consequently, every examination candidate had to take the test again. With the new knowledge that the god had given him, the student passed with honors.

# CREATION FROM AN EGG

## *Japan*

I N THE DAYS OF OLD, HEAVEN AND EARTH WERE NOT yet separate. And the feminine, In, and masculine, Yo, were also not divided. Only a mass without form, but something like an egg, existed. The egg substance was without clear limits, and it contained germs.

One part of the egg was purer, and it became heaven. The heavier, grosser part settled down to become earth. The particles in the finer portion easily united to make heaven. The union of the grosser particles was accomplished with difficulty, which meant that heaven formed first.

Once heaven and earth were formed, Divine Beings were produced. It happened in this manner. When the world began to be created, the soil of the lands floated about like a fish floating on the surface of the water. In the realm between heaven and earth, the shoot of a reed took form. The reed transformed into a god. The god was called Kuni-toko-tachi no Mikoto, which meant Land-eternal-stand-of-august-thing. As august, the god possessed majestic dignity.

There were seven generations of the age of the gods. Including Kuni-toko-tachi no Mikoto, eight deities in all were formed. They came into being by the mutual action of heaven and earth, and they were made male and female.

The last god and goddess to be formed were Izanagi no Mikoto, or Male-who-invites, and Izanami no Mikoto, Female-who-invites. Together they stood on the floating bridge of heaven and looked down.

"Is there not a country beneath?" they asked each other.

So they thrust the jewel-spear of heaven downward, and after some groping, they found the ocean. The brine that dripped from the spear's point coagulated and formed an island. They called the island Ono-goro-jima, or Spontaneously-congealed-island.

The two deities dwelled on the island. They stated their wish to become husband and wife and to produce countries. Ono-goro-jima became the pillar of the center of the land. By circling the pillar in opposite directions, and meeting at the same place, they were married.

Izanagi no Mikoto and Izanami no Mikoto began to produce islands. Their minds took no pleasure in the first they created. So they called the island Ahaji no Shima, or the island which is unsatisfactory. They tossed it away.

Next they produced the island of Oho-yamato no Toyo-aki-tsu-shima, or rich-harvest-of-island. The two islands of Iyo no futa-na and Tsukusi followed. The twin islands Oki and Sado came next, as the precursors of the twin births that were to come later among humans.

The islands of Koshi, Oho-shima, and Kibi no ko were the sixth, seventh and eighth islands, which they created and kept. They called the country Oho-ya-shima. It meant great-eight-island country.

Two islands called Tsushima and Iki, along with some smaller islands, came into being afterward from the foam of the salt water. The two deities continued creating until they had made the sea, rivers, and mountains. Then they produced Ku-ku-no-chi, the ancestor of the trees, and Kaya no hime, the ancestor of herbs.

Izanagi no Mikoto and Izanami no Mikoto consulted each other. "We have made the great-eight-island country, the mountains, rivers, herbs, and trees. Shall we not produce someone who shall reign over the universe?"

In response, they produced the sun goddess. They called her Oho-hiru-me no muchi, or Great-noon-female-of-possessor. So resplendent was the sun goddess's luster that she shone throughout the six quarters of the North, South, West, Above, and Below.

Next they made the moon god as a companion to their wondrous daughter. He was as radiant as she was. And they sent the sun goddess and the moon god to rule in heaven.

Afterward they produced the leech-child. However, after three years, the leech-child could not stand upright. So they abandoned the child to the winds. The next child was Sosa no wo no Mikoto, called the Impetuous One, because this god possessed a fierce temper and was prone to cruelty. He caused great damage to the people and the lands of earth.

"You are exceedingly wicked. You are unfit to reign in the world. Therefore, depart to the land of Yomi, or Hades," said the two deities that created the Impetuous One. And they banished him to the Underworld.

Their next child was Kagu tsuchi, the god of fire. Kagu tsuchi burned her mother, Izanami no Mikoto. As she lay dying upon the earth, Izanami no Mikoto gave birth to the earth goddess and the water goddess. Kagu tsuchi, god of fire, and the earth goddess mated to produce a child named Waka-musubi, or young growth. Upon this god's head were produced the silkworm and the mulberry tree. In her navel were the five kinds of grain.

# A Taste of the Food of Hell

## *Japan*

FTER THE GOD OF FIRE BURNED HIS MOTHER, IZANAMI no Mikoto, the Female-who-invites, the goddess descended into Yomi, or Hades, the place that was the Underworld. The god Izanagi no Mikoto, the Male-who-invites, went after his wife to bring her back to earth.

"My husband, why have you come so late?" asked the goddess Izanami.

"I have just followed you," said Izanagi.

"But I have already eaten from the cooking furnace of Yomi."

Izanami reminded her husband that it was impossible for anyone to leave the Underworld after eating the food there. But Izanagi would not hear his wife's words. He protested that she should speak to the god of Yomi and obtain his permission to leave.

"I am about to lie down to rest now. I pray you, do not look upon me," said the goddess.

But Izanagi grew impatient. He took his many-toothed comb, and he quietly broke off the last tooth. Then he lit it and used it as a torch to look upon Izanami. Putrefying matter gushed from Izanami's body, and maggots swarmed over it. Eight Ugly Females watched over the decomposing goddess Izanami.

Izanagi was horrified. "I have come unaware to a hideous, polluted land," cried the god.

"Why did you not listen to my request?" demanded Izanami.

When her husband began to flee, the goddess cried after him, "You have humiliated me!"

So she sent the eight Ugly Females of Yomi in pursuit of Izanagi. The god drew his sword and brandished it behind him as he continued to run away. He flung his black headdress upon the ground, and it changed into grapes. The Ugly Females stopped following momentarily and ate the magical fruit. When they renewed their pursuit of Izanagi, the god hurled his many-toothed comb. The comb changed into bamboo shoots, and the Ugly Females paused again, this time to eat the bamboo.

Finally Izanami herself assumed the pursuit of Izanagi. But, by now, the god had reached the Even Pass of Yomi. He blocked the entrance to the Underworld with a huge boulder, and Izanami was forced to relinquish the pursuit.

Back on earth Izanagi realized he had brought bad luck upon himself for having visited the Land of Yomi. In an attempt to wash it away, the god proceeded to the Aha gate and the Haya-sufu-na; the first known for its rapid tides, and the second, meaning Quick-such-name gate. Seeing the strong tides at the two gates, Izanagi went instead to Wodo, or little gate, in Tachibana to cleanse himself.

Entering the water at Wodo, Izanagi exhaled and produced Iha-tsu-tsu no Mikoto, or Rock-of-Elder. Exiting the water, he exhaled again and produced Oho-nawo-bi no Kami, or Great Remedy Person. Then he entered the water a second time. Repeating what he had just done, he produced Sokotsutsu no Mikoto, Bottom-elder, and Oho-aya-tsu-bi no Kami, Great-

Pattern-of-Person. Izanagi entered the water a third time. When he exhaled, he made Aka-tsutsu no Mikoto, Red Elder. When he exited the water and exhaled, he produced the various deities of heaven and earth and of the sea plains.

Izanagi washed his left eye with the water of the sea. And he gave birth to the great goddess of the sun, Amaterasu. He washed his right eye. So doing, he produced the goddess of the moon, Tsukiyomi. He washed his nose. And he gave birth to the god Susanoo.

To Amaterasu, Izanagi gave a necklace of jewels.

"You will rule the plain of heaven," he said.

"You will rule the kingdom of night," Izanagi said to Tsukiyomi, goddess of the moon.

"And you will rule the plain of the seas," he said to Susanoo.

Upon the words of Izanagi, Amaterasu and Tsukiyomi took leave to obey their orders. But Susanoo did not move. He stood where he was, weeping and groaning.

"What is the meaning of your weeping?" asked Izanagi.

"I wish to go to the kingdom of my dead mother," responded Susanoo, ruler of the sea plains.

Susanoo's words aroused a fury in Izanagi, who had barely escaped the Land of Yomi. Before the ruler of the sea plains departed for Yomi, he paid a visit to his sister, the goddess of the sun, in heaven.

Izanagi no Mikoto knew that his divine task had been accomplished. His spirit had forever changed. So he built for himself an abode of gloom on the forsaken island of Ahaji. He decided to dwell there always, hidden and in silence.

# The Orders of Cagn

## *Southern Africa (Bushmen)*

AGN WAS THE FIRST BEING. HE WAS AN ANIMAL SPIRIT. He ruled on earth as the great magician and organizer. His orders caused all things to be made, including the sun, moon, stars, wind, mountains, and animals. Cagn's wife was Coti. They had two sons. Cogaz was the elder and the chief. The younger son was Gewi.

When Cagn ordered all things and animals to be made, he made them fit for the use of humans. He ordered snares, or traps, and weapons. Next he made the partridge and the striped mouse. He ordered the wind so it could carry the smell of game. And so on.

Here are two of the many myths about Cagn.

One day Cagn's daughter grew angry with her father because he scolded her. She ran away, intending to throw herself among the snakes, the qabu. In the world that Cagn made, snakes were also men and they ate snake's meat. The chief of the snakes married the daughter of Cagn. But the chief served his new wife the meat of eland, or African antelope. He did this because he knew no child of Cagn could eat an evil thing.

Cagn knew what was in the far distance. He enlisted his first-born Cogaz to go to the land of the snakes and to bring back his daughter. With his father's tooth to make him strong, Cogaz gathered an army of young men to accompany him on his mission.

Seeing the party of Cogaz approach, some of the snakes grew angry. They began to hide their heads.

"Do not be angry. They have come for Cagn's child," said the chief of the snakes.

The sister of Cogaz gave her brother and his army the meat of eland.

"Tell your husband we are here to take you home," said Cogaz.

After doing so, Cagn's daughter prepared food for their journey. The next morning Cogaz, his sister, and the army found some rushes that grew in the nearby marshes and bound them around their limbs and bodies. They departed for home while three snakes followed closely behind them.

First the snakes tried to bite Cogaz and his party. But the rushes protected them. The snakes tried to beat them with reins, but the rushes served as a shield. When the snakes threw sand at the foreigners in an attempt to drive them into the water, they failed once more. They did not know that Cogaz carried Cagn's tooth for strength.

Meanwhile, the snakes that were at home with their chief knew that when the three snakes returned, they would fill the country with water. Upon willow poles, they built a high stage. The wives of the three snakes took their husbands and threw them into the water. The water rose to the height of the mountains. But the high stage kept the chief and the other snakes dry.

Cagn bid Cogaz to return to the snakes with an invitation to come to him. Cagn ordered the snakes to lie upon the ground. With his stick he struck each one. Every time he struck, the body of a person emerged from the snake. The new people saw the ground littered with the skin of the snakes they had been. Cagn sprinkled the snakeskins with the oil of canna, a tropical herb. In this way the snakes turned from being snakes. They became Cagn's people.

Another myth about Cagn tells of the thorns, or dobbletjes. They were called Cagn-cagn, and they were dwarfs. One day Cagn came upon the thorns, and he saw them fighting among themselves. When Cagn went to separate the thorns, they turned their anger upon him. And they killed him. The biting ants who witnessed the killing devoured Cagn.

Time passed, and the biting ants and the thorns collected Cagn's bones. They arranged the bones in order, and they attached Cagn's head with cord. Thus assembled, Cagn stumbled home. When Cogaz, his elder son, saw his father, he cured Cagn. Once Cagn was whole again, Cogaz asked what had happened. On this occasion it was Cogaz that gave Cagn advice and power.

"The best way to fight the dwarfs is to pretend to strike at their legs. When they move to protect themselves, hit them on their heads," said Cogaz to his father.

As Cogaz instructed, Cagn killed many of the evil thorns. And he drove them into the mountains.

# QUETZALCOATL

## *Central America and Mexico*

 UETZALCOATL LIVED IN TOLLAN IN A GREAT HOUSE constructed of gleaming silver. The house was surrounded by sweet gardens with flowers of every color of the rainbow. The fields of his land were filled with maize, or corn, that grew so tall that the stalks cast shadows on the full moon. The rooms of Quetzalcoatl's palace reflected the red of the mountain peaks, the greens and blues of turquoise stones, and the yellow of wildflowers. A thousand brightly colored birds flew among the clouds over his house and landed in the trees, where they sang songs to the people all day long.

The people of Tollan learned many useful crafts from Quetzalcoatl. He taught them about the stars and constellations of the skies. They learned how to work with silver and gems, how to build a house, how to paint and carve and sculpt. Everything they learned was taught in the spirit of peace, for Quetzalcoatl only shared the knowledge of things that were creative and beautiful. There was no war in Tollan, no fighting or jealousy or hunger.

Far away in the distant mountains, where the gray storm clouds rested from their long journey across the sky, there lived a sorcerer called Tezcatlipoca. Unlike Quetzalcoatl, he lived his life in pursuit of trouble and strife. He found pleasure in bringing heartache to others. Looking down from his dark perch, he sent a chilling, destructive wind into the valley where Quetzalcoatl's house was situated. The flowers in the garden felt the cold blast of air, closed their blooms and died.

Quetzalcoatl looked out the window of his silver house and saw what had occurred. His heart was filled with sadness. He called to one of his loyal servants and spoke to him.

"There is someone who wishes to harm me. If I am to protect this place, I must leave here today."

The servant was confused by Quetzalcoatl's words, though he packed some food for him and some warm blankets. Then he took many bags of precious jewels and gems and packed them, too. As the cold winds continued to blow, Quetzalcoatl left Tollan and went to the mountains. Several of his servants followed him.

As he traveled into the wilderness, he was tracked by a jaguar. He attempted to change his path many times to avoid the animal, but it was no use. The jaguar, who was really the evil Tezcatlipoca, had Quetzalcoatl's scent and was intent on hunting him.

Quetzalcoatl grew weary. He began to age, and the muscles of his arms and legs ached with fatigue. After he had crossed a great mountain range, he found a quiet valley, where he stopped for a while to rest. From one of the sacks, he took a mirror and looked at his reflection. Looking back at him was the face of an old, tired man. Homesick and discouraged, Quetzalcoatl threw the mirror into the tall grass. He thought of his beautiful home in Tollan, and the memories of it caused him to weep. His tears fell down upon the earth and left lasting marks on the stones.

The servants who accompanied him tried to raise his spirits by playing music on their flutes. For a time he forgot the bittersweet memories of his home and the constant sound of the jaguar who stalked him.

The sacks that Quetzalcoatl and his servants carried seemed to grow heavier and heavier with each mile they traveled. Quetzalcoatl decided to dump one of the sacks in the fountain Cozcaapan. It was the bag that contained his most precious treasures.

The men climbed higher and higher into another mountain range. It snowed and sleeted and hailed for days and nights. Eventually the loyal servants who had remained with Quetzalcoatl died from the bitter cold. He was left with only his memories and the taunting wind that came from the breath of Tezcatlipoca.

On the other side of the mountain, Quetzalcoatl found the sea. Upon seeing the great waters, he built a raft from snakes that he wove together. He sailed far away from the land, out into the middle of the ocean until he arrived in the land of Tlappallan, in the country of the sun. The jaguar spirit of Tezcatlipoca finally stopped pursuing him.

In Tlappallan he drank the waters of everlasting life and threw himself into a brightly burning fire. When the fire died, only the ashes of the kind and good Quetzalcoatl remained.

Some believe that Quetzalcoatl will return one day as a young, happy man, eager to teach the people of the world the good crafts of life, like weaving and spinning and painting and creating beautiful things. In the meantime his spirit appears as brightly colored birds, soaring and diving high above the treasure he cast in the fountain in the mountains.

# PELE, GODDESS OF FIRE

## *Hawaii*

B EYOND THE CRYSTAL-BLUE WATERS OF THE HAWAIIAN islands, inside a crescent of warm white sand, is the great volcano Kilauea. It stands proud and tall, spitting fire and sparks at the sky. The people of the islands have long believed that the protector of the mountain Kilauea is Pele, the goddess of fire.

Like Kilauea, Pele was fiery and powerful. She could become angry quickly; nearly as quickly as the ocean could turn from calm to stormy. With her temper tantrums she could cause the volcano to spew forth hot, molten lava and poisonous gases. The people were afraid of Pele's moods and tried to appease her with sacrifices and music whenever they could.

One day Pele and her sisters and brothers were visiting the shores of the island. They relaxed in the golden sand. They collected shells and looked out at the deep, beautiful blue waters as graceful dolphins jumped in the foamy waves. Contented, Pele asked her favorite sister, Hiiaka, to watch over her as she slept. She spread a soft blanket in the sand and curled up to take a nap, while Hiiaka kept her cool by waving a palm leaf over her body.

Pele fell into a deep sleep. Soon the images of a dream called out to her. She dreamed of another island, not far from her own. The people on the island were dancing and celebrating. They feasted on wonderful food. They danced the hula. In the middle of the dancing, Pele saw a beautiful young man, who had commanded the attention of all the women around him. She was astounded by his skill as a dancer, and his graceful motions.

Without waking, Pele turned herself into a spirit and went to find the handsome man of her dreams. Hiiaka kept fanning her sister, believing that she was enjoying her sleep. She didn't know that Pele was traveling away from the peaceful seashore, toward another island.

Pele's spirit came to the island in her dreams. There she found the prince of Kauai, as tall and graceful as she remembered him to be. Pele changed herself into a beautiful, young woman and approached the prince.

"Prince Lohiau," she said to him, "I have come here to dance with you."

The prince, not knowing that the woman was really the goddess Pele, said to her, "Welcome to my island. I am glad you are here. Please, know that I must dance with all of the young women here."

Pele was not pleased with Lohiau's words. She had hoped that he would find her more beautiful than any other woman. She cast a spell on him so that he could not resist her charms. The spell worked its magic. Prince Lohiau fell in love with Pele.

Pele spent many days with the prince as his wife. They were happy together. However, Pele knew that she had to return to the volcano and her sisters and brothers. One day she told Lohiau that she had some errands to take care of in another land, but would return to him as soon as they were completed. She bid him good-bye and went on her way.

Many, many days passed and Pele did not return to her husband as she said she would. The prince grew weak with sadness. His people tried to cheer him up, but it was hopeless. He refused to eat or drink. He would not leave his house. Finally he crawled into his bed and died of a broken heart.

Pele had returned to the spot where she had been taking a nap under the watchful eyes of her sister Hiiaka. When she woke, she told her sister of the dream in which she fell in love with the Prince Lohiau.

"I have heard that the prince is dead," Hiiaka told her sister. "Some say he was in love with a beautiful woman who left him, and he died of a broken heart."

Pele was moved by the story Hiiaka told. "If this is true, Sister," she said, "then you must travel to the land of the dead and bring him back to me, for I am the one that he loved."

Hiiaka did not understand Pele's words, but she did as she was asked. She went to the fiery underworld to find Lohiau. Many months passed before she succeeded in finding the prince and restoring him to life.

Lohiau was grateful to Hiiaka. He was touched by her kindness and her devotion to her sister Pele. Hiiaka explained that it was Pele who wished for him to return to her in Hawaii. He left the land of death with Hiiaka.

Just as they were approaching the beautiful shores of the home of Hiiaka, the two saw a terrible sight. The volcano Kilauea had erupted many times. The sands of the beach where Hiiaka loved to walk were covered with black, smoking lava. The trees were scorched and burned; all the brightly colored flowers that grew on the hillsides had been reduced to ash.

Hiiaka knew that this was the handiwork of her sister Pele. She approached Pele and asked her why she had done such a thing.

"I thought that you would never return," Pele replied, embarrassed at her own jealousy. "I thought you might fall in love and keep him for your own."

"I cannot understand your cruelty to your sister!" Lohiau cried out loud to Pele. "She risked all kinds of danger to find me among the dead. She was always kind and good to me."

Pele thought about her actions. She asked Lohiau and Hiiaka to forgive her. "The land will soon return to its former glory," she told them. "The trees and flowers will grow back. The sand will become white again. Let us celebrate tonight that you have returned safely, and I will be content that you are alive, Lohiau."

That night there was a great festival on the island. Torches burned brightly into the night and the people all danced and sang in joyous celebration. Lohiau danced the hula for Hiiaka, and even Pele remained calm and content, happy that she had been forgiven for her terrible temper.

CREATION

# HOW THE WORLD BEGAN

## *Thompson Indians, North America*

HERE ARE MANY NATIVE AMERICAN MYTHS TO EXPLAIN how the world came into being. The Thompson Indians of the Pacific coast in North America told a tale about five women who were responsible for the creation of the natural world and its people. The tale begins with the Old One.

Old One lived in his kingdom in the clouds. He floated through the universe and observed all the phenomena of the heavens. He saw the stars and the moon, the sun and the comets as they streaked through the skies. The things Old One saw were beautiful and interesting, but the old man felt that something was missing.

Below Old One's cloud, nothing existed except for a lake, or watery wasteland. He looked at this nothingness for a long while and then plucked five silver hairs from his head. He threw the hairs down to the surface of the lake. Each one floated on the calm water, spinning in a different direction.

Suddenly the hairs were transformed into five women. The women swam to the shores of the lake, and pulling themselves out of the cold, murky water, they rested and looked around at the nothingness.

Old One descended from his cloud and approached the women who had appeared from his hair.

He walked to the first woman, who was rubbing her legs to keep warm. "Woman," he said to her, "what would you be?"

The woman thought for a while and then replied to Old One, "I would be a woman who will bear many, many children. They will grow to be big and strong. But my children will be bad and enjoy violence. They will fight with each other and cause wars. They will commit murder and do many terrible things."

When Old One heard this, he shook his head. "That is too bad," he told the first woman. "You will upset my new world with trouble and strife and violence."

Then Old One turned to the second woman, who was sitting on the shore of the lake.

"What will you become?"

The woman looked at Old One and then answered, "I will also bear many, many children." She told him, "My sons and daughters will be big and strong, too. But they will also be kind and intelligent and wise and good. They will invent many useful things and nourish the earth and spread goodness wherever they walk."

Old One was pleased when he heard these words. "I am grateful to you," he said to the second woman, "for you shall begin a righteous race of people to live in my new world."

The third woman was braiding her long hair when Old One came to her.

"Have you given any thought to what you will do?"

"Yes, I have," she replied carefully. "I will become the earth. That way, I will become a mother to all living things. They will all grow from my soil and swim in my oceans. Everything will come from me, and after these things have lived upon me for a long time, they will die and return to me."

"This is a very good thing," Old One said to her. "I am pleased with your decision."

The fourth woman, overhearing what had been said by the other three, replied to the Old One without being asked.

"Old One," she said, "I will become the element of fire. I will exist in all things for the good of people. I will light the way in darkness and I will warm the food that people eat. I will keep the wild animals away from the caves."

"This is an important thing to be: fire!" Old One exclaimed.

Finally he approached the fifth woman, who had sprung from the hair of his head. "Woman, what will you be in the scheme of things?" he asked her.

"I will be water, Old One," she replied. "I will quench the thirst of every living thing. I will cleanse all things and I will provide a place for the fish and all the creatures of the ocean to live."

This reply also pleased Old One. He stood on the surface of the lake and changed the five women into the creations they had described to him. They became the mothers of good and bad, the earth, fire, and water.

Old One spoke to them once more before he returned to his cloud.

"Be the things you are. At first there will be much trouble and unhappiness in this world, because of the First Woman's choice. Eventually, however, the world will return to a good state and all of you will live in harmony in the universe."

And so, the Old One left the lake, and the world was born with the elements of fire and water and people who were both good and bad.

CREATION

# THE CREATION OF HUMANS

## Zuni Indians, New Mexico

HE ONLY LIVING THING THAT EXISTED AT THE BEGINNING
of time was Awonawilona, or the Maker. The universe was
shrouded in darkness. The Maker, being wise and powerful,
transformed himself into the sun. As the sun he cast light
and warmth, where there had only been darkness. A great mist rose from
the warmth mixing with the cool darkness, and the mist gathered together to form water. Then the Maker spread seeds, that he had plucked from
his own flesh, upon the water, and the seeds gathered together to form
land. Two great beings sprang from the creations of the Maker, and they
were Awitelin Tsita, or Mother Earth, and Apoyan Ta'chu, or Father Sky.
They were joined together in marriage, a perfect union.

Before long, however, Mother Earth grew larger and larger and separated herself from Father Sky. When the time came for Mother Earth to give
birth, she became concerned about the destiny of her children. She kept
her unborn children within her until she could consult with their father.
She asked Father Sky how the children would come to know one another,
and know the things of the world. The Maker heard her question and sent

her a great terra-cotta bowl. Mother Earth took the bowl in her two large hands and looked inside it. It was filled with water. Mother Earth pronounced, "Each country in this world will have a rim, as this bowl has a rim, and then our children will know the boundaries of all the lands. They will know when they have left one country and entered another." And so the mountains of the world were formed.

She stirred the water within the bowl until it made foam. The foam grew bigger and bigger. Mother Earth blew gently across the foam, which drifted through the air. The foam became clouds and delivered mist and rain to the earth.

The Sky Father thus declared, "As the foam waters the earth, it will make things grow. All types of plants and vegetation will grow in the world to feed our children." Then he opened his hands wide, and from the wrinkles and crevices in each one, he took some corn grains. He sprinkled the grains onto the surface of the water in the bowl and from the grain, tall stalks of maize, or corn, grew.

Finally the offspring of the world were born. Mother Earth gave birth to many creatures: worms, insects, flowers, toads, serpents, and humans. The living creatures all multiplied very quickly. They did not communicate in the same language, nor did they walk the same way, nor eat the same food. The earth was a place of great confusion.

One of the offspring was filled with great wisdom. His name was Poshaiyankya. When he saw that his sisters and brothers were constantly fighting and causing disruptions, he appealed to the Maker to help. The Maker looked down and saw what was occurring. He knew that he had to help creation once more. He encouraged Mother Earth and Father Sky to give birth to twins. The twins were to become the ancestors of all humans. They were to be wise and intelligent, and restore order to the earth.

At first the humans lived on the first level of the world, which was cold and dark. Mother Earth and Father Sky created a straw ladder for the people to climb upon so that they would reach another level. Those who could not climb to this new level stayed behind and became monsters and demons. The second level was still dark and cold, but more spacious than the first. Many generations of people were born here, and their skin colors were wonderful shades of white and red and bronze and yellow and black. The people continued to climb until they reached the third level. Here they found warmth from the cold. They separated into nations and tribes and wandered over the land, each claiming a place for their kind in the world.

The final level was a cave called Tepahaian tehuli. The sun rose above the crests of the mountains, and the air was filled with singing birds. This level was sacred and was entered by those who were good and kind. The people learned of their heritage from the Sky Father and Earth Mother and respected them. They obtained valuable knowledge from their parents and were good, obedient children. This was the place known as Tek'ohaian ulahnane, or the world of Light, Knowledge, and Seeing.

# THE SEARCH FOR FIRE

## Yana Tribe, Native American

IN THE BEGINNING OF TIME THE YANA PEOPLE OF Clover Creek had fire, but it was only in the form of a glowing ember—warm, but not very hot. They could not cook the meat of the animals that they hunted, nor could they see very far in the dark.

Au Mujaupa was a powerful god who was the master of fire. But he kept the secret of the flames to himself. He lived in the south of the land, far away, across the currents of a powerful river.

One day a member of the Yana tribe named Gray Wolf decided to depart from his village in search of the fire that could roast venison and cure fish. He traveled to the peak of Lassen's Butte, which was called Wahkanopa. High above the land, he looked out into the darkness for flames that might belong to Au Mujaupa. There was no sign of fire in any direction. He returned home.

The chief of the village advised Gray Wolf to climb to the top of Mount Shasta for a better view of the world. He introduced Gray Wolf to Sigwegi, "Little Bird," who had a remarkable gift of sight that allowed him to see through trees and even down to the core of the earth.

The two men climbed Mount Shasta. In the evening they looked to the north, the east, and the west in hopes of finding Au Mujaupa's fire. There was nothing but darkness, and a few stars.

Then they looked toward the south. Suddenly Gray Wolf spied a small orange glow in the distance.

"I think I see fire!" he said to Little Bird.

"I see it, as well, Gray Wolf!" Little Bird replied.

The men descended Mount Shasta and returned to their people. Gray Wolf addressed the chief.

"Little Bird and I have seen where Au Mujaupa keeps his fire. It is far away and to the south of this land. We will need many people to recover it."

Fifty people volunteered to go with the men. The journey to the south was long and very difficult. By the time they reached the outskirts of Au Mujaupa's village, there were only three people left in the expedition: Gray Wolf, Metsi, and Shushu Marima, the old woman.

Au Mujaupa kept the fire in a large sweathouse in the middle of his village. The fire was guarded by several powerful warriors; among them were Patcha ("Snow"), Chil Wareko ("Big Rain"), and the winds of the four directions.

When the people of Au Mujaupa's village were fast asleep, Gray Wolf, Metsi, and Shushu crept silently toward the sweathouse. They climbed onto the roof, and Gray Wolf went inside to hand out pieces of the fire to his friends. Gray Wolf gave them to Shushu first, who put them in her ears for safekeeping. Then he gave some to Metsi. After filling his own ear with pieces from Au Mujaupa's fire, Gray Wolf and the other two stole away in the night.

Not long after they had left the sweathouse, Au Mujaupa woke from his sleep. He quickly noticed that the fire pile in the center of his hut had been disturbed.

"Someone has stolen my fire!" he cried to his guards. Au Mujaupa did not want anyone else to possess the powerful element of fire. The guards jumped up from their sleep and began to pursue the three. Chil Wareko drenched them with torrents of rain. Patcha covered them with biting frost, and the winds blew gales at them.

Metsi became so frozen that the fires in his ears were extinguished. Gray Wolf's fire died, as well. But Shushu kept her hand over one ear. She managed to prevent the fire from going out. Several pieces fell to the earth from her other ear. Au Mujaupa's guards found the pieces and thought they had foiled the thieves from leaving with fire.

Gray Wolf and Metsi struggled back to the village, leaving Shushu trailing behind. When they arrived, they explained to the chief and his people that they were not able to prevent the guards from recovering the precious pieces of fire that they carried in their ears. The people were disappointed.

"Where is Shushu?" the chief asked the two men.

"I am afraid she is frozen dead," Gray Wolf solemnly replied.

That evening as the village gathered in the hut of the chief, a person appeared out of the dark shadows. It was Shushu, frozen and nearly dead.

She walked to the center of the hut and shook her head over a pile of wood dust. Soon the pieces of fire she had stored in her ear fell onto the dust and ignited it. Excitedly the villagers scrambled about to bring more wood to the beautiful golden flames that were lighting the interior of the hut. The fire grew and grew.

The people then selected pieces of red meat and roasted them in the flames. The cold meat became hot and sweet. There was a great feast for many days, and all of the villagers returned to their huts with pieces of the flame that Shushu had so bravely stolen from the sweathouse of Au Mujaupa.

# The Seven Corn Maidens

## Zuni, Native American

 AIYATUMA, THE FLUTE PLAYER AND THE GOD OF THE dew and the dawn, gave many great gifts to the people of earth. Among the most sacred gifts he gave them was the corn that grew in the field. And with the corn Paiyatuma gave people the seven pure maidens who danced and nurtured the corn and made it grow.

The people were grateful for the work of the corn maidens and treated them with enormous respect. When the annual season for growing came, they built a special bower for the maidens that was constructed of cedar and covered with wood from the mountains. They also built a bonfire for the maidens to dance around.

The maidens danced to insure the healthy growth of the corn plants. Each maiden would embrace a stalk of corn, and as she did, she would pray that the stalk would climb upward toward heaven. The fire would grow brighter and brighter as each maiden touched a stalk of corn, until it burned so brightly that it exhausted itself. Into the dark night the maidens would continue to dance in their beautiful gowns to the music of the drums.

Once when the maidens were performing their ritual, a sound came down to the people from Thunder Mountain. No one had ever heard such a sound before, like beautiful music. Several of the young men of the tribe left the celebration of the corn maidens and made their way to Thunder Mountain to see why such sounds were being played. When they arrived, to their surprise, they found another celebration occurring. There were maidens dancing here, as well, beautiful and tall and as graceful as the corn maidens from their own land.

There were also flute players everywhere they looked. They played sweet music on their instruments and danced with the women. The young men were captivated by all they saw and heard.

Paiyatuma looked down from the clouds and saw what was happening. He appeared as a messenger to the young men and asked them why they had come to seek the dancers and flute players on Thunder Mountain, when they had their own music and beautiful corn maidens to celebrate with at home. The men could not answer Paiyatuma, but knew they had done wrong by leaving their people. They ventured back to their own festival, bringing the flute players with them.

When they arrived home, they instructed the musicians to play for the seven corn maidens. The flute players did as they were asked, but the young women refused to come out of their bower. No matter how many times the people asked for them, they would not emerge. Finally someone went inside the bower to ask the women to return to their dancing, only to find that the seven maidens were gone.

The people were deeply saddened by the news that the women had deserted them. This would mean that no corn would grow during the season and there would be no food. They turned to the great eagle to help them.

"Have you seen where the corn maidens have gone?" they asked him.

The eagle replied from his perch in the treetop. "I have flown everywhere, but I have not seen the maidens. Ask the falcon to help you, for his eyesight is better than mine."

The people sought the wise counsel of the falcon. Unfortunately, the falcon could not help. "I have not seen your maidens," he told the people, "perhaps you should go to the raven and ask him."

The people found the black raven near a heap of trash. He was angry that they came to see him. "When I am hungry all you give me are your scraps of garbage. Now, you expect me to help you?"

With this, the people fed a delicious meal to the hungry raven. After he had finished eating, however, he, too, announced that he had not seen the corn maidens.

"I know of only one person who can help you," he told the people. "He is the god of the dawn and the mist, and his name is Paiyatuma."

The people gathered together to consult with each other. They decided to send the young men who had visited Thunder Mountain, and had turned their backs on the corn maidens, to ask for Paiyatuma's forgiveness. The tribesmen went to seek Paiyatuma. When they found him, they asked him to forgive their sins and to restore the wonderful maidens to their land.

Paiyatuma felt sorry for the young men and agreed to lead them to Summerland. There the world was lovely and green, filled with butterflies and snapdragons and flowers. There, too, were the corn maidens, all seven of them, dancing in the fields.

The young men apologized to the maidens for being distracted by the music from Thunder Mountain. They promised to always appreciate the women who helped to make the corn grow. The maidens left Summerland and returned with the men to the village.

Once again they embraced the corn and sent the fire growing ever higher into the sky. They danced and sang and brought great joy to the people. This time, however, the maidens sent their spirits into the grains of corn growing in the earth. In this way, they could never be separated from the plants and would always remain within the corn to assure its health and growth.

CREATION

# TURTLE AND EARTH SPIRIT

## *Maidu Indians, North America*

T THE BEGINNING OF TIME THERE WAS NOTHING IN the sky and there was no earth. There were no stars, no moon, and no sun. Everything was covered with water, and everything was in darkness. One day a raft came floating in the water and in the raft were two beings. One was Turtle and the other was Father of the Secret Society. As they sailed along in their tiny raft, a rope of feathers dropped from the sky. It landed in the boat, and a being called Earth Spirit climbed in with Turtle and Father.

The two looked curiously at the Earth Spirit. "Where do you come from?" they asked him.

"I come from above," Earth Spirit replied, "from the heavens."

"That is well and good," said Turtle, "but do you think you could make me a piece of dry land so that I don't have to swim around all the time, or float on this lazy raft?"

Earth Spirit thought for a minute and said, "I would make you some land, but I have nothing to use for the foundation."

Turtle smiled. "Tie your rope of feathers to me and I will dive to the bottom of these waters and I will bring up the mud and soil you need to build some land. Be sure to pay attention to the rope. If I tug on the rope once, it means that you are to pull me from the water. If I tug twice on the rope, you must use all your strength to pull me up from the bottom of the sea, for I will be carrying a great load of dirt."

Earth Spirit and Father agreed and lowered Turtle over the side of the raft. He descended down into the dark, murky waters until they could no longer see him.

Days and months and years passed, and still Turtle did not rise from the bottom of the water. Earth Spirit and Father began to worry until one day they felt a tug on the rope of feathers.

"It is Turtle!" cried Father, "Quickly, pull him out!"

Earth Spirit and Father grabbed the rope and began to pull Turtle from the water. It took many hours, but finally he emerged from the surface of the water, dripping with slime and algae. They pulled him into the raft and helped him to scrape the gooey mess from his shell. When Turtle finally caught his breath, Father asked him, "Where is the soil that you were diving for, Turtle?"

Turtle looked at Father sadly, then replied, "For days and weeks and months and years, I dug at the bottom of the water. I gathered a very large amount of soil together in a great pile. I started to swim with this load on my shell, which took a long, long time. When I reached the top of the water, I noticed that the weight on top of me was not as it had been before. I knew that everything I had carried was gone. I have only this dirt that is under my nails. The rest slid off of my shell. All that work—for nothing."

Earth Spirit took a knife and removed the dirt from under Turtle's nails and collected it into a pebble. Then he placed the pebble at the end of the raft and left it there for several days. Turtle and Father were amazed when they went to look at the pebble the next day, for they found that it had grown ten times its normal size. Each morning after that, they found that the pebble had grown again and again until the raft could not contain it.

It grew and grew and grew until it became a massive piece of land on which the three could walk.

"This is wonderful!" Turtle exclaimed as he crawled about the land. "Do you think we might have some light so we can see where we are going?"

Earth Spirit agreed to the request and asked Father to call out to the heavens. Father did just that, and the sun appeared and sent its beautiful rays all over the earth.

"I am so happy," Turtle cried. "Is there more you can do?"

With that, Earth Spirit blew his breath upward into the heavens, and a thousand stars came out of the skies, each with a name and a special light.

Turtle and Father were happy because they had been given land and day and night. Earth Spirit was not finished, however. He caused a great tree to sprout from the ground, a tree with enormous branches and filled with many green leaves. Turtle and Father sat beneath the tree, which provided cool shade and many acorns to eat.

# ISHTAR VISITS THE UNDERWORLD

## *Babylon*

HAMASH, THE SUN GOD, LOOKED DOWN FROM HIS place high in the sky and beheld the earth below him. Where there were once green fields, there was now barren land. Where there had been horses and cows frolicking in the fields and producing offspring in the spring, there were bones and flies. Where there had been lovers walking in the moonlight and gazing into each other's eyes, there were the empty stares of people who no longer loved each other.

Shamash felt great despair and wondered why things were so. He went to the great god Ea, and told him what he had observed. Ea looked closely at the world and saw that it was barren and cold.

"Bring me the queen of the gods, Ishtar," he told the sun god. But Shamash simply shook his head. "No one knows where Ishtar has gone," he reported sadly. "No one has seen the great lady."

Far below the world was the land of the dead. Cold, dark, foggy, and filled with the smells of decay, it was the kingdom of the goddess of death,

Irkalla. At her command the hopeless souls of the dead lived in squalor and darkness, eating mud and dirt.

In this kingdom was the soul of Ishtar's beloved husband, Tammuz. Ishtar missed Tammuz. She missed him so much that one day she made up her mind to go to the underworld and bring him back.

She climbed down into the cavern of death and was greeted by the watchman Nedu, who guarded the great iron gates of hell.

"Let me pass," Ishtar commanded Nedu. "There is one I must find here."

Nedu looked at the queen of the gods, but did not answer her.

Finally Ishtar threatened to curse Nedu and break down the gates of hell with her bare hands.

"Stop!" Nedu cried out. "I must consult with the queen of the underworld, who is Irkalla, and get her permission before you may enter." He went into the depths of hell and looked for the queen.

When Irkalla heard who was at the gates, she became very upset. She did not want the great goddess in her kingdom. She gave strict instructions to Nedu. "Do as I say, and bring the lady to me." Nedu bowed and obeyed.

Returning to where Ishtar was standing at the entrance to hell, Nedu asked her to remove her splendid crown. "This is the will of Irkalla," he told Ishtar.

Ishtar took off her crown and handed it to him. He opened the gates of hell and let her in. After they had traveled only a few steps, Nedu turned to Ishtar and asked her to remove her beautiful necklace. "This is the will of Irkalla," he told her. Ishtar did as she was instructed and gave the necklace to the watchman.

Before long, they descended into Irkalla's kingdom. Nedu again turned to the queen of the gods and asked her for her gold bracelets. Ishtar was becoming impatient with Nedu's requests, but did as she was told. He took the bracelets.

Without her jewelry, Ishtar began to appear plain and ordinary. She became tired and discouraged as she and Nedu walked over sharp rocks and through treacherous streams on their journey to the throne of Irkalla.

"Give me your veil and your garments," Nedu finally told Ishtar. "We are about to approach Irkalla."

Ishtar was angry. "If I give you these things, I will have lost everything that marks me as the queen of the gods!"

"This is the will of Irkalla!" Nedu told her. "This must be done, or you cannot be received by her."

Ishtar removed her veil and her clothing. Naked and cold, she finally approached the queen of the underworld.

"I come to you naked," she told Irkalla, who sat upon her dark throne, happy to see the great lady disrobed and powerless before her.

"Very well, Ishtar," Irkalla spoke. "You have succeeded in entering the kingdom of hell. What is it that you want?"

"I wish to recover the soul of my beloved, Tammuz." Ishtar whispered.

Irkalla laughed an evil laugh. "You cannot recover his soul!" she announced. "Further, you cannot ever leave this place. You are destined, as are all who come here, to eat dust and mud and dwell without hope."

And so Ishtar, the once powerful queen of all the gods, was made to eat the soil of hell. She no longer walked in finery and jewels, but was covered with dust and dirt from the top of her head to her toes.

Meanwhile, Ea conducted a great search. He had a hunch that Ishtar would pine for her Tammuz. He created a creature called Ud-dushu-namir to go to the underworld to bring the water of life to Ishtar and bid her return to the earth.

The creature did as he was instructed. He traveled to hell and told Ishtar, to drink the water that he carried on behalf of the great god Ea. Irkalla was livid when she saw the creature approach, but knew that she had no power over Ea.

Ishtar drank from the water, and then poured it over her dusty, dirty body. It washed away the soil of hell, the despair, and sadness, and made her body clean again. Then she put on her clothing and her jewelry and her crown and followed Ud-dushu-namir to the earth.

Ishtar was grateful to return to the world. Upon seeing her, every living thing rejoiced and produced offspring. The crops returned to the fields and the lovers fell into each others' arms once more. Ea was pleased, knowing that the world was returned to its former way. Yet, even with the flowers and birds and budding trees surrounding her, Ishtar's heart was still heavy, missing her husband, who could not return from the underworld.

UNDERWORLD

# THE CRUEL BIRD

## *Aranda Tribe, Australia*

 N THE LAND OF ILKANARA, IN THE SOUTH, THERE were many giant red rocks. The rocks formed mountains and caves and crevices. From one of these crevices, from deep within the earth itself, a woman reached her hand up to the sky and crawled out onto the warm rocks. She was soon followed by another woman, who glanced up at the blue sky and the mighty rock, and was a little frightened. She, too, climbed out of the crevice in the earth.

A third woman followed. Behind her a fourth woman climbed out, and then a fifth woman did the same until they were all upon the rocks. They sat in the warm sunlight.

When the women had all ascended from the land below the earth, a group of men began to emerge. The men began to argue about who should climb out first. One of the five men to come from the crevice in the rock scampered before the others and sat next to the five women. After a short time the other four men climbed up and out of the earth. Finally they were all out.

The men were angry at the first man, who had managed to get out before they did. They shouted at him and called him insulting names. He lit a large bonfire that could be seen from everywhere. He sat near the fire for warmth and protection. But it was of no use. The other men took magic bones and pointed them at the first man and continued to chant and call him names. The man grew weary of all the noise and the name-calling. The magic bones caused him to become very tired. He lay down next to the fire's orange flames and fell into a very deep sleep. He slept for two days, and then he died.

The four remaining men and the five women were astounded. They could not believe that the first man had died. They only wished to admonish him for his behavior and rudeness. They found a place, safe from the wild animals that came in the night, and buried the man. Then they were filled with grief and sorrow about what had happened. One of the women went to Tjolankuta; another went to Lkebalinja. The rest stayed in that place where the man had died, and began to dance a magic dance. They danced around the fire all night long, under the stars and the moon. The four men chanted and sang.

Then an amazing thing occurred right before their eyes. The dead man's fingertips began to appear out of the soil. Next his hand appeared, followed by his arm up to his elbow. The top of the dead man's head appeared, then his forehead was noticeable. Before long the group could see his eyes. He continued to emerge from the grave until he was out of the soil up to his shoulders. The group rejoiced, for they believed that the man had escaped death. For some reason, however, he could not move his shoulders out of the earth.

From a distant mountain, Urbura, the magpie, could see what was happening among the great rocks. He knew that this event was against the laws of nature. Urbura hurriedly flew to where the dead man struggled to rise from the dirt. He circled the dead man's head several times, then flew off to the mountain Urburinka. He swooped down on the mountain and picked up a spear in his beak. Urbura flew back to the site where the man was attempting to leave his grave. Urbura thrust his spear into the man's neck and killed him, instantly. To insure that the man would never rise again, the magpie instructed the women to dance on his grave until the dead man was stomped back into the depths of the earth.

He called out to all those who would listen, "This man shall remain in his grave. He shall not rise again."

All of the women and men who had crawled from the rocks were instantly turned to birds. They screeched and cawed and flew in every direction of the earth. As they flew, their tears fell below onto the earth. They were saddened to learn that death was so final.

Urbura left the area, as well, and flew back to his home, where he remained for the rest of time. Many people consider Urbura to be a cruel bird, for he did not allow the dead man to rise from his grave. Yet Urbura knew in his heart that if the man had succeeded in leaving the world of the dead, he would live forever, and all men would be able to live forever. And Urbura knew that this could never be.